Not Exactly As Planned

A Memoir of Adoption, Secrets and Abiding Love

Linda Rosenbaum

DEMETER

DEMETER PRESS, BRADFORD, ONTARIO

Demeter Press logo based on the sculpture "Demeter" by Maria-Luise Bodirsky <www.keramik-atelier.bodirsky.de>

Cover design: Allyson Woodrooffe (go-word.com)

Every effort has been made to contact the photographer who took the photograph used on the cover of this book. The author and the publisher welcome any information that would allow them to acknowledge the photographer in subsequent editions.

Printed and Bound in Canada

Library and Archives Canada Cataloguing in Publication

Rosenbaum, Linda, author
        Not exactly as planned : a memoir of adoption, secrets and abiding love / Linda Rosenbaum.

ISBN 978-1-927335-91-8 (pbk.)

        1. Rosenbaum, Linda. 2. Adoptive parents--Canada--Biography. 3. Mothers--Canada--Biography. 4. Adopted children--Family relationships--Canada. 5. Children of prenatal alcohol abuse--Canada. I. Title.

HV874.82.C3.R68 2014   362.734092   C2014-906273-7

Demeter Press
140 Holland Street West
P. O. Box 13022
Bradford, ON L3Z 2Y5
Tel: (905) 775-9089
Email: info@demeterpress.org
Website: www.demeterpress.org

MIX
Paper from
responsible sources
FSC
www.fsc.org   FSC® C004071

For Alberta

Der mentsh trakht un got lakht.
Man plans and God laughs.
—Yiddish Proverb

Prologue: The First Secret
Detroit, 1958

THE FIRST FAMILY SECRET unravels on the holiest day of the Jewish calendar. It is *Yom Kippur*, the Day of Atonement, 1958. I am ten.

My oldest sister and I return home from synagogue after the ritual prayers of repentance and forgiveness. Our mother and father stay for *Yizkor*, prayers of remembrance for the dead. *Yom Kippur* is one of the few holidays treated with reverence in our home, powerful enough to lure the whole family to *shule*.

Soon after we come into the house, the phone rings. My sister and I look at each other. "Who would be calling on *Yom Kippur?*" It is such a solemn day for us. Most people we know are at synagogue or busy with family.

"Answer it." Barbara says. "It might be important."

The voice on the other end is matter-of-fact. "Mrs. Belle Rosenbaum, please."

"My mother won't be home until later."

"I'm calling from Eloise Mental Hospital to inform her that Mrs. Esther Koenigsberg passed away this morning."

Eloise? Even at the age of ten I know that Eloise is the place for crazy people. I have overheard enough stories to know they lock people up there, tie them to beds, and shock them with electricity.

"Esther Koenigsberg?" I ask. "Sorry, we don't know..." I stop myself. The name is familiar.

"Our records say she is the mother of Belle Rosenbaum."

"That's my mother."

"Ask her to call when she comes in."

I hang up the phone and sit down at the kitchen table. My head is swimming.

"Who was it?" Barbara asks, looking alarmed.

"Our grandmother just died…" I tell her, and then fill in the details, still piecing them together myself. "But it can't be. She's dead. But the lady says it was Mom's mother. The woman's name was Esther Koenigsberg. Wasn't that our grandmother's name?" My voice tapers into silence. I lower my head and stare at the flecks in the green linoleum floor, then look up, hoping my big sister, ten years older, will help me.

Though she is with me that day, Barbara lives with her husband and baby in their own home. That means she is a grown-up. It will make sense to her, right?

At first, only silence. "It must be her," she finally says. "I have vague memories of driving out of town to a big hospital with Mom when I was little, but I don't remember visiting anyone or even getting out of the car. I'm not even sure I knew why we were there. We never talked about it. I guess mom assumed I was so young I wouldn't remember anything. But the place must have been Eloise. If it was, that's where our grandmother was living all these years." She shakes her head. "This is crazy."

Her response adds to my confusion. Barbara has been to Eloise? What about Sharon, my middle sister, five years older than me? Has she been there, too? Did she know our grandmother was alive? The only thing I knew about my grandmother was her name, Esther Koenigsberg. And Esther Koenigsberg was long dead, according to my mother.

After wearing out the conversation with my sister, I sit alone in our book-lined den, going over and over what the lady said. If she really was talking about my grandmother, it means my mother has kept her a secret. She has lied. My grandmother hadn't died before I was born, like she said.

How could my mother send her own mother away? How

could she deprive me of me my grandmother? Worse still, how could she deny my grandmother *me*? I was so mad, my chest began to ache, like an anchor had been tied to it. I practise aloud how I will punish my mother when she comes home. I am never going to forgive her.

Late in the afternoon, my parents return, looking tired and solemn after a day of fasting and prayer.

I run up to my mother, barely through the front door. "You never told me about my grandmother," I shout, with rehearsed fury. "How could you keep her a secret from me?" As an aside, I throw in, "Oh, I forgot. They called from Eloise. Your mother died this morning."

I am surprised how good it feels to say something so cruel, but the pleasure doesn't last more than a few seconds. I am too aware that it is The Day of Atonement, also of forgiveness.

My mother stands by the door, expressionless. Her two worlds, the one with her daughters and the one with her mother, have collided. "It's hard to explain," she eventually says, unable to look at me. "You can't understand. It was different then. There were things you didn't talk about."

She is right. I *couldn't* understand. It will be a long time until I learn that the "thing" people don't talk about is mental illness in the family.

My sister and I try to get details from my mother, but she won't reveal much, no matter how we pry.

"What was wrong with her?" we ask.

"She had problems."

"Come on, Ma, what kind of problems?"

"She was ... sick."

"But why was she in Eloise?"

"We couldn't take care of her."

"How old were you when she went in?"

"Young."

The more we press, the more she closes down. We ask our

father for answers, but he defers, letting us know it is not his domain. "Ask your mother."

My sister gives up on the inquisition before I do. With each unsatisfying answer to our questions, my fury rises. It isn't right that I can close my eyes and imagine what Eloise Mental Hospital looks like, but not my own grandmother. Were her eyes blue like mine? Was her hair grey, wrapped in a braid around her head like my father's mother? Did her hankies smell of lilies of the valley? What did her dresses look like? Would she speak English or Yiddish when I visited? Did she ever ask about me or know I was alive?

I have no compassion for my mother. I only feel betrayed.

That night, my mother walks into my room, unsolicited. She sits down on my bed. She doesn't hug me, try to console me or tuck me in.

"I used to visit my mother," she says. "I drove to Eloise every week to see her. I'd bring containers of cottage cheese and eggplant that I cooked the way she liked. She'd only say a few words, and mostly rocked while I was there. I'd stay for a while, then drive home." She sits for a few minutes more, then stands up and leaves the room.

Somehow, these few words break the floodgates. They allow me to fantasize, imagine myself sitting in the car with my mother as we drive to Eloise every week. When we arrive, I head straight to my grandmother's room. "Hi Grandma," I say, and give her a hug. We hold hands until my mother says it is time to leave. I kiss my grandmother on the cheek and say goodbye. I know she is sorry I have to go. "It's okay, Grandma," I say. "I'll be back next week. Don't worry."

I lay in bed brooding that night. I'm not old enough to run away, so make another plan.

Just like my sister, I will move away from home and have a family of my own by the time I am twenty. I will never, ever be anything like my mother.

No secrets. No lies. I will hide nothing and no one from the people I love.

1.
New Baby / New Reality
Toronto Island, 1987

"WE DON'T KNOW what happened," I said to the doctor. "I didn't think it was possible, but Michael's crying is worse than ever.

"Besides his ear-piercing screams, he stiffens his limbs when he's crying, arches his back and clenches his fists. His arms are flailing again like when we first brought him home. His tummy's bloated and he sometimes draws his arms and legs up to it."

"He has colic," the pediatrician pronounced.

Colic was defined as long, unexplained bouts of crying in an infant that could last over three hours at a stretch. About twenty percent of babies had colic, considered the by-product of a not yet fully developed nervous system.

"How can it be colic? I thought babies got colic when they were two or three weeks old," I said. Michael was now six months.

It was the summer of 1987. I was thirty-nine and living with my husband on Toronto Island, on the Lake Ontario waterfront. Robin and I had been married for three years and, after trying unsuccessfully to conceive a child, we had made the decision to adopt. In May, we brought Michael home when he was seven days old. Since then, as parents, we had become desperate. We didn't know what was happening with our child, and no one seemed any wiser than we were.

"It can appear this late with preemies, but this is quite unusual," the doctor admitted. Michael was born full-term. "But it's colic nevertheless. It should last about three months, then miraculously disappear." It wasn't reassuring to know we would have three months of this, but the diagnosis subdued our fears that it was something more serious.

"If it's any comfort, I don't think Michael is in any pain," the doctor said. I wish it were comforting, but I didn't believe him. Michael looked and sounded like he was being tortured. A few days after the doctor's, a friend told me her own doctor admitted using the term colic as a five-letter word to say, "I don't know." That I could believe.

As the intensity of Michael's cries mounted, so did my frustration. I was back to feeling completely helpless again, like the days when we first brought him home. I didn't know the causes of my son's distress or how to relieve him. There were days he was so inconsolable, we were both in tears, hurting together.

I remembered my dad once saying when I was young, "This is hurting me as much as it's hurting you." At the time, he was digging out a bad sliver in my index finger. I didn't believe him. Now I thought maybe my dad was telling the truth. Michael's colic was killing me.

Robin and I tried doing the things we had done right after Michael was born to calm him. We swaddled him as a form of gentle restraint. We held him tightly against our chests or over our shoulders to put firm pressure on his tummy. We tried hot water bottles. We kept him away from light or too much stimulation. We gave him gripe water and homeopathic remedies. Everything helped a little, but not much and not for long.

I read everything I could about colic, but found little to explain why it happened. Then, while browsing the Internet for the ultimate colic cure-all, I read something by a doctor that shocked me. The root cause of colic? What else? The mother! I had grown up in a time when conventional wisdom held mothers responsible for homosexuality because we were overbearing; schizophrenia because we gave double messages to our children; and ulcers and asthma because we were creating too much stress. And now colic? I had to hear this crap at a time I was already vulnerable about my parenting skills?

What the doctor was saying, in essence, is that babies develop colic to get the attention of their otherwise distracted mothers. After "the miracle of a new birth," mothers want to revert to their previous activities and schedules — if only their newborns would let them! But "colic demands attention," the doctor continued, forcing mums to "leave their previous ruts and develop new dynamics that include this new individual." According to this logic, babies wouldn't develop colic if mothers were giving them what they needed and wanted. Bullshit.

My energy and spirits were slowly wearing down from the constant attention Michael needed. I began doing things I had sworn never to do. It made me afraid of what might be next. Plopping Michael in front of a video to get a few quiet moments was the least of it.

I was home alone with Michael on a dreary, rainy day. He was crying for what felt like hours and probably was. All the tenderness in the world couldn't get him to stop wailing. I held him, rocked him, coddled him, petted him, fed him, rubbed his tummy, turned on soft music, walked him in the stroller, sang to him, whispered soft sounds. Nothing worked.

I always assumed Michael's crying signalled something was wrong, that he was saying, "Help me, mommy, help me." The crying both pulled on my heartstrings and drowned me in guilt. The feelings escalated with each successive attempt to help him.

I snapped. My sympathy had run dry. Wham! I couldn't listen to him any longer. I took Michael into my arms and raised him above my head. I screamed at him in fury. "Why are you doing this, Michael? Stop crying! Stop it! Stop it!"

I must have been feeling what parents I read about in the *National Enquirer* felt before they did unspeakable things to their children.

My screaming scared the wits out of Michael. He cried even harder. I got even madder. Yet I must have held on to a gauze-thin veil of control. I knew enough, somehow, to get Michael out of my arms, fast. If not, I'd soon be shaking him. I could feel it coming.

I ran with him into his bedroom. Without lowering the sides of the crib, I threw him down into it. It wasn't a violent toss, but it wasn't friendly, either.

I had no idea how close I was to my breaking point until I reached it. I ran out of Michael's room and headed upstairs to the bedroom. I threw my own self on our bed, covered my head with pillows and cried myself to exhaustion. When I came back downstairs an hour later, Michael was asleep. I told myself he wore himself out. That was the expression used by the head nurse at the hospital where Michael was born. That's the way she said he fell asleep each night before we brought him home.

I felt ashamed and terrified. I had to ask myself questions I preferred not to. What separated me from the *National Enquirer* mothers? What kept me from doing worse? Could it happen again? Why wasn't I aware of my anger and frustration being on the rise until it was too late? And the bigger questions: Why didn't I call Robin? Why didn't I ask one of my many neighbours to take Michael out of the house for a walk?

I remembered nothing else from that day. Not even what happened when Robin came home or if Michael seemed affected by the experience. It took time before my shame lifted. When it did, I made a promise to both Robin and myself. If I ever felt anything like that again, I would call him at work or ask a friend to come over. I hoped I didn't have to.

The colic disappeared on cue after three long months. Other challenges didn't.

One morning, a few weeks after Michael's arrival, I startled awake and bolted upright in bed. I felt completely alarmed, though not sure about what. I was petrified. My stomach clenched. My heart was racing, pounding loud and fast. The palms of my hands were slick with sweat. I shook Robin, curled in his favourite position, his face buried deep in the pillow. "Wake up, wake up," I said, my voice quaking. "I think I'm going crazy."

He was dozy, not yet registering what I was saying. "Robin, something's wrong."

Just barely awake, he tried to calm me. "It must be lack of sleep, or post-adoption depression."

"It's nothing like that." Robin and I took turns feeding Michael through the night, so I didn't get that little sleep. And he probably made up the term post-adoption depression so I could feel like other new mothers in case I did get depressed. But I wasn't.

When Robin saw I was shaking, he pulled himself upright and put his arms around me. Holding me tightly, he tried to stifle the shivers rolling through my body.

"I'm scared to death of something," I said. "My head is whirling." My voice became louder, less controlled. I pleaded with Robin to tell me what was happening. "I think I'm going crazy. What's wrong with me? Will it go away?"

He looked straight into my eyes. "Linda, you told me you had these symptoms before, before we met. Remember?"

"Is it a panic attack?"

"Probably," Robin said. "Maybe your body is trying to tell you something, just like before."

I pulled myself away. "Like what? What could it be telling me?" Certainly nothing I wanted to know about.

"That you're trapped. You're stuck. That's what it was telling you before, so maybe it's telling you the same thing now. You have a child you can't ever leave."

I was sickened by what he was saying. "I love being a mother. I love Michael," I said. I've waited all my life to be a mother and have a child. Now I'm ungrateful and worried I might not be able to escape? How shameful is that?

"What if you're right?" I whispered, looking away in embarrassment.

It wasn't hard to see that there might be connections between my previous panic attack and what I'd been feeling since Michael's arrival. I let myself admit that below the surface, despite all the love, I was feeling trapped, something beyond garden-variety new-mother jitters.

"Before we brought Michael home," I said, "there was never anyone in my life I couldn't run away from if I had to. Even you, my husband. If I ever had to leave, I could. People get divorced. It happens. But you can't run away from a child, ever." What if this doesn't work out? What if I have to get away?

"You won't have to escape," Robin said. "I know you. No matter what happens with Michael, you'll never run away. You'll be a devoted mother. You were made to be a mother." He reminded me that I wasn't the first mother to feel trapped by a new baby, but they had nine months and a whacking good set of hormones to help them get used to the idea. "Still," he said, "being trapped has more meaning to you than it does them. You may have to take a look at that."

"You can just forget about that," I snapped, thinking he was suggesting a trip back into therapy. I couldn't bear the thought. I'd done my time.

Robin backed off. We sat and talked for the few moments we had before Michael's next feeding. Identifying the source of my fears was making me feel slightly better. I was becoming noticeably less anxious. My heart was beating more slowly, I had stopped sweating and thoughts weren't galloping through my head at breakneck speed. "Maybe I actually do have some control over my feelings," I said, feeling myself becoming calmer. I couldn't do that after my previous panic attack. It took years of blistering self-analysis to heal.

I felt better knowing that my past was playing havoc with my mind as much as the present, "but it's not fair," I said to

Robin. "I've spent years on this and I'm still haunted by the notion of being trapped."

Yes, caring for Michael so far had been tough, but it was early times. If we were lucky, Michael's needs would lessen and disappear altogether. But raising Michael wasn't a horror I had to escape from, anyway. It wasn't like my student experience in Washington where the danger was real and I couldn't run from it. Nor was it like being trapped in the airplane during the trip back from Florida.

I didn't need to analyze anything further. There was no way in hell I was going back to revisit the past, particularly the event in Washington close to thirty years before. As long as I could put one step in front of the other to take care of Michael, I would.

I just didn't know how hard that would be.

A few days later I jumped out of bed as if I was about to miss a meeting with the Pope. It was just after six in the morning. Before walking ten steps to the bathroom to brush my teeth and have a much-needed pee, I started frantically picking up clothes lying on the floor, rearranging the dying red roses on my night table and fluffing the duvet — with Robin still under it.

"What are you doing?" he asked, annoyed. Robin has always loved his sleep. "The rare morning Michael is actually sleeping and you're running around like a maniac."

I tried to sound reasonable. "The other new mothers are coming for coffee. I want to get everything cleaned up. Then, maybe, I can relax enough to bake muffins or something nice like that."

"What time are they coming?"

"Ten."

"You're kicking me out of bed, cleaning up a room they won't see, getting yourself into a frenzy, and they won't be here for four hours? It's a little crazy, don't you think?"

"Only on the surface," I said. I knew "getting everything in order to bake muffins" didn't touch on what my frenzied activity was about. I tried to quickly change the subject. "How about a cup of tea?" I asked, as I headed downstairs to the kitchen. "Wow," Robin said, nicely surprised. "That would be lovely."

Every morning of the three years we'd been married, at his own doing, Robin brought a cup of hot tea to me in bed. It was such a sweet, generous gesture, most likely inherited from his English upbringing. I never had the heart to tell him I didn't really care for tea in bed in the morning. If anything, it was coffee I'd like. With time, however, that cup of tea meant more to me than you would think a cup of liquid ever could.

Such sweet thoughts I had, but the minute I entered the kitchen, my mood was punctured. Before I filled the kettle, my good intentions were sidetracked. There was stuff everywhere. Dirty dishes piled in the sink. Leftover Greek salad in an uncovered bowl on the counter. Breadcrumbs hovering around the toaster. Yesterday's *Globe and Mail* lay on the butcher-block kitchen table. And there, in the middle of our kitchen's hardwood floor, sat a pile of dirt, right where I'd left it after sweeping up the night before. Distracted by a screaming Michael, the pile never made it into the dustpan, let alone the wastebasket.

I had been awake for fifteen minutes, but already my enthusiasm for the day was waning. I wasn't sure what to tackle first, and this was only the kitchen. I had three other rooms to do. Making Robin a nice cuppa was losing importance. I was trying desperately to beat the clock. Michael could be up any minute and I hadn't brushed my teeth yet.

I was so worked up, it was pathetic. What was such a big deal, for god's sake? I'd had six-course Turkish-themed dinner parties without making such a fuss. Yet here I was crumbling just thinking about a few moms dropping by? Sure I wanted the house to look nice, and sure I would have loved to bake something to welcome my neighbours. But honestly, they probably couldn't care less. As new moms, we were mainly looking for good adult company, weren't we?

The self-talk didn't work. I walked into the living room and became further overwhelmed. The carpet was covered with rattles, stuffed animals, blocks and books. This was the one room, minimum, I had to get organized before my friends arrived. I started hurling the toys into the wicker chest on the other side of the room like a quarterback making a pass.

That job done, I was ready to make Robin tea. Too late. I could hear him walking around upstairs and Michael making noises in his bedroom. Though only three hours since his last feed, I knew it would be minutes before he started crying for his next. It was already 7:00. Robin would have to leave to catch the 7:45 ferry for work.

"I guess you forgot the tea," he said, coming down the stairs.

I wanted to say "I had to finish the kitchen, sweep the floor, then put the toys away," but I kept my mouth shut and walked over to him instead. He opened his arms.

"It's not about the women, is it?"

"It is, partly. I love company, and you know I like to make things nice when people visit."

"Linda, it doesn't matter; they just want to be with you," he said.

I had been meeting with the same four new mothers and their boys every week. We formalized weekly get-togethers soon after the babies were born. It would be fun, good for stimulating under-used grey matter and sharing parental advice. We assumed the boys would be going through developmental stages at relatively similar times, and we liked the idea that the boys would bond from this early contact growing up together on the Island.

Initially, I really looked forward to these get-togethers. They were everything we intended. Yet, without telling Robin, I'd recently become increasingly anxious about them. Though I enjoyed everyone's company, I didn't feel good by the time I left for home.

At first I couldn't figure out why. Then, slowly, it began to dawn on me. My experiences as a new mother and theirs were diverging. They were sharing tips about taking their children to restaurants, concerts and friends' homes — places I couldn't imagine taking Michael. They spoke of babies starting to sleep through the nights, gaining weight and growing an inch or two. Their lives were becoming less topsy-turvy. Mine was getting steadily worse. I was jealous.

"Michael is really different than the other boys," I said to Robin, trying to help him understand at least part of my frenzy.

I could feel his body tighten the second I said it. "All kids are different," he said. "You know that. You mustn't compare him to anyone else. He's having a bit of a rough go right now. He's fine."

I expected him to say exactly that, though I wasn't sure if it was denial or that he actually believed what he was saying. We both knew that all children develop differently, and at their own pace. Yet I still felt concerned. I didn't, however, want this to become an argument, so I pulled myself away, not knowing whether to pursue the conversation. What good could come of it?

It wasn't as if Robin didn't know how sensitive Michael was or how his body continued to startle and his arms thrash with changes of sound or light. He knew Michael shook and fidgeted, was never easily soothed. He saw that he wasn't putting on weight. He knew what a huge proportion of time was taken up trying to comfort, console and calm Michael. That was why the dishes didn't get washed, the newspapers read or the piles of dirt removed from the kitchen floor.

"The doctors say he's fine," Robin reminded me. He was right. We had taken Michael repeatedly to the pediatrician for check-ups, vaccinations and advice. He had been checked out from head to toe when he was born, and by other experts since then, including a neonatologist, a specialist in newborns. There was nothing to be concerned about, they assured us.

"And," Robin added, "don't you remember how furious you

got when your sister suggested something might be wrong? That he might be going through withdrawal or something? You wanted to throttle her."

I could see the conversation could go nowhere good. I was feeling utterly lonely and separate from Robin. To feel otherwise, though, would mean Robin would have to see things the way I did about Michael. That would be awful, too.

I was about to say, "Robin, I think something is wrong with Michael. I'm afraid he may have a tenuous hold on life. I really do." But I held back. I decided that feeling alone in my husband's presence was far better than voicing that thought and having him agree with me.

"You're right," I said. "He's probably fine. It's just hard sometimes seeing him make such a fuss, particularly with the other boys. They seem happier, more settled than he is." The other boys had recently begun lying happily on their backs in the playpen and gaining more control of their bodies. Some were turning over by themselves, holding rattles and other toys while Michael continued to squirm, moving randomly and indiscriminately, any way he could.

Robin and I felt terrible that we couldn't make our son comfortable or happy, and worried we might be doing everything wrong. Perhaps we were bad parents. But I was lying when I said to Robin that I was afraid the mothers would think I was a bad parent and that was why I was anxious that morning. My usually good instincts were telling me something was wrong with Michael. For the first time in my life, I prayed for those instincts to be dead wrong.

I left Robin to get ready for my guests, then to fetch Michael. His face lit up when he saw me and he stretched out his arms. It was a moment every morning I always adored. Nothing could beat that. But once I picked him up, the chance of getting anything done before the women came was kaput. The day had begun. Who was I kidding when I said "I want to get things in order so I could bake some muffins"?

The mothers arrived soon after. Everything went smoothly on the surface. We chatted, drank tea, watched the boys. No one would have had the slightest idea of the angst I was feeling. The get-together confirmed my desire to stop going to them. I called one of the mothers to tell her I didn't think I could continue with the weekly gatherings. Though I hedged about my reason, she said she understood. Several other mothers were also finding it hard to find time, too. They were getting out more and moving on with their lives, so needed less formalized support. I let her believe I was thinking the same thing.

Days later, Yolanda sat down next to me on the ferry. "I might be able to take Michael," she said. "I've got room for one more."

"I thought you were full," I said. "What happened?"

"I'm afraid this might sound self-serving," she said, "but I'm worried Michael might not be getting the attention he needs."

Yolanda was the Island's childcare worker extraordinaire. She "raised" half the kids in our community. Yolanda didn't need me. I needed Yolanda. The waiting list for the daycare she ran out of her home was a mile long. Opportunity for Michael to spend time with Yolanda would be a godsend, for both Michael and me.

Yolanda wouldn't specify why she was concerned, but I suspected it was about the woman I hired periodically to give me a break. It had been difficult to find someone on the Island to look after Michael, so I had been thrilled to find Soraya.

With Yolanda's comment, though, I had to ask if I'd grabbed too quickly at the opportunity. I was already developing a few of my own doubts. After Soraya had been out with Michael a few times, she told me how good his spirits always were. Everything a mother wanted to hear, right? But really. Michael?

Yolanda eventually confirmed my suspicions. Soraya was letting Michael cry for long periods without comforting him — she believed he should not be coddled, needed more discipline and had to learn who was boss. Yes, it would be tough on him at first, but best in the long run. Several other moms at the Island's Parenting Centre agreed. Michael needed a firmer hand. The reason he wasn't sleeping and eating well was because we hadn't enforced a routine. We'd been too soft and were paying for it.

It wasn't the first time I'd heard comments about how we were raising Michael. I was disconsolate, but took comfort knowing that Yolanda was no softie and she was dumbfounded by such talk. She'd seen a lot of babies in her years of daycare. She felt Michael's physical fragility alone told her he needed extra doses of TLC, not neglect. But who really knew? I was new at this parenting thing. My friends were caring, but as dumbfounded by Michael's behaviour as I was. They were also busy with their own children.

But now I had Yolanda. She always said something good when I picked Michael up. I felt comfortable enough to talk openly about Michael's problems. We could acknowledge his differences from other children his age, yet I never felt guilty that Robin or I were the cause.

Learning to care for Michael was an ongoing challenge, but I was managing, for the most part. I tried to take it day by day and do what I needed to connect myself to my present life and not my past. As I had reminded myself during my panic attack a few days earlier, I didn't want to go back into fear mode, especially now with a baby depending on me for safety and security. Safety and security: something I had temporarily lost at an earlier point in my life and thought I had found.

In spite of or maybe because of the troubles with Michael, Robin and I became more and more attached to this vulnerable little soul, if such a thing was possible. We were both mad for this strange boy taking over our lives. I couldn't get enough of the delicious smell and velvety feel of Michael's smooth white skin. I marvelled at the perfection of his inexplicably long, tiny fingers and toes. During his naps and at night, I would often sit by his sleeping basket. As I watched the ebb and flow of his breath while he slept, I found each rise and fall nothing short of a miracle.

It didn't hurt that Michael was new-puppy cute. He had the smile of a seraph, first revealed on the diaper table several weeks after his homecoming. Robin called it, "The smile that could launch a thousand camera clicks." In time, the smile was accompanied by a great gurgling chuckle. It emerged one day while blowing bubbles on his tummy and playing peek-a-boo. Another endearing attention-grabber of Michael's was his preposterously thick, dense head of hair, slowly turning from its original strawberry to blond — a guaranteed crowd pleaser.

Strangers in grocery stores, scanning my tight curly brown locks and Robin's dark hair, would come up and casually ask, "Where did your son get a head of hair like that?" We spared them the complexity of the real answer and enjoyed the shared laughter.

2.
Panic and Fear: Tracing the Origins
Florida, 1980 / Washington, DC, 1968–1970

M Y FIRST PANIC ATTACK happened on Christmas Day in 1980, four years before I married Robin, seven before Michael was born. I was on a Wardair flight returning to Toronto after visiting my parents' retirement home in St. Petersburg, Florida. I boarded at Tampa International, feeling lucky as the stewardess led me to a window seat. I stretched my long legs out, placed my *Harper's* into the pocket compartment on the seat in front of me, held on to the *Maclean's*, arranged the small white pillow I had grabbed from the overhead compartment, then buckled up. I was all set for the next three hours.

After being airborne for forty-five minutes, I looked up from my magazine and glanced out the window. Two engines on the plane's wing were spewing bright red flames.

No one was sitting next to me and the flight was sparsely filled. I looked around to see if anyone else was looking at the fire, but everyone seemed perfectly engrossed in whatever it was they were doing, mostly sleeping. I reached up and pressed the white button, calling for the stewardess. When she approached my seat, I spoke with remarkable calm, then pointed: "The plane is on fire."

Her eyes widened. She looked terrified, but checked herself immediately. "I'm sure it's nothing. I'll speak to the pilots," she said in a lollipop-coated voice. She turned and walked briskly towards the front cabin.

The pilot came on the intercom. His deep voice was initially commanding, then faltered.

"Ladies and gentlemen. We seem to be having some engine difficulties. Nothing to be concerned about. We're ... we're going to attempt to return to Tampa. If that proves impossible ... we will look for another location to land. I will keep you posted. Keep seatbelts fastened and do not leave your seats."

No mention of the bright red fire flaming out of the engines. No explanation as to how or if an airplane could fly another forty-five minutes with two of its four engines on fire. The stewardess never returned.

I sat calmly, inexplicably riveted to the article in *Maclean's* debating whether Calgary or Edmonton was Alberta's hottest new city. As if I really cared. But that's what I did. I read, keeping my head buried in the weekly newsmagazine. I stayed calm all the way to our safe landing back in Tampa. Upon arrival, I didn't mention to the other passengers what I saw, nor call my parents to tell them I was back in town.

Wardair rescheduled our flight for the next day. I happily dined that evening on rib eye and Merlot, compliments of the airline, before nestling into sleep, wrapped in white Egyptian linen.

I woke early the next morning with my heart pounding. I was so shaky when I pulled myself out of bed, I didn't know if I'd make it to the bathroom, let alone out the hotel door. I didn't know what was happening to me, but whatever it was, I had to get myself to the terminal and back to Toronto. No way could I stay in Florida and be with my parents feeling like this.

I managed to dress myself and pull myself down to the front desk to checkout. I then slowly and carefully walked from the hotel, dragging my suitcase, until I reached the terminal.

The moment I walked through the sliding glass doors, my physical symptoms grew worse. I began to sweat, my heart beat faster, and I felt light-headed and dizzy. But these symptoms paled in comparison to the near-unbearable terror consuming me — terror from what, I didn't have a clue. My palms were soon soaking and my heart wouldn't stop racing.

Fearful thoughts darted chaotically through my mind in every direction. I had no control over what they were saying. It felt like I was going crazy. My thoughts were telling me the same thing.

I was alone, utterly afraid and desperately in need of someone to help me. I walked towards the check-in line for my flight and parked myself in front of a complete stranger standing at the end of the row. "I think I'm going crazy," I blurted. "I don't know what's happening to me. I'm supposed to be on this flight too, but I can't get on the plane." I was now pleading. "Can you help me?"

I wasn't screaming, but from the look on the gentleman's face, the poor guy didn't have a clue what hit him. This lunatic had approached him out of nowhere telling him she was crazy, then expected him to do something about it. Sure, lady. He raised his arms in the air and motioned wildly for an airline employee to come quickly.

"I saw the engines on fire yesterday," I said to her, flat as the nearby tarmac. "I think I'm going crazy."

It didn't take long for the woman to make the connection. "You're probably having a panic attack," she said reassuringly. I had never heard the term before, but welcomed it. If my condition had a name, it meant at least one other person in the world, maybe even two, had had the same thing happen.

"Sometimes it takes a while to register the affect when you've had a big scare," she continued. "Most likely you're reacting to yesterday's flight."

She was convinced my body was telling me how deeply scared I was about getting back on the plane. "You don't want to be in a situation again where you feel you can't escape."

Eureka. My body was telling me I was scared out of my mind. I was experiencing viscerally what I had blocked emotionally: if I'm in an airplane that's on fire, I can't escape. Fight or flight. I'm trapped. There's no way out. Until I land, that is. If I do.

My body had to scream to get my attention. "Get me out

of here," it was telling me in a way that forced me to listen. Unfortunately, that meant board the plane and go home.

With the handholding of a stewardess and anti-nausea medication she hoped would deliver mild sedation, I forced myself onto the plane. It took all the will I could muster. If I was going to be a crazy person, it certainly was not going to be in Florida.

Back in Toronto, I phoned my best friend Barbara the second I walked into my Toronto Island house. I was living by myself at that time, and didn't want to be alone. "Something's wrong," I said. "Can you catch the next boat over? I really need you right now."

My symptoms hadn't abated when she arrived. Surviving the airplane trip home wasn't good enough for my body to tell itself "you can settle down already." Instead, it felt like a gush of fear was flooding my gut, then dripping drop by drop through my body until every cell was permeated with the message: stay on guard.

But scariest of all was what was happening with my mind. My thoughts were obsessively self-absorbed. I couldn't get away from myself. Nothing distracted me. I was consumed by my crazy, darting, uncontrollable thoughts. Being so scared made me more scared. I plummeted further. One of my uncontrolled thoughts was telling me, "You're going to be like this the rest of your life."

I kept asking Barbara, "What's happening to me? Why do I feel like this? Why can't I make it go away?" And my biggest worry: "Will it last forever?"

She was as confused as I was.

"I'm calling Michael," Barbara said. Our close friend Sybil had moved to Vancouver with her boyfriend, a therapist. "Maybe he can tell us something."

"It's anxiety," he told her. "She's still in panic mode. Make her drink lots of chamomile tea," he recommended. "Take deep breaths and soak in hot baths. If that doesn't do it, she may have to see someone."

The symptoms remained, unbearable. My panic increased every time we tried something that didn't work. "What if this *never* goes away?" I kept asking.

"Please take me to the Clarke," I begged Barbara. The Clarke Institute of Psychiatry was Toronto's mental health facility, not a place people normally beg to be.

"Please take me there. They can shoot me up with heroin to make it all go away. Please." Barbara wasn't taking me to the Clarke.

"I'll find a good therapist. It's time."

She didn't want to worry me more, but there was another problem. It was Christmas Day. What doctor works on Christmas?

Hours later, I approached the tall, heavy oak door with trepidation. A kind-looking elderly Jewish man with grey hair and white beard answered my knock. He stood there, wearing a thick wool tweed suit with matching vest and dangling gold pocket watch. A *pince-nez* fit snugly across the bridge of his nose. He welcomed me in with what I assumed to be an Austrian accent and ushered me into his office. I later learned that he had studied under Sigmund Freud in his youth. I had no idea if this was a plus or minus. I just knew this man had to save my life.

He seated me in a large soft brown leather chair facing him in a book-lined office. His desk was a cliché, covered with messy piles of medical journals, books, correspondence, files and half-drunk coffee cups.

"Tell me about your symptoms," he said in his thickly accented voice. "When did they start, and do you know why?"

After my short synopsis about the airplane fire, he said, "I believe you have not dealt with some past trauma in your life. The experience in the airplane has brought back feelings from that former experience. The airplane was traumatic, of course, but that is not the root of your problem." He said I had to deal with the *real* experience before these symptoms could go away. "Feelings don't stay down forever. They usually come up when a person is ready to deal with them," he explained, "or when forced back to the surface, as in your case. Down or up, they still cause suffering. They are here for you to deal with now."

Though he spoke gently, I lowered my head into my lap, covered my face and sobbed.

"So I now ask. Have you ever been in a situation before where you felt the need to escape? Or trapped?"

I sat in silence for a while. I finally took a big breath and gathered the strength to mumble. "Ten years ago. In Washington, DC."

I stopped. I wanted him to say something. I wanted him to tell me I wouldn't have to go back "there."

"Do I really have to talk about it? I don't want to."

"I'm afraid so." He was firm. "You must look at your life before, during and after this incident. You need to see where it took you and why. It will be hard, but essential. I'm sorry."

"Don't be sorry," I whispered.

I moved to Washington, DC, in 1968 when I was twenty, after two years at Michigan State University. I decided to leave on April 4, the day after Martin Luther King, Jr. was assassinated in Memphis, Tennessee. It was one month before the end of my second year at college.

My first move away from home had been to an "experimental" liberal arts college at Michigan State called Justin Morrill College. Justin Morrill's *raison d'être* was quintessential 1960s. The school hoped to teach their students to think, love knowledge, lead a life of self-discovery and become broad-minded, socially conscious citizens of the world. According to the Justin Morrill website developed years after the school was integrated into the larger university, the college had been the "Legendary Proving Ground for Wandering Minstrels." I was eighteen, earnest, eager, curious, empathetic and impractical. I was made for Justin Morrill, and it for me.

The school attracted bright, politically conscious students from all over the United States. Many were black, longhaired, politically radical or living outside mainstream society. While other college students stayed up nights playing bridge, going to frat parties and participating in panty raids, we draped ourselves across deep-cushioned green leather couches in the student lounge sipping chocolate malts, smoking cigarettes, talking politics, reading excerpts aloud from James Baldwin's *The Fire Next Time* and feverishly debating with our comrades whether non-violent tactics could *really* bring our brethren and native sons home from Vietnam.

Going away to college wasn't only a move away from family. I was also parting ways with Judaism, or what I thought at the time was Judaism. So, unlike other Jewish students I started college with, I didn't join Hillel, the campus organization where Jews go to meet Jews of the opposite sex while pretending they're there to participate in community service. I didn't choose a residence with large numbers of Jews, nor did I pledge a Jewish sorority.

This was partly because I approached the world with an increasingly unrestricted heart, and was ready for a break from elements of the post-Holocaust Jewish world in which I grew up. I did not yet know that by leaving the stifling parts of my childhood world and religion behind, I was relinquishing the precious security, familiarity and comfort both had also given me.

It was sunny and hot the day after Dr. Martin Luther King was murdered. Classes at Michigan State had been cancelled, allowing students to mourn or attend rallies, speeches, lectures, films and demonstrations in honour of Dr. King. I was one of many on campus whose world had been rocked five years before by Dr. King's fiery rhetoric in his inspirational "I Have a Dream" speech made on the steps of the Washington Monument. Beyond being devastating for us personally, we knew his murder would be a turning point in the country's black–white relations.

As I made my way across the university's huge campus from one tribute event to another, I saw hundreds of students sprawled out on the grassy greens, clad in bathing suits or madras plaid Bermuda shorts — laughing and playing in the sun, throwing Frisbees and footballs, treating the day like any other.

What stood out most were all the white people lying on beach towels using the sun-tanning fad of the time to darken their skin. As they held self-made cardboard and aluminum foil reflectors against their faces, the sun's rays hit the reflectors and bounced back with intensified rays to brown them faster.

The irony of their action on this particular day did not escape my twenty-year-old earnest mind. I wanted to get away. I needed somewhere else to go. Justin Morrill, for all its liberal and open-minded ways, was still an ivy-covered academic enclave in the middle of rural Michigan.

I had been to Washington, DC, several times when I was young, and more recently for anti-war demonstrations at the Washington Monument. Front and centre, in the thick of turbulent American politics, was just where I wanted to be. I applied and was accepted to George Washington University for my third and fourth years of college.

Washington was an elegant city, with a grandeur and energy that felt more European than American to me. It was just what I was looking for. But as in love as I was with the public face of Washington, I didn't have to look far to know there was another Washington — the one whose neighbourhoods had gone up in flames to the cheers of "Burn Baby Burn" on the

April night Martin Luther King was murdered, five months
before I arrived in the city. Crime rates, including murder, were
staggeringly high. Guns were easy to buy. Sections of the city
weren't considered safe, especially at night.

When my parents asked me, just before I moved down, "Where
will you live in Washington?" my answer was rebellious and
petulant, "I don't have a clue."

"You know we just want you to be safe," my mother said.

"I do too, but that doesn't mean I'm going to close myself
off in some lily-white suburb."

I knew I should take racial tension and crime into consider-
ation when looking for a place. But ever since I was thirteen,
I had been marching, campaigning and verbally fighting at the
side of black people. When push came to shove, what did it
mean? That I didn't want to live next door to them?

"I'll figure it out, Ma. It's hard to know from here what I'll
do."

The first year, still new to the city, I moved into an apartment
downtown with a fellow student. Living in an unfriendly high-
rise didn't feel right for me, but it did have one perk. Through
my roommate, I was introduced to a handsome, curly haired,
opera-loving graduate student from Washington State who
had recently arrived at GWU for a master's degree in history.

At the age of twenty, I had my first real boyfriend. It was
about time. My childhood dream of having a family by that
age had been steadily vanishing due to the choices I was making, as was any trajectory towards marrying a Jewish man.
Maybe Jeffrey might help me get back on track. Or maybe
not. Though he was non-practising, Jeffrey, my first love, was
raised by Christian fundamentalists.

My second year in Washington, I was ready to find somewhere else to live that better suited me. My first taste of living
in a commune brought me closer to the university.

I was happy living in a racially mixed neighbourhood, too.

It had a lot more buzz, street life and visiting back and forth between houses than in my previous neighbourhood. Our commune was in a once-elegant three-level Victorian brownstone with hand-polished staircases and twenty-foot-high plastered ceilings with thick wooden moldings and trim (the latter painted, in a moment of psychedelic madness, day-glo orange and purple).

Life on our street was intense and fun. Busy front porches played an essential role. At our own house, the porch seldom emptied. Before, during and after classes and usually way into the night, at least three or four out of the nine of us living there would move outside to watch the world go by. We sat, sometimes eating, sometimes drinking, sometimes making music and sometimes smoking marijuana, but always laughing, arguing, debating and plotting how we would fix all that was wrong in the world.

Like everyone else I knew, I kept inching away from mainstream politics, attitude and dress. We young people were cranky in our rebellion, and our disdain for government, war, police, corporations, capitalism, money and materialism was loud and overt.

My father was philosophical about how I dressed during that period. My rag-tag hippy look wasn't working for my mother, however.

"Why can't you be proud your daughter looks like a poster child for *Hair*?" I half-joked, referring to the hit musical on Broadway. She thought I looked horrible. My long, thick, frizzy brown hair hung down my back and out to the sides like an unpruned hydrangea. I wore floor-length, Indian-print gypsy skirts with scarves, bangles and hand-embroidered peasant shirts from Morocco and Mexico — usually braless underneath. I always wore large, ornate earrings and left my face make-up bare. Like all the other young, budding feminists around me, I was defying corporate America's cosmetic industry.

On trips home from university to visit my parents, I'd get a relatively warm smile when my mother first greeted me. Within seconds, though, she'd put me through her full frontal visual body scan, resulting in a look of marked disappointment on her face. What was she thinking? That Mamie Eisenhower or Jacqueline Kennedy had somehow become my role models since I was last home?

On one return from school, my mother opened the front door, and before even saying hello, let the refrain "We'll go shopping tomorrow" slip from her lips.

"Thanks, Ma. It's really nice to see you, too." I said, seething. Sarcasm was my usual mode of defense with my mother.

"You know I'm glad to see you. I don't have to say it. I just want to make sure we have enough time to shop and get your haircut. You'd look so much better with that hair off your face."

That hair? That hair told the world who I was and what I believed in. "Ma, we've been through this a million times before. You don't stop, no matter what. You're acting like you're from Mars."

"Well at least on Mars they know how to make themselves look good."

I began to think seriously about staying in Washington after graduation, at least for a while, to see what I could make happen. After two years together, Jeffrey and I had moved into an on-again, off-again stage. Even though he still had another year of grad school at GWU, I wasn't going to decide where to live or what to do based on our relationship.

I had no plans for the future, nor did I think I needed any. My degree in French literature hadn't prepared me for a job, but it was 1970, the spirit of the sixties lived on, so who cared? The words "upward mobility" and "ambition" hadn't yet made their way into my vocabulary. It never entered my mind to think seriously about how I'd pay rent or buy my next Joe Cocker album.

I felt I could do anything. Not only was I white and educated, I was also young, smart and enthusiastic, all of which would help me in the world. As Crosby, Stills, Nash and Young reminded us burgeoning baby boomers: We are stardust. We are golden.

So who cared if I had a job?

My parents, naturally.

I began to dread routine calls home to Detroit every Sunday. I couldn't bear to hear my mother ask for the zillionth time, "Do you have a job yet?" But one Sunday my mother surprised me. "Daddy and I want to come to your graduation."

"My graduation? I wasn't even thinking of going. No one I know is going." I spared her the rhetoric, but going to your graduation wasn't something you did in those anti-establishment days. We had more important things to do, but of course, I couldn't name them.

"Ma, it will be stupid. They're not going to talk about anything important."

"What is it you want them to talk about?"

"About *real* issues on everybody's mind. Like the riots, like Vietnam, about the students shot at Kent State, the assassinations of President Kennedy, Malcolm X, Robert Kennedy and Martin Luther King."

"We just want to see you graduate, Linda. We're very proud of you."

They were proud of me? That's all she had to say.

"… Sure, Ma. If it will bring you and Daddy *nachas*, come. We'll go to my graduation." I had planned to come back to Detroit when classes let out, but I'd stay the extra week. I even had the grace to add, "I think it's nice you want to see me graduate."

They were my family, and I truly hoped to bring them a little pride. It wasn't easy considering the life I chose. My parents' friends had been *shepping nachas* for years from their children's law degrees, marriages, babies and good jobs. Though they liked Jeffrey, he wasn't bragging material.

"I'm still hoping you'll date Jewish guys," my mother said whenever the subject of Jeffrey came up in conversation, which wasn't often.

During the years I ignored their preferred script for me, my parents still kept up with phone calls and visits, put up with my politics, general moodiness, griping and political rhetoric. And, to my great delight, my father never once stopped sending his legendary "care" packages.

I was always curious to see what new gems my dad added to his usual monthly mix of regulars — cans of tuna and sardines, boxes of wholegrain Wheatena cereal, white-shelled pistachios and bags of figs, dried apricots and lima beans. What surprise would be in his package this month? Mothballs and rubber bands again like last month? Or perhaps another hard-boiled-egg-slicer and apple-corer like the month before that?

I always wanted to know how and why my dad decided what new items to put in. Did he see a melon-ball scooper in a hardware store and decide his college student daughter desperately needed one? Or did he think, "I bet Linda could really use a ball of jute twine," and then go shopping specially for it? Whichever, those boxes were always precious to me.

Other than fairly decent marks throughout my college years, there had been little else my parents could boast to their friends about. And to my mother, particularly, boasting meant the world. So I booked them a nice hotel close to the auditorium where commencement was being held. I then crossed my fingers that they wouldn't ask to see where I was living.

It wouldn't be long. To graduation I would go.

With a week to go before graduation, houses on our street emptied as classes ended and students trickled home to summer jobs. Six of my housemates were gone. Three were left behind. Lorne, who lived upstairs; Rosie, a close girlfriend; and me. I would be the next to go. In one week, after graduation, I would pack my worldly belongings into my parents' car, and drive back to Detroit to spend the summer sorting out what came next.

One night, four days before graduation and three before my parents' arrival, Rosie, Lorne and I walked out our front door onto the raised front porch. It sat atop an elegant wrought-iron staircase with railings that led up many stairs from the street-level garden below. I crouched down on the top step, Rosie took the lone chair. Lorne leaned against the railing.

We sipped iced coffee and nibbled watermelon, spitting seeds into the garden below, noting how different the street felt without the usual hubbub.

Looking down the street, I saw Tom, the neighbourhood cop, coming towards us on his nightly beat. Washington's police department was trying to improve community relations to cut down on crime, and beat-walking cops were part of the program.

"Hello up there," Tom yelled to us. Normally, we'd respond with an invitation for a chat and cold drink. But not that night. We were too hot to engage in even the minimum of chitchat. Tom hung around for an offer, but when none came, started to move on. Before disappearing, he called up, "It's a hot one, all right, so be careful. Things are different around here these days."

We didn't really know what he meant and were too hot to care. "I can barely see him walk down the street," I commented, only seconds after Tom moved past the house. Though the streetlights were on as usual, it was unusually dark and noticeably quiet, making me feel slightly unnerved.

A while after Tom left, I saw the silhouettes of five young men across the street. They were coming our way, acting loud, crude and badass. When they noticed the three of us sitting on the porch, they stopped and huddled in conversation, too far away for us to hear. When they broke out of their huddle, they turned around and started walking away.

With my relief came white-person's shame. Shame for feeling

afraid. Shame for being afraid because the men were black. Shame I felt unsafe because they were black. Shame because I thought they were drunk, maybe high and possibly dangerous. Shame because it meant I was guilty of racial stereotyping. It was what anyone with a conscience in 1970 was desperately trying to rid the world of. We were all too aware of our country's history of stereotyping, falsely arresting and lynching black men for crimes they did not commit. In my head, Billie Holiday was singing:

Southern trees bear a strange fruit
Blood on the leaves and blood on the root
Black body swinging in the Southern Breeze
Strange fruit hanging from poplar trees.

I was busy chastising myself when I saw the men turn around once more. They were crossing the street, running in our direction. Without a word, Rosie, Lorne and I jumped up, turned towards the door and reached for the handle. The men were at the bottom of our steps.

They started running up. Only ten steps to go before they reached us. We had one, maybe two seconds to get in the house. It looked good. We would make it.

"Hey, man, be cool," one of them yelled up, friendly-like. "Why you all runnin' way like that? We just lookin' to score pot."

In the nanosecond we paused to listen, our grace period slipped away. Three men pulled revolvers from their pockets. One, cold and hard, was pressed to my right temple. Shoving me towards the door, its owner yelled, "Get in the house."

Rosie and Lorne were told to lie on the bed in the front bedroom and cover their faces with pillows. I was led to a back bedroom, told to do the same. As footsteps approached me, lights in my head began to darken. I had the feeling that my body was separating from my soul right then, whisking me into some inexplicable state that would help me survive the horror of what came next.

Despite a vagueness engulfing me, I had one moment of remarkable clarity. I experienced the "life passing before me" moment. I *knew* in a way I had never known before or since, how much I wanted to live. Life wasn't something I was casually passing through. There was so much more yet to be. For all the ugliness the world held, it also offered good. I knew more was yet to come.

If I came out alive, it would be a blessing. No matter what happened.

I closed my eyes and prayed to the same god I prayed to as a child. It was the one I asked to make my parents stop fighting and keep the bogeyman at bay. Please dear god, keep me safe to see the morning light.

I lay on the bed afterwards for what seemed like hours. Were they still in the house? I thought I heard them leave, but maybe they were upstairs, rummaging around. What if they came down and heard me calling 911? I was paralyzed with fear that they'd come back. I had no sense of how much time was passing. I just lay there, not moving. Rosie and Lorne, still in the other room, did the same. We didn't even call out to each other.

What may have been half an hour later, I heard Rosie yell out meekly. "Leenda?"

I got up slowly and went to them in the next room. I gasped when I saw Lorne. He had been tied up in the same room with Rosie, obviously helpless, unable to protect her. He couldn't look at either of us. It was then I knew Rosie had been raped, too.

A cruiser came and sat in front of the house, lights flashing red circles through the night's still impossibly thick air. Two uniformed policemen led Rosie and me out of the house. They were taking us to the hospital. They headed Lorne to another car, to the station.

The days, even weeks that followed, disappeared from memory. Only a few moments remained. Being mocked by a nurse when I arrived at the hospital because I had put my shirt back on inside out. The pained, helpless sound in Jeffrey's voice when I called the next morning. The mean, jeering taunts hurled at Rosie and me from police suspects piled behind bars that we were forced to look at in the back of a paddy wagon.

The only thing keeping me sane were the lyrics I kept singing over and over in my head from a song James Taylor had just released. Using his words like a mantra, I kept repeating *Fire and Rain*, rain, fire, lonely times, find a friend, see you again, fire and rain, rain and fire. His lyrics gave me much-needed solace, the way a jilted lover takes comfort in songs of heartbreak. I was also trying keep my mind filled every single second, hoping to block it from screaming... "I've been raped."

My sister Barbara and childhood friend Sybil flew down from Detroit to Washington to handhold me through the round of hospital examinations, police interrogations and line-ups that lay ahead. They did the right thing. Being 1970, the world was still not a kind place for sexually assaulted women. Neither my roommate Rosie nor I were treated well by the many cops, doctors or nurses. I badly needed someone to speak for me and remind everyone I was the victim.

I never told my parents what happened. I had been sparing them the details of my life for years. They missed out on my first kiss, dalliance with drugs, hitchhiking mishaps and serendipitous late-night trysts. Children keep things from their parents. But not telling them about the attack was different. I knew that secrets this big held power. It would separate me from them forever. They could never possibly know or understand me again.

I didn't think I had a choice about keeping the secret. Perhaps there was some hidden shame, even guilt behind it. Rape victims often feel both. If so, I wasn't aware of either. I just felt I was protecting myself. Protecting myself from them. I knew from past experiences that my father would become bitter. Instead of lamenting what the world had done to him, this time it would be what the world had done to his baby girl.

My mother would have somehow made me feel bad, no matter how unintentional. She wouldn't have blamed me for what happened exactly, but would somehow plant seeds leaving me with self-doubt.

So I did what my mother did — what I promised as a child I would never do. I kept a big, dark secret. I was doing what I had come to believe my mother had done about my grandmother: I was protecting myself from what other people, including the people I loved, might think, say or feel. For the first time in my life, I understood what may have motivated my mother. Telling the truth wasn't worth the risk.

I never doubted the wisdom of keeping silent. Yet I often longed for the comfort I know a parent can give a hurting child. I wished I'd had a relationship that didn't demand secrecy. Perhaps telling my parents might have helped me to release, then incorporate my pain rather than repress it. Maybe that would have kept it from tearing its head unexpectedly when I least expected it on that flight from Tampa so many years later.

My parents arrived for graduation right after my sister and Sybil left. I was uncommunicative, though not altogether different from how I had been for years. My parents chalked up my sullenness to being sad to leave Washington and worried about my future. I never said otherwise.

I went to my graduation. I had absolutely no memory of who spoke or what was said. I could not remember shaking hands with the dean or accepting my diploma. My parents told me I was there.

I never once looked at my parents' many snapshots of the occasion. When they both died more than twenty years later, pictures of Linda's Graduation Day 1970 also died, unclaimed and unlamented, along with them.

3.
Seeking Safety and Solace in a New Country
Detroit to Toronto, 1970

I WENT BACK TO DETROIT that summer to heal, as if healing is something you *do*. But the Detroit I went back to was different from the one I had left. My parents had experienced their own trauma in the intervening years.

While still at Michigan State University, I had gone to Europe with Sybil, my childhood friend from Detroit. At an outdoor café, I glanced at the newspaper sitting on the next table. "Detroit in Flames" read the headlines in the *International Herald Tribune*. I knew what it meant. Newark, New Jersey, had already gone up in smoke from racial riots that summer. Thirty-five people had been killed.

I called home. My dad answered. He was barely able to talk. "What's wrong?" I asked.

"We'll talk when you get home," he said.

"What about the store?" His jewelry store was downtown, right where the riots were.

He handed the phone to my mother.

"There's nothing to tell you, Linda." She was firm and un-convincing.

"I hate it when you keep things from me," I said. "If there's something I should know, I want to know now. Not when I come home."

"Daddy was hit pretty bad," she eventually conceded. "They smashed the front windows and took everything out of the display cases. They ran inside, took what they could carry or stuff in pockets — watches, wedding rings, gold necklaces, even

NOT EXACTLY AS PLANNED

the light-up Madonnas." Lit canisters were thrown in the store, so it was damaged by fire and smoke. "Daddy's heartbroken."

To help end the riots, Governor George Romney ordered the Michigan National Guard into Detroit, and President Lyndon B. Johnson sent Army troops. After five days, 2000 buildings were destroyed; 1139 people were injured, and 7200 arrested. Forty-three people died. The youngest was Tonya Blanding, aged four, killed by gunfire from a National Guard tank when her father lit a cigarette near the window of their darkened apartment.

Max's Jewelry Company on Detroit's Chene Street was the ma-and-pop jewelry store my grandfather opened in 1910 after fleeing pogroms in Poland. Next to his family, the store was the love of my dad's life. He worked hard, never got rich, never intended to. He doted on his customers, mainly Polish, black, Italian. There were also the "hillbillies," the men from Mississippi and Alabama who came to work at Chrysler or Ford, who asked to put their wedding rings on "lay-away" so they could pay a few dollars each week until the ring was paid off. "I never ask them to do any paperwork," my dad once told me. "Most can't read or sign their name except with an X. I don't want to embarrass them."

My dad was a gentle, unworldly, idealistic man who believed family was all. Though marital bliss wasn't much evident in our household considering my parents' frequent fights, my dad still extolled family life and cherished its sweetness. I knew he hoped I would marry young and have children soon after. He undoubtedly planted seeds for the domestic future I invented for myself. My oldest sister Barbara had married at eighteen. I knew my dad hoped the same for me.

Like me, my dad loved children, was shy and sensitive. Whenever I needed help figuring out the world, I would join him after dinner in our book-laden den where he'd recline in his Lay-Z-Boy. I'd plop myself down near the TV table beside him. While he cracked walnuts and cut apples for us, I'd ask: "Why did kids at school say I would burn in hell?"

"Why were the women who cleaned houses all Negro?"

"Why did the lady at the fruit store have blue numbers painted on her arm?"

"How many trees are there in the Amazon?"

Though I never got an acceptable answer about the trees, my dad's other answers taught me about being Jewish, about being "other" and why some people don't like you because of it. I knew my dad was happy when I asked what he called "your hard questions." I was proud that everyone said I took after him. And not only because we both had the same big, bright blue eyes — eyes I once heard referred to as the legacy of a thousand pogroms. I was proud I inherited his idealism. I always felt loved and protected by my father. I used to think my dad saved my life when I was a child, though I was never sure from what.

I hung up the phone after talking to my mother about the riots and returned to the table in the café where Sybil was waiting.

"He's too fragile for this," I said. "My dad doesn't have good survivor skills. You know how idealistic he is. I'm afraid he won't recover." My father saw young men he knew break his windows, reach in and take loot, set his store on fire. Never in a lifetime could he understand what would bring someone to do that.

Though I was nineteen at the time, I was already becoming aware of something my dad didn't seem to know. Our lives are not solely determined by what happens to us. How we deal with what happens is what matters.

Several weeks after my return home in Detroit, I received a letter from the courts in Washington. They had arrested possible suspects. Would I come testify? I was pleased to hear they had followed up on our case, but knew it would be a mistake to go. My sister and friends agreed. I had already been poorly treated by police and health professionals. I didn't need one more person hurting me.

In 1970, the law, cops, courts, jurors or judges seldom took the side of a rape victim. Five years later, in 1975, Rape Shield Laws were passed in the U.S. Before then, an accuser with any previous sexual history in a rape case was *not* presumed innocent. That changed with the law, which also prohibited publication of the identity of an alleged rape victim, and threw out the requirement that rape victims *prove* they had resisted their attackers. We owed these changes in the law to the women's movement of the 1970s. Reform of rape laws was one of its top priorities. I wished those changes had come sooner.

So I stayed put in Detroit. Gone were plans, thoughts and dreams for my future. Also gone was any semblance of my confident, adventurous way of being in the world. Interest in any political cause vanished, too. It was me I had to take care of now.

I stayed with my parents in the apartment they moved into after three home robberies sent them fleeing to the suburbs. My childhood bedroom was only a memory. This new, gated complex in suburbia felt foreign and cold, but it was now the only home I had.

I took refuge in a spare bedroom, watching TV and reading old copies of my mother's *Ladies' Home Journal* and *Woman's Day* stored in an old nightstand. My parents were smart enough to keep away from me. They still had no idea of the trauma I had just been through, and chalked up my moodiness to post-graduation confusion. I joined them now and again for meals at the kitchen table when the familiar smells of my mother's chicken soup, chopped liver or brisket permeated the hazy miasma I was orbiting in.

I spent little time that summer talking about what had happened. My friends Barbara and Sybil and my sister Barbara knew, but I seldom spoke about the rape to them. They were patiently waiting for me to unload. It never happened. For the first time in my life, something felt beyond words. I was shell-shocked. What was there to say?

I tried to avoid thinking about it, let alone talking about it. It wasn't easy. It was the first thing that entered my consciousness every morning, ducking mercilessly in and out until I lay down on the pillow at night. It didn't only appear in the form of words or even images. I had a visceral reaction, as if the psychic aftermath of my terror had seeped into my gut and was metastasizing throughout my body until it colonized every cell and pore.

I spoke to my roommate Rosie several times during the summer, but neither of us could find much to say. Each of us was full-up with our own pain. We couldn't take on each other's. We just wanted assurance the other was doing fine. It never came.

"I'm still upset it was stolen," Rosie said during our initial call, referring to the first serious camera I ever owned, stolen in Washington. My Ricoh 35mm SLR. In it was a fully exposed roll of film shot the weekend before, documenting a happy, carefree Linda and Rosie visiting Coney Island, the last remaining evidence of girls who no longer existed.

I also spoke to Jeffrey periodically, still in Washington, but neither of us knew what to say. We both needed a script, mine telling me how to get someone to think I was listening even when I wasn't because the screams inside my head were driving everything else away.

I was sad we had not made it through to this period, yet realistic enough to know any relationship with a man, particularly physical, would be more burden than comfort.

After a couple of months at my parents' apartment, I began to feel a shift.

I phoned my sister. "I feel ready to move on, but I might be blocking stuff I should be dealing with." She made an appointment for me with a well-known psychiatrist. I answered

NOT EXACTLY AS PLANNED

questions he hurled at me, more voyeuristic than therapeutic.
I wasn't strong enough not to. After twenty minutes he took
his glasses off, leaned forward in his chair and pronounced
with great certainty, "You're fine. The experience wasn't that
significant. You're handling it well. Congratulations."

Idiot.

At the end of the summer, I received a call from my friend Barbara. Barbara had been living in Toronto since she graduated
from Michigan State. She loved Toronto and was making a
life there.

"I've been waiting until you were ready before I asked," she
said. "Why don't you come up for a while and check it out
here?" She was working on our friend Sybil to do the same.

I liked the idea of the three of us being together again. And
no small thing, anti-war Americans like me had a warm spot in
our hearts for a Canada that had opened its doors to our draft
dodgers and military deserters. I could make a loud statement
of thanks with my feet.

I called Sybil.

"Let's do it," she said.

Days later, in early September of 1970, I announced to my
incredulous family that we were moving to Toronto. My dad
offered his station wagon to haul our stuff, mostly tie-dyed
T-shirts, jeans, work shirts, Indian skirts and Moroccan bead
jewelry; my Motown collection; cherished books by James Baldwin, *Les Fleurs du Mal* by Baudelaire and Thoreau's *Walden*.
I bought myself a brand new Pentax 35mm SLR camera.

Sybil and I hit the road. We planned to get landed at the
border. Being landed meant the Canadian government would
grant us official status as permanent residents. It would allow
us to live and work in Canada indefinitely. Most hopeful
immigrants did not try to get landed at the border. It was
seldom successful. The usually long-drawn-out bureaucratic
procedure took months, even years to complete. It was best

undertaken at home through the mail.

We drove my dad's car through the tunnel underneath the Detroit River to the border checkpoint in Windsor, Ontario. Nervous, and unsure, Sybil walked up to the immigration officers behind the desk, "We'd like to get landed, please."

"Just like that, eh?" one of the officers asked. The others looked on, smirking. The men sat us down, and pulled out forms. We had to answer a series of questions, including work prospects, whether we spoke French, where we would live in Toronto, and how much money we were bringing in. Depending on our responses, the officer would assign a certain number of points. At the end of the interview if we had enough points, we were in. Landed. If not, homeward bound. They never asked for any proof or documentation, not that we had any. They put their papers down, and one of the officers looked at us.

"You hit the jackpot," he said. We were landed.

We had no real, useful job skills, little money and no evidence of future employment to prove we wouldn't be a financial burden to our new country. What *did* we have going then? We were young, white, smart, cheerful females. What harm could we possibly do?

I pulled my dad's car onto the MacDonald-Cartier Highway 401, the long, flat stretch of road that would take us to Toronto in four hours. While I drove, Sybil reeled off the names of places we were passing with British-sounding names.

"Chatham," she first said, then "Ingersoll, Woodstock, London and Stratford." We even passed the river Thames outside of London.

It made me hopeful. Maybe this new country would be far enough and foreign enough for me to leave my recent past behind.

Or so I had hoped.

Toronto was a peaceful, welcoming city. It gave me exactly

what I needed, a feeling of safety. I was still a city girl, and no major city in the United States at that time came close to fitting the bill.

Sybil and I moved into a downtown neighbourhood near Kensington Market on a street lined with narrow, single-family Victorian row houses. Our house was one of the many communes in the burgeoning American ex-pat ghetto developing smack in the middle of a Chinese neighbourhood.

Toronto wasn't exciting like Washington, but I was no longer looking for exciting. I was looking for a safe haven.

Many of the estimated 50,000 young Americans who came to Canada during the Vietnam-war era lived in communes near me around Beverley and Baldwin Streets. We created a tight, counterculture community packed with draft dodgers, deserters, students and other wayward souls who weren't quite ready to get on with the practical matters of their lives.

At night, Sybil and I would often go for dinner at Grossman's Tavern, the slightly down-on-its heels union-style beer hall and restaurant on the corner of Spadina Avenue and Cecil Street. We always found a little bit of home there. The elderly Jewish Mrs. Grossman gave many of us what was missing from our lives at the time — the feeling that someone cared. She'd load up our dinner plates with greasy potato knishes and cabbage rolls *mit* extra dollops of sour cream, always followed by kind words and a big smile.

Later in the night, with the dishes cleared away, we'd line our arborite tables with sudsy-looking pitchers of draft beer and listen to The Downchild Blues Band or David Clayton-Thomas. We'd loudly debate American foreign policy and inadvertently pick up bits and pieces of the Canadian culture we had come to embrace.

Despite all the wonders I was discovering, Toronto still didn't feel like home, whatever I needed home to be. I had no past, no history or cultural references to the city or country. I was uprooted and disconnected. I was lonely, afraid of the night, unsure of what I was doing, what work I should look for, who I wanted to be with and who I wanted to be.

Within a month of my arrival, I had landed a sales job at Britnell's, a bookstore where Barbara was working. I was hired to help out until Christmas, but it was a miracle I managed to keep the job considering my performance within a month after starting.

Britnell's was a quiet, library-like, traditional English-style bookstore on busy Yonge Street, with floor-to-ceiling oak bookshelves and sliding ladders to retrieve books from upper shelves. It was known for its quiet, genteel ambiance, which one day I managed to seriously betray. Screaming "Oh, my god," I frantically ran through the store, back to front, having just spotted a handsome, slightly dishevelled Jeffrey walking through Britnell's front door, with guitar case in hand and grinning from ear to ear. He had arrived unannounced and unexpectedly from Washington to be with me. I was shocked, flattered and ready to give the relationship one more try.

The mostly elderly saleswomen at Britnell's thought our dramatic, happy front-door reunion was charming, romantic and straight out of a Harlequin romance novel. The senior Mr. Albert Britnell, the store's owner, who came to work each morning in spats and a pin-striped suit, didn't share the saleswomen's sentiments about my embrace with Jeffrey. He didn't fire me, but I was "reassigned" unceremoniously one day shortly after Jeffrey's arrival. I was released from covering the store's *Fiction* section and banished to the Siberian hinterland of *Nature* and *Cookbooks*.

Jeffrey and I lived together for over a year, for the most part happily. A musician and serious opera buff, Jeffrey eventually found work in the classical music department at Sam the Record Man at Yonge and Dundas Streets. It kept him happy for a while.

In time, though, we knew things weren't going to work.

He had fast-tracked his master's degree in history at George Washington and longed to teach in his field. He didn't have the right papers to "officially" work in Toronto and wasn't sure Toronto was where he should be, anyway. Like other people I knew from the West Coast, Jeffrey was terribly homesick. These were parts of his life he understandably couldn't give up for the uncertainty of what Toronto and I could give him.

He moved back to his hometown, Seattle. I didn't go with him. My life was still sketchy, undefined and too fragile to pack up and start over again. I was beginning to feel I belonged in Canada, not in the States. Maybe if I believed Jeffrey was *the one*, I would have gone. And maybe if I were *the one* for Jeffrey, he might have stayed. But timing was everything. Our ability to commit to one another, or in my case, to anyone at all was still way off. Washington, DC, still held a tight-fisted grip on me.

After Jeffrey left Toronto, I flitted from one guy to the next.

"You're making up for lost time," my mother said. "You didn't have a real boyfriend until you went to college."

"Maybe that's it, then," I responded. But I was lying. My mother didn't know what happened to me in Washington, so was missing an important piece in the Linda puzzle. It was becoming more and more clear to me that what happened in Washington continued to affect my relationships with men, and that included Jeffrey. Though my desire to be married and have children began bubbling up again in my early twenties, it was only in the abstract. The reality seemed further away than ever.

Four years later, in 1974, I met a man named Alexander Ross who would put in motion the chain of events that dramatically changed my life. I was twenty-six when I met Sandy, a charmingly boyish, brilliant, mildly eccentric journalist of legendary short attention span.

Sandy was thirteen years older than me and at a significantly different stage in his life, particularly regarding work. Since my degree in French literature wasn't getting me anywhere in the job market, I had gone back to school the year before Sandy and I met and earned a Diploma in Public Health from the University of Toronto. But even with my new specialization, I was still floundering about what to do with my life. Sandy, on the other hand, already had a successful career behind him. He had recently become editor of the trendy city magazine *Toronto Life* after years as a columnist for the *Financial Post* and *Toronto Star*. Before that, he was London correspondent for United Press International (UPI), and managing editor of *Maclean's*.

To my horror as well as that of my friends, Sandy, for all his ostensible charm, intelligence, wit and good looks, was a political small c-conservative.

Sandy, known to be extremely generous with young talent, encouraged me to write. He assigned me my first commissioned magazine piece, an article for *Canadian Business*. Edited by his then managing editor Margaret Wente, it won a National Magazine Award. On the strength of the article, I was hired to work on a public affairs talk show at CITY-TV. It proved to be a major stepping-stone in my work life.

One late summer night, fairly soon into our relationship, Sandy said he wanted to take me someplace special, a place he was surprised I hadn't already visited since I had come to Toronto. We drove down to a dreary, relatively undeveloped industrial area along the city's waterfront on Queen's Quay, parked the car, and walked to the dour cement-grey ferry docks run by the city government. We bought round-trip tickets for two dollars and boarded a large two-storey black and white ferry. At the toot of a horn, the dockmen lifted the gangplank and the ferry drifted slowly into the shimmering waters of Lake Ontario.

Just over ten minutes later, the captain pulled into the docks at Wards Island, one of fifteen little islands that comprise an archipelago called Toronto Island. It didn't take me long to realize I had landed in another world.

Coming off the boat, we walked towards the nearby club-house, passing through the perfume of linden trees planted along the path. At the side of the blue-painted clubhouse, adults were lawn bowling while barefoot children and untethered dogs ran playfully around the village green. To my left, I could see a large cluster of cottage-like houses nestled cheek to jowl in rows separated by sidewalks. Drifting around us were the sounds of people talking, dogs barking and the slight hum of the city.

"Considering all these sounds," I said to Sandy, "there's a remarkable quiet here."

"Look around," Sandy said. "Do you notice anything missing?"

"No streets, no traffic ... no cars." For a girl from Motor City, this was astounding.

"Wards Island," Sandy said. "One of the few carless communities left in the world."

Sandy and I walked into the area where the houses stood, past freshly washed laundry hung out to dry on lines tied from tree to tree across tiny yards. People were walking up and down the streets, interrupting their chats to smile and say hello to us. A pod of children's tricycles sat parked in the middle of a sidewalk while excited owners exalted in the black and yellow garter snake soaking up warmth on the sun-drenched pavement.

"Wanna see a live snake?" they asked as we passed.

"Sure do."

The word charming didn't begin to describe what I saw. Of course I had heard about the Island and this community, but I had been so entrenched in my narrow little corner of Toronto's landscape that I hadn't branched out much. I now thought it unfathomable that I hadn't come to the Island before this. I was in love with the place.

"Let's find a place to rent," I said.

As luck would have it, Sandy's managing editor at *Toronto*

Life lived full-time on the Island. She and her boyfriend were soon leaving for a holiday.

For the month of August, Sandy and I lived in a two-bedroom cottage facing an inland lagoon. Month's end came too quickly. We wanted to live on the Island full-time. Sandy was outgrowing Rosedale, his upscale downtown neighbourhood, and ready for this new adventure. As for me, the time had come to leave the security of my ghetto behind.

In 1974, competition for houses to buy or rent on the Island was stiff, surprising since the local government was making serious noise about demolishing the Island community to make way for development. But Sandy and I had a better chance than most people to find a place. Islanders had a warm spot for Sandy because of his *Toronto Star* columns railing against the government's planned demolition. So when an elderly Island couple decided to retire to the country, they telephoned Sandy and offered us first shot to rent their tired-looking Insulbrick bungalow of no apparent charm. We grabbed it.

The fit was good for me on the Island. I could start building a new life for myself. I thanked my lucky stars that not only did this anachronistically charming village exist, but also that I was led to it. It was a long way from Detroit, even further from Washington, and had all the makings of home.

We moved into a community of roughly 650 people at last count, though no one knew for sure when the last count was or if anyone was actually counting. Islanders inhabited 250 small, wood-frame, cottage-like homes nestled on a twenty-seven-acre sandbar, roughly one and a half miles long and a ten-minute ferry ride across the bay from downtown Toronto.

We had meadows, a beach, two community clubhouses, a café, a canoe club and enough community meetings fuelled by fire and brimstone to rival electoral debates in a New Hampshire Town Hall.

The community sat on two islands, Wards and Algonquin,

at the eastern end of a collection of seventeen small islands covering 591 acres called Toronto Island Park. Close to a million people visited the park every year, mainly in summer and mainly to the two other major islands in the system — Centre Island and Hanlan's Point.

Our community was separated from the hullabaloo of summer visitors by a buffer of woods, meadows and unmowed grassland that kept our space light years away from the crowds and urban-like atmosphere in the larger park.

Yet for all my love of the place, there was nothing convenient about living on the Island. City people who came in summer said, "You live in Paradise."

I laughed. "Come back mid-February during a snowstorm," I said. "Maybe we can house trade." There were no stores. Nowhere to buy food or toilet paper, or pick up an extra pair of socks on a cold day. We had to bring everything we owned, ate or drank by boat from the city.

No motorized form of transportation was allowed on the Island other than garbage or maintenance trucks, a school bus and a snowplow. It left us dependent on our feet or bicycles to get from place to place. We relied on carts, wagons and shopping buggies we called "bundle buggies" to *shlep* all manner of goods from the city back home to the Island. Whether bringing home a new fridge, case of twenty-four, a watermelon or a first-born child, that's what you did. It didn't matter if it was raining, sleeting, hailing or snowing, we *shlepped*.

Sandy and I lived together on the Island for three years, until the late 1970s. Somewhere along the way we realized the inevitable: we were at very different stages in our lives. It was time for each to move on.

I had gained confidence from our relationship and for the first time in years felt safe enough to dream again about having a family. But Sandy, at that time, did not share those dreams. He already had a family. I would have to find someone else to share my domestic dreams with — I knew I could never be happy in a marriage without children. When Sandy and I broke up, he returned to the city, a practical decision considering his career demands. I stayed on the Island. Alone, but unafraid. My past long behind me. Or so I thought.

After the airplane debacle in 1980, I opened up the Washington memory and could not easily close it. Therapy had begun in earnest. During the year of gruelling, gut-wrenching sessions, I relived my night of terror in Washington. I wept, screamed, cried and pounded. All to let out the horrors that had been locked inside for so long. It had taken me ten years to face them.

When I began my weekly appointments, I was still living alone on the Island. I was trying to lead my life and function day-to-day as best I could. On the surface I carried it off, but it was hard. I had become claustrophobic and couldn't go anywhere I felt trapped or couldn't escape from if I felt danger. Meaning, I was afraid to get into elevators (which could get stuck between floors) or onto the subway (which often stopped in between stations). I needed both to get to work.

Sometimes I became so physically drained and emotionally weak after a session, I couldn't make it back home and would have to stay in the city at Barbara's or at the house of another close friend, Ellie. They fed me and put me to sleep. I lost more than forty pounds over the course of the therapy. Thinner than ever before in my life, I spared people my discomfort when they'd say "You've never looked better." I'd never felt worse.

Miraculously, I didn't stop working. Three months before my trip to Tampa to see my parents, I had started a demanding job at CITY-TV. I was a researcher and story producer for *The Shulman File*, a one-hour public affairs talk show hosted by television personality, politician, city coroner and prankster, Dr. Morton Shulman. Amongst many other duties, I had to become an expert in whatever current issue we chose for Shulman to debate on air.

A prescription of Valium made all of this possible. Without it, I wouldn't have left the house. Part of me wanted to do just that, not leave, but everyone advised against it. Their judgment was good. So was the Valium.

I landed the job at CITY-TV following the investigative article I had written for *Canadian Business*. The producer of *The Shulman File* happened to read it. She decided my skills were exactly what she was looking for. Would I like a job? I would, indeed.

When my panic attacks began, I was mid-season into production of the show. As long as I could keep up the façade at work, I would. The job paid my bills and stopped me from constantly thinking about myself. I swallowed a five-mg hit of Valium with coffee in the morning to send me off to work, another with a sandwich at lunch to get me through the day.

I made it through the production season, sure that no one at the TV station, including the producer, had a clue about my inner turmoil, though I may have been kidding myself. Showing a stunning lack of ambition, I never made any attempt to work my way into a higher position or asked to learn editing, directing and production skills.

Though I had made considerable progress reducing my anxiety in therapy, I knew that working in television was too fast-paced and stressful for me, even without my present problems. Fortunately, I was offered a job at City Hall doing health promotion and communications work.

The feeling "I'm going crazy" had slowly subsided during the first year in therapy, but by the second year, while in my new job, something else replaced the fear. The butterflies were back in my gut, though they were falling into a pit rather than fluttering. It made me feel as though I was sinking into a dark, gloomy hole, flapping through my body with despair, slipping into a clinical depression. I experienced dark, dark days. Coupled with a genetic propensity for the illness inherited from both my mother and father's family, the rigours of such intense therapy had been too tough. Forcing me to dig so deeply into my pain had exhausted me. Pulling up the residue of anger, fear, and powerlessness from years past sent my body chemistry haywire, downhill haywire.

It was time to find someone else who could put me back together. Again. Barbara, Ellie and I called anyone in our network we thought might know a therapist who would be right for me in my present state. We were now wary.

After a month, Ellie found the person we were looking for at the Clarke, the same institution I had begged Barbara to take me to two years before, after the airplane debacle. But if I had gone with Barbara then, entry would have been through the backdoor emergency entrance. This time, Ellie and I pushed open the institution's plate-glass front doors off College Street, and headed straight to an outpatient office for an appointment with a world-renowned psycho-pharmacologist who specialized in treating depression.

I noticed very quickly that while the doctor was asking basic questions about my depression and its origin, he wasn't pressing me to go into any great detail, or to go back too far into my life history. He gave me a standard chart to fill out to determine just how depressed I was, asking questions about sleep and eating patterns, thoughts of suicide, whether I wanted to be with people or withdraw, whether I suffered from guilt or shame and if I saw the future with optimism or pessimism.

Whatever the doctor needed from me on the chart, he got. Results from a blood test helped him reaffirm that the heavy-duty psychoanalysis I had been through played havoc with my body, contributing to my depression. Putting me back together was now a matter of raising serotonin levels back to normal. Enough talk therapy. It was time for medication to build me up.

The psycho-pharmacologist tried me on several drugs at different doses until he found the right combination with the least side effects. I could feel the Prozac kick in after three weeks.

By one month, I was back to being me. Neither high me, nor low me, just me. I had forgotten who that was.

The doctor slowly weaned me off the Valium I was still taking to help me function — not daily, but often. I still carried one pill in my purse, just in case I got caught in an elevator or subway. My past feelings of being trapped without an escape hatch still lurked. One year after starting the anti-depressants, I took the Valium vial out of my pocket and threw it into the wastebasket.

To my great disappointment, though, I needed a five-mg hit of the anti-anxiety medication to get me through one of the happiest evenings of my life. I had been nominated for a National Magazine Award for my article in *Canadian Business*. I was still a little shaky, worried that such a big public occasion might overwhelm me. I was doing well, but still haunted by the horrible years I had just come through. I worried about being in a room with hundreds of other people; having to smile, walk, talk and act normal. And what if, by any chance, I won and had to walk up on stage to receive the award with the whole room looking at me? What if I went crazy in the middle of it or had to escape?

One week after the awards dinner, the postman shoved a large manila envelope through the mail slot in my front door. I ripped it open, knowing what it was: a glossy photograph of me beaming as I accepted the Award. The picture also exhibited my smiling face framed on a too-skinny body wearing the dazzling pink, purple and red floral silk wrap-around dress I had bought at Holt Renfrew for the occasion. Only I knew that my convincing smile and beautiful dress hid a still fragile, vulnerable soul.

4.

Toronto's Safe Harbours: Marriage and Adoption
Toronto and Toronto Island, 1983

A FTER A YEAR ON ANTI-DEPRESSANTS, I became stable. I put on weight, had a social life, but most importantly, I could think about the well-being of people other than myself. Instead of wondering how I was going to make it through the next day (and whether I wanted to), I could start thinking about my future.

I realized in therapy that I had been afraid to get too close to a man for the last decade — specifically, since Washington. Even with Jeffrey and Sandy, men I cared about deeply, I wasn't able to make a real commitment. I was afraid of being trapped. I wasn't the first woman, or man, to equate signing a marriage register with trepidation. But the trepidation only represented part of me. Through all the zigs and zags in my life, I never stopped longing for the day I'd be married and have a family.

It was time for a change. Enough time had passed. I was ready to find the person referred to in those days as Mr. Right. My single life on the Island had become too comfy-cozy. I wasn't reaching out to new people. People, as in single men. I had to get strategic.

"I'm moving to the city for a year," I told my Island friends.

"You're what?"

"Don't worry, I'll be back," I said. "I'm only moving off for a year. I'll meet a guy and bring him back to the Island," I added, with the false certainty of a first-time politician running against the incumbent.

A month later, I moved into a renovated attic in a charming, red-brick Victorian row house in the Annex area of the city. I loved the ease of a city life with buses, subways, hardware stores, cleaners. A 24-hour pizza joint at my doorstep was all a girl could ask for.

One night, several weeks after my move, I received a phone call from my friend, Judy. She had a plan. Did it have anything to do with my search for Mr. Right?

Yes, in fact, it did. Judy, also single, suggested we take out a personal classified in our national newspaper, *The Globe and Mail*. A writer for the paper, she received free ads as a job perk. We should muster the courage and do it, she said.

Courage was right. Running a personal was not something anyone we knew did, unless looking for a used vacuum or chesterfield. It was 1983, after all, light years before the advent of Lavalife, J-date or eHarmony.com.

We chose not to write a regular "personal," one requiring us to describe ourselves and the type of men we were looking for. Both Judy and I were writers. We had dated and lived with writers. In her case, she had previously married a writer. We both knew, too well, you don't really know someone from the snapshot of words they string together, no matter how appealing those words might be.

We needed a twist. I was reasonably fluent in French from my university days and travels, but in need of practise; Judy, recently returned from a *Globe*-sponsored French-language intensive in Quebec, also needed practice. Why not put together a French conversation group? We would write an ad asking men to join us. What a great way to meet guys without pressure on anyone, we thought. We might even improve our French.

Judy called in the ad.

Single, professional women in their 30s looking for single men between the ages of 30 and 45, interested in forming a French conversation group. No Parisian snobs need apply...

One week after the ad went in, Judy called. "I'm ready. I'm going to the box now. I'll see if anyone responded."

Ten minutes later, the phone rang. "There are over one hundred letters. I peeked at a few," Judy added. "There are some good ones."

"Now what do we do?"

"I don't have a clue. Let's start by reading the letters. We'll figure it out from there."

I ducked out of work. When I got to Judy's office, she pulled out a stack of letters from a drawer and plopped them on her desk in front of us. The envelopes were of every conceivable size, mostly white, some blue, one yellow, one light green. A few were typed. Most were hand-written. I flipped through, aimlessly trying to analyze the handwriting.

We decided to read the letters aloud, taking turns, discussing each one before we moved on to the next.

"We'll make a 'yes' pile for people we'd like to meet," Judy suggested. "A 'maybe' for ones we're not sure of. And a 'no' pile for the creeps," she added. "There are bound to be some."

We knew immediately when we hit a "no." The giveaway usually reared its ugly head in the first sentence, if not paragraph. More often than not it contained mention of a male body part, in descriptive, florid language. We tore up all ten of those on the spot and tossed them in the wastebasket.

Then, every once in a while, something would go zing. It told us maybe we weren't such goofs after all. If Judy was reading, she would start, then pause. She would look up, smile. I would already be smiling by the time our eyes met. The same word, phrase or sentiment that had caught her fancy had caught mine. Our hearts were going simultaneously boom.

There were fifteen "yes" letters out of the hundred. One was from a thirty-seven year-old producer of documentary films at the CBC who had recently returned from southern France. His name was Robin Christmas.

"I'm 38, a TV producer with the CBC. Beyond things French, my interests are quite eclectic: music (Pat Metheny to Mozart), sport (sailing, baseball and tennis), films, the theatre, good food and fine wines — the usual stuff.

I work as a field producer for a public affairs TV show, travelling all over the place making documentaries on any subject that might interest an audience. Fortunately, given the nature of my job, I love travelling and have seen a large part of the world.

I was born in London, England, and came to Canada when I was five ... I'm five foot eight, fit and healthy, love canoeing and camping; I read quite enthusiastically and follow the flow of world events with keen enthusiasm..."

Robin became one of the fifteen "yes" men we called for a 7:00 p.m. rendezvous at La Bodega, a French restaurant downtown. At 7:30, Robin walked through the front door. He had a kind, gentle face that registered panic upon noticing everyone at our table staring at him. Judy promptly kicked me under the table. I kicked her back. It was our way of saying "Two Thumbs Up" to his outfit. He was dressed in properly worn jeans, a tweed sport jacket, blue workshirt and nicely worn-in cowboy boots. Judy gave me a look that meant "go-for-it."

"No you. He's too short," I whispered back. I'd long since learned that most men feel uncomfortable around women who are taller than them.

Judy ignored me and made room for Robin beside me at the table.

I took it slow with Robin. The first month we saw each other only at our weekly French group. It was the perfect way to get to know someone without pressure, and it required minimal personal disclosure. He slowly began to open up, telling me about his brother Stephen's congenital illness, his father leaving home when he was nine, the ups and downs of living with his erudite stepfather, about his work and his desire to have children one day.

I eventually trusted him enough to open up about what had happened to me in Washington and how, after thirteen years, its ghost was still there, but fading. There were now days when it wasn't my first thought upon waking each morning.

It took time before we held hands, longer to kiss. Then, several months into the relationship, Robin was given an assignment to produce a documentary in Nicaragua for the CBC. His departure significantly heightened our feelings. His letters to me were beautifully written, passionate about the struggles in Nicaragua. Best of all, the letters were romantic, almost yearning. Being lonely in the middle of a war zone, far from home, is known to do that to a person.

I read Robin's letters over and over in bed at night. I couldn't wait for his return. When he came back, we began seeing each other daily, then nightly. He cared about me in a way that made me believe him when he said, "I just want you to be happy." If there was something he could do to make that possible, he did.

One summer evening, as we were eating on the outdoor patio at the site of our first official date, Robin asked me to marry him. My answer to Robin was an enthusiastic yes.

We flew down to Florida so my parents could meet Robin. Both my mother and father embraced him with open arms, literally. They of course knew he wasn't Jewish, but surprisingly, only made one small peep of disapproval. My mother pulled me aside to ask, "If you had to marry a non-Jew, couldn't you at least have found one with a name like Smith or Harris? Did it have to be Christmas?"

"Fair enough, Ma. I ask myself the same thing."

While in Florida, my dad would wake Robin at sunrise to take him out for breakfast at a nearby bagel joint, the supreme compliment from a man who normally liked sipping morning coffee solo. I was never invited to join them, which secretly pleased me to no end. I loved thinking my dad had someone new to love.

My mother noticeably brightened up around Robin, acting just shy of flirtatious. I liked that he brought out this schoolgirl side I had never seen before. She cooked and fussed, so much so I found myself mildly jealous, especially when she shared her private stash of Heavenly Hash ice cream, strictly *verboten* to her daughters.

"They clearly adore you," I said to Robin on the plane ride home. "They can both rest easier now," I said. At the ripe old age of thirty-five, their baby daughter was heading towards the altar. My father, particularly, could relax. In his way of thinking, it meant, finally, *someone* would be taking care of his Linda.

Robin and I decided to officially live together just around the time we became engaged. I had remained enamored of the ease of life on the mainland, so much so, I was willing to stay in the city if that's what Robin wanted. He didn't. His visits to the Island with me during the year worked its magic. He wanted us to move back there together.

The half-hearted joke I uttered before leaving the Island that year kept ringing happily in my ears. All you have to do is say "I'm going to the city to meet a guy and bring him back," and it actually happens? I didn't think life worked like that. Maybe the Yiddish expression "Man Plans, God Laughs" wasn't always true. No laughter here.

I had much to be thankful for: my sweet little Island home, my wonderful neighbours, a welcoming community to live in, flora and fauna at our doorstep. At last, with Robin by my side, I was beginning to understand what my 1960s mantra of "peace and love" was really all about.

It wasn't easy for Robin to move into "my home," "my Island"

and "my community." But we were lucky to have a house to come back to. For over twenty years, and at least ten since I had arrived, Islanders had been fighting to save their households, which the local government and developers threatened to dismantle. No one knew whether they'd have a house to live in from one month to the next. Time was running out. Bulldozers were revving their engines. Hundreds of homes on Centre Island and Hanlan's Point (where some of the most beautiful Victorian gingerbread-style homes once stood) had already been razed. The homes in our 150-year-old community were next in line.

We fought back with a vengeance. With strong support from mainlanders and the media, we lobbied the metropolitan government to reverse its plans. After a two-decade fight that included drawn-out court cases and a showdown with eviction notices from a real live sheriff complete with badge, we finally saved our Island homes. In 1989, the newly elected NDP government stepped in and passed legislation to save our Island community, giving us a 100-year lease on the parkland our houses sat on.

By the time the legislation was passed, Robin and I had purchased a different house, two Island blocks away. With our future clear, we settled in and headed to the garden to plant asparagus, lilacs and apple trees — plants that would take time to mature and bear fruit.

Three months after our move to the Island, Robin and I married. The ceremony was held outside our community clubhouse on the water's edge, overlooking the Toronto bay and city skyline. It was a beautifully clear fall day in September, the air alive with the sound of cicadas and the scent of sweetgrass in the surrounding meadow. Sailboats cruised past and Canada geese squawked overhead as we said our vows under the folds of a homemade cloth *chupa*, the traditional Jewish marriage canopy.

Though my father had grown frail, I knew nothing would keep him from coming with my mother to Canada for our wedding, and it didn't. I truly believed he was keeping himself alive for the day. I chose not to tell him at the time, just in case, but I was also planning something else he'd want to stick around for. More grandchildren to add to the four my sisters Sharon and Barbara had already given him. Becoming a mother was suddenly high on my agenda again.

All was not perfect in Paradise, though. I did not find a rabbi who would marry us because Robin was not Jewish. I was upset after unsuccessful attempts to find a rabbi in Toronto or nearby Buffalo. Not a good thing for a bride-to-be. I had the good sense to stop looking.

For the Jewish rituals I wanted in the ceremony, I asked a friend to stand next to the minister and provide Jewish content. One of my specific requests was to recite the Priestly Blessing from the *Book of Numbers*, a blessing I had loved since my childhood.

"You look beautiful," my teary-eyed father said, seeing me in my white knit wedding dress with fresh purple, pink and white Lisianthus blooms woven through my thick curly hair. We were standing in the Island clubhouse, waiting to hear the homegrown Island string quartet play its first notes, telling us it was t-i-m-e.

"How are you feeling?" he asked.

"I have never been as sure about anything in my life."

He took my arm, wrapped it around his and walked me out the door into the open air. Family members and friends stepped aside as we slowly weaved through a self-styled aisle until we reached the *chupa*. My father kissed me, unwrapped my arm from his and passed me to an equally teary-eyed and smiling Robin.

To my great joy, after the official bits of the service were over, Gerry stretched his arms in the air over both Robin and me and recited:

May the Lord bless you and protect you.
May the Lord shine His face upon you and be gracious
unto you.
May the Lord lift up His countenance on you and
grant you peace.
Amen.

I never expected to change my last name when I married Robin. It went without saying considering Robin's last name being Christmas. How exactly could I spend thirty-five years as Linda Rosenbaum, which when you introduce yourself is tantamount to saying, "Hello, I'm Linda Jewish," then overnight switch to "Hello, I'm Linda, Jesus' birthday?"

I wasn't going to give up *my* name when we married, but what about our future children? I had always been clear with Robin that I wanted to have children and I wanted to raise them Jewish.

As Robin wasn't practising any religion, I didn't think it would be a problem. He knew how much it meant to me. I didn't know for sure what I would have done if it had been a problem; something would have had to give and I didn't think it could be me.

Robin had long been a committed atheist. He believed the world's fractious, bigoted and war-like ways were and remained founded in the slurry of religious zealotry of one kind or other. How was I going to argue with that? I secretly hoped that he was going through an extended, rebellious adolescent stage and would eventually come around.

I would have liked to marry a Jewish man, but obviously not enough to make sure it happened. Nonetheless I was determined to raise my children Jewish and have a "Jewish home." I believed with Robin it could be possible. I made it clear that it was a need, not just a hope. Without a moment's hesitation, Robin gave this to me with grace.

He did, however, have one thing to ask in return.

"I would like the children to have my last name."

I was startled. I figured the worst-case name scenario would be the ridiculously attenuated "Rosenbaum-Christmas."

"You mean Christmas?"

"That's the one."

Christmas? Little Jewish children running around with the name Christmas? Registering for Jewish Sunday school with the name Christmas? The rabbi blessing our Christmases at their *bat* and *bar mitzvahs*? My parents taking the kids to *shule*, beaming proudly as they introduce their little Christmas grandchildren to friends? Hard to picture.

I had to work fast. "Why don't we compromise," I said.

"I give up Rosenbaum, you give up Christmas, we both take the name ...Tannenbaum ... like in the song 'O Tannenbaum.' It means Christmas tree, so it's very close."

"I'm surprised the name means so much to me," Robin responded. "Especially since my father left home when I was so young." Yes, difficult to understand the loyalty. Yet, as far as Robin knew, the Christmas name was not held by any of his dad's living family members other than his younger brother Stephen. Stephen, however, didn't expect to have children because of his chronic medical condition. It would be up to Robin if the family name were to continue.

"So Tannenbaum isn't going to work?"

"Wasn't even in the running."

I had known Robin long enough to know he gave much, asked little. When he did ask, I took it seriously. It was clear we were not to become a gaggle of Tannenbaums. I didn't give up completely, however. I would make sure our children's birth certificates carried the name Rosenbaum as an additional middle name. Either they, or I, could whip it out when, and if, we desired to do so on any given occasion.

5.
Our Baby's Homecoming
Toronto Island, 1985–1987

I WASN'T GETTING PREGNANT, but it didn't come as a complete surprise. At sixteen, my mother hauled me off to a gynecologist because my periods had only just started. The doctor diagnosed polycystic ovarian syndrome (PCOS), a common hormonal disorder among women of reproductive age and a leading cause of infertility.

I didn't pay much attention to the condition at the time. When you're sixteen, babies seem so far off. And becuse my girlfriends were complaining about mood swings, cramps and bloating, what was I missing, anyway?

The reproductive part of my body had never worked well. I began to doubt it ever would. I actually became scared of what would happen if I *did* get pregnant because of what my messed-up organs might do to me or my unborn child. Why would "down there" suddenly start working properly just because I wanted to get pregnant? Fortunately, by the time I met Robin, I knew it was *being* a mother I cared about, not how I got there. I still hoped to give birth, but didn't bet on my chances.

"I might not be able to have babies," I told Robin when the relationship began to deepen. I was so worried about his response that I blurted the words out quickly, hoping if I said them fast, he wouldn't notice them. Everybody takes for granted they will bear their own children.

Robin was quiet momentarily, then took my hand. "We'll try, see what happens. Of course, my first choice would be to have our own child. I'm sure it's yours, too," he said. "But if we can't, we can't. Like you, I want children. I won't care how."

I believed he meant it. If so, it was a godsend, since the news must have come like a wrecking ball. If he really believed what he said, it could spare us the grave sadness, disappointment and marital misery many infertile couples live with. I wasn't naïve, though. Only time would tell.

We went from one fertility specialist to the next. After twelve months of pills, prodding, and procedures, the prognosis was not good.

The fertility business seems to have become just that since our experience in the 1980s. I presume customer service has seriously improved because of it. But at that time, the doctors we ran into were cold, distant and perfunctory.

I'd walk into a treatment room and a doctor I never met before would say, "Lie down and put your feet in the stirrups, please." Uh, could you tell me who you are first? A name would be nice. Even a hello would do. Nice you said please, though.

While examining me, doctors would speak to students they had invited into the room, not to me. "This patient has one of the most common female endocrine disorders. It affects approximately five per cent to ten per cent of women of reproductive age. She's extremely high risk for infertility, and in later years, obesity and diabetes." I wished I had a hankie to wave in the air at him and say, "Yoo-hoo, doc! Sorry to interrupt, but I'm over here! I was just overhearing your conversation about my body and thought, Hey, I'm kinda interested too."

I was seldom, if ever, introduced to a student about to give me an internal, a fairly intimate encounter, even for a PCOS woman like myself who had endured many. Nor was I told why he or she was in the room in the first place. No one seemed to have yet taken a course in bedside manners. I would be passed from one unnamed professional to the next. Each asked the same, highly personal questions, which included details of my sex life with Robin.

I never had the courage to tell them how I felt about my visits with them. I "should have," but I was vulnerable and at their mercy.

Sometimes I walked out of the examination room in tears. An anxious, sympathetic Robin would be hunched down in his seat in the waiting room with a stack of abandoned magazines piled on the chair next to him, waiting to hear how I was. I wouldn't have cared so much about the doctors' social skills if I were there for a tonsil swab or tetanus booster. It wasn't meant to be a social call. Seeing a fertility doctor was different. I was dealing with my sadness and dreams.

On the day I came out from what would turn out to be my last appointment, Robin was again in the waiting room. His lower lip curled above the upper and every muscle on his face was furrowed. A thick line of sweat hovered above his upper lip. I knew it meant, "Enough. There's too much unhappiness going on here." And that was that.

We'd have to try something else. I wanted to be a mother. I adored children, always had. Though I had always questioned social and political conventions, I was a sentimental sucker when it came to family, the most traditional social convention of all.

Fortunately, Robin and I were both open to adoption. We were no longer youngsters. Traditional notions we once entertained about how old you were when you got married, who you were supposed to marry, what a wedding dress was to look like and when and how you made a family had vanished somewhere with the passage of time.

"You'll have to find your own baby to adopt," said Alan, the adoption counsellor on our first visit in 1986. "There are few available. Children's Aid has a three-year waiting list. Considering your age, I think it best you start looking now."

We were stunned. Find our own baby? Like from where? Alan might as well have been telling us to go to Borneo in search of the rare Asian Slipper Orchid. We didn't have a clue where to begin.

"The best I can do is make suggestions on how to go about it," he continued. "Then, if you find a willing birth mother, I'll meet with her, counsel her and arrange all the administrative aspects of the adoption."

I saw Robin's body tighten and his eyes become moist. Before I even registered how *I* felt about what Alan said, I wanted to make his disappointment and sadness go away. "We're only looking for *one* baby," I said with false cheerfulness. "Really, how hard can *that* be?" Both Robin and Alan turned towards me quizzically, neither bothering to respond.

Fortunately, Alan was full of ideas. "Let everyone know you're looking, from your butcher to your hairdresser," he stressed, "*especially* your hairdresser. Write letters to doctors, particularly rural physicians or those in small towns." Put ads in newspapers. Talk to people at teen health clinics, high schools and community centres. Get on the Children's Aid waiting list. Start thinking about adopting from another country and be open to a special needs child. Alan didn't say it, but I was sure it would be smart to make friends with fundamentalists, anti-abortionists and other people I would normally not make nice to.

"Sure thing," we said to all the suggestions, and then basically did nothing.

For some inexplicable reason, we didn't act like we were in any rush. Other than going weekly to our appointments with Alan to get ourselves approved for adopting, we kept on with our lives, including our work.

When we decided to adopt, I was doing communications work for the Ontario provincial government. I was in my late thirties and still held other career possibilities in the back of my mind, which included opening "Linda's Detroit Bagel Shop," modelled after the store in Detroit I went to every Sunday morning with my dad.

I was also flirting with the recent and unexpected offer made from a television producer at a start-up cable TV network, courting me as an on-air host for a new talk show about health issues. I said, "Great, I'll get some head shots taken," then did.

All speculation about future careers abruptly stopped the night we received a telephone call.

"Will you be around tonight?" asked Lynn, our neighbour. "I'd like to talk to the two of you." Her voice was particularly no-nonsense. Having known Lynn for thirteen years, it meant business. It was Lynn's house that Sandy Ross and I stayed in our first summer on the Island.

Lynn arrived with a bottle of red wine and a look on her face that said there would be no small talk. "Kira is five months pregnant," she said.

I had only once met Kira, the daughter of Lynn's partner. However, in the three years Lynn had been with Don, I had repeatedly heard stories about his troubled daughter from a previous marriage. This pregnancy was not happy news. Kira was not in a steady relationship with the baby's father, and had already given birth to two daughters when she was sixteen, now being raised in Czechoslovakia by her former husband's parents.

"Kira plans to put the baby up for adoption. She's due in May." Lynn then paused. "Would you like me to talk to her about the baby?"

Robin and I looked at each other and froze. "Oh, my god," was all I could say. Robin couldn't muster that.

Asking Lynn to speak to Kira was neither simple nor automatic. In some ways it seemed like guardian angels were channelling down a child. But could Kira be trusted not to change her mind? Was her decision to give up the baby a momentary whim while things were sour with her boyfriend? What if he sauntered back tomorrow, next week or six months after the baby was born? If she wanted the baby back, could we live through that kind of heartbreak?

Such stories are legion in the adoption world. Though not completely avoidable, we wanted to minimize chances. Ontario law said a birth mother could change her mind up to twenty-one days *after* the child is placed with the adoptive parents — a reality we'd have to live with, but it would be hell. We needed to know how definite Kira's decision was.

We had other questions, too, harder to ask, even harder to answer. Kira had been leading a walk-on-the-wild-side life. Even her father didn't know all the details. She had given birth to two other children she wasn't raising; she was in and out of bad relationships, wasn't working and had little money. Was she taking care of herself during the pregnancy? Were the two other children she gave birth to healthy? Was she drinking alcohol? Doing drugs? We had read terrible stories about crack babies. And, as it was now 1987, what about the recently identified HIV?

We called our adoption counsellor.

"We don't know what to do," I said. "There are so many reasons to say yes. I believe in taking chances. No baby comes with guarantees. Not even one you give birth to yourself." Every child deserves a loving home, yet what if we make the wrong decision?

"Have Kira make an appointment with me. I'll get the information you need to decide."

Alan's job included spending time with Kira, asking about her decision to give up her baby and to collect a full background history. He'd find out about drugs and alcohol, illnesses in her family, what kind of home she wanted for her child, if she cared about siblings...

If Kira wanted to move forward, Alan would tell her about us. She would decide if we were the people she wanted to give her baby to. There was a long line out there. We would be given first choice as we "found" her, but Kira had no obligations to anyone but herself.

If we went ahead with the adoption, Alan would provide whatever support Kira needed, including being at the hospital when she gave birth and with us for the handover of the baby.

For our part, if we were approved and decided to move forward, Alan would give us support too, and file the myriad of government documents required in adoptions. He would speak with the birth father, find out about the family medical history and request written approval for the adoption. Having his approval in writing would help avoid potentially nasty custody conflicts in the future. Birth fathers are not always told they have sired a child. If and when they find out, it can become an unholy mess, often landing in the courts to determine who gets custody.

Kira and Alan met several times. He thought she was bright and charming, was taking relatively good care of herself and clear about giving the baby up — he didn't foresee any reversal. She said she was confident her baby would be going to a good home (meaning us!).

Kira was twenty-two, said she was a smoker, drank alcohol a few times before she knew she was pregnant and had only taken prescription drugs since. She was drinking milk constantly, felt great, and her previous pregnancies were easy. "I stay in touch with the girls and they're both in good health," she said, referring to her two children in Czechoslovakia. With respect to AIDs, Alan assured us the government required testing of all babies at birth, "and the hospital will perform a battery of tests before releasing the baby. You'll know if there's any problem." More good news: the birth father agreed to the adoption. "Kira is asking him to sign the official release papers and provide his family history."

It was time to make the decision, yet it took days of considering and reconsidering. "Let's do it," I said one minute. "Maybe we shouldn't," the next.

Robin was also vacillating. "What are we waiting for?" he asked. Neither of us believed another child was coming our way anytime soon. Especially a newborn.

Robin and I were painfully aware there *were* actually children immediately available for adoption through Children's Aid, not chosen because of disability, age, colour or ethnicity. They weren't white or newborn. Yet, like other prospective parents who dream one day of having a child, we too initially hoped to begin parenthood with a newborn, a healthy newborn if possible, and a child with skin or hair similar to our own. Parents who give birth take these expectations for granted. They never have to give them a second thought.

We weren't rescuing pups from the pound. We had to give serious thought to what might lie ahead. We had no doubt that we would love any child that became ours, but were we really up for adopting a child from a different race or with a disability? Could we handle the extra challenges? Would this be the best way for us to do our bit to repair the world? Were we made for it?

No, we decided, we weren't. Our non-youthful age had something to do with it, but we had also heard too many disturbing stories about well-meaning adopting couples with high ideals and social consciences like ours. They had adopted children different from them in colour, who were older or had known emotional or physical problems. The challenges were often tragic. We were old enough to know that raising children was sufficiently tough without those extra dimensions. Some of us are better made for the challenges than others. We were not what my friend Barbara calls "God's people," the ones who take on the work of angels.

Couples wanting to adopt privately have to hire someone, usually a licensed social worker like Alan to lead them through the long, laborious and expensive legal process to parenthood, which included a "home study." The government-required a round of in-depth interviews and home visits to determine if we were fit to parent.

Good thing I liked Alan because I quickly became resentful about everything we had to do to become legally approved. I found the required questions like "Tell me about your mother?" irksome. As for the home visit, how clean did the house have to be, and should the freshly baked muffins I popped out of the oven on Alan's arrival be banana or blueberry? (I went for blueberry.)

I hated trying to figure out what the authorities were looking for. Anybody can have sex, bring a child into the world and be a lousy parent if so inclined. We, on the other hand, had to bake muffins and go through a long bureaucratic rigmarole to *prove* we would be good parents. It made sense to have to follow this process, but I had just spent a year with fertility specialists and now, with the home visits, I was dwelling way too much on what was and wasn't fair.

We couldn't make up our minds. Should we or should we not adopt Kira's baby? We'd go back and forth, never settling on a yes or no. Were we waiting for a better offer? Who were we kidding? Alan had a long list of parents who couldn't find babies to adopt, and who were counting the years slipping by. Would we be nuts to turn down this opportunity? Probably. But we were only clear on one thing. No baby comes with a guarantee.

After several weeks of this indecision, my final words to Robin were "Let's go for it." He agreed. Many of our doubts had little to do with Kira or her baby. We were scared to become parents, particularly this way. There's nothing natural about deciding to have a baby with your brain instead of your body.

We called Alan and told him we wanted to go ahead. Kira did too.

We were not surprised to hear she was opting for a "closed"

NOT EXACTLY AS PLANNED

rather than "open" adoption. It meant she didn't want any contact with the baby or adoptive family after the birth. In those days, "closed" was the most common form of adoption arrangement. Everyone would move on with their lives after the baby was handed over, independent from one another. All arrangements would be handled through Alan. Kira wouldn't receive any identifying information about us, like our name or address. Though she knew we were friends of Lynn and her father and could easily find us, she was clear with Alan. She had no such intention.

Robin and I weren't against open adoptions, where birth parents and adoptive parents stay in contact. When adoption was still in the abstract, that's what we hoped for. But from what we knew about Kira, we felt she could be a wild card. We weren't sure whether or not she might decide to pop in and out of our lives or the baby's on a whim. We were relieved when she said "closed." But of course, closed adoptions required keeping secrets. We wouldn't be able to tell our child who his or her birth mother was or anything revealing about her other than what we got from Alan. That was part of the deal.

But it also meant I was now in a situation leading me to betray the vow I made as a child when I uncovered the terrible secret my mother had kept about my grandmother — my grandmother who was supposedly dead. I swore that as an adult, I would harbour "No secrets, no lies." But this adoption would change all that.

I wasn't too upset, though, about keeping Kira a secret. I didn't believe the secret would last forever. I was sure we'd connect someday.

I had always been surprised that some adopted people had no desire to know who their birth parents were. I couldn't imagine not wanting to see the genetic line I descended from, checking out what traits I might have inherited or being able to ask a few questions. Feeling that way myself, I assumed that day could come for our child.

I also knew Kira would not disappear from our lives the moment we walked out of the hospital with her newborn in our arms. There were too many threads connecting us. Lynn was a close friend: it would be natural for her to talk about Kira. Even if Lynn didn't initiate a conversation about Kira, I would most likely ask how she was doing, either out of curiosity or concern.

My biggest concern was that Lynn and Don lived nearby. In other words, close. The Island was different from most neighbourhoods because there are no streets, just sidewalks that separate rows of houses. Whether we were out for a walk or going to a community meeting, we were always walking past one another's homes. And, we rode the boat together to and from the city. It wasn't easy to avoid running into people. So when Kira came to visit Lynn and Don, it was possible that she might see us with the baby on the boat or walking somewhere. What if she recognized the baby? As Kira and I had once met, what if she saw me with my new baby and came over to say hello?

"Oh, hi, Linda. What a cute baby! Lynn didn't mention you were pregnant. When was your baby born?"

What a deceitful web we weave. Lynn and Don promised their best to ward off chance meetings or unplanned overlaps in our lives. But really, who trusted this plan to be foolproof? I had a sense that the Yiddish saying "Man Plans, God laughs" would soon become operative.

"You're not eligible for maternity leave like other new mothers," said the human resources officer at the Ontario government office where I was working. "You're adopting."

The adoption was starting to feel real, so it was time to discuss parental leave from my job that would kick in once the baby was born. The HR woman was so dismissive, I looked at her incredulously. She looked back with the same expression of surprise.

"It's not like you're going to be sick or anything," she added. Well, whadya say to that? I called my union rep, assuming he would be outraged as I was. Dead wrong. "We don't represent enough adoptive mothers to make it worth our while to take up with management. We've got bigger fish to fry."

Not much I could say to that, either. Robin and I tried to decide how far I should take the issue. We both thought that it was a union concern, so that's where to put the pressure. At the same time, I was waffling. How much energy did I want to put into fighting the idiotic policy? I didn't want anger to mess with my happy state waiting for our child to be born.

I decided not to get too roused, but made several phone calls, calmly threatening to get a lawyer and make a stink. In that day and age, there was no way to deny adoptive mothers the same rights as birth mothers. My baby would need as much mother love as any other baby.

"I believe the *Human Rights Code* would be on my side," I said, not really knowing if it would be or not. "Want to test it?"

"We'll get back to you," the union rep said.

Soon after, he did. They took the issue to management and the maternity policy was amended. I was granted adoption leave with benefits. I could take up to a year off after the baby was born, like any other new mother working for the Ontario government. This ruling would now apply to all adoptive mothers within the civil service. What a sweet victory.

I said goodbye to the television job offer and put the bagel factory on hold. How could I be unhappy abandoning either career dream? I was about to have a baby.

I will never forget the moment I became a mother, because that's what it was, a moment. The phone call from Alan had finally come. Kira had left the hospital, and all the medical tests were complete. Except for a minor heart anomaly considered inconsequential, the baby was deemed healthy. Kira's seven-day-old, five-pound-thirteen-ounce baby boy would soon be ours.

"Everything's all set. You can come and, well, *meet him,*" Alan said, acknowledging how strange the words sounded.

Robin, my best friend Barbara and I took the next boat to the city and drove out to the suburbs. We virtually jumped out of the car the second it stopped, ran through the parking lot, then flashed through the revolving front doors of Scarborough Centennial Hospital in search of elevators. After what felt like an interminable wait, we arrived on the fifth floor. As the doors opened, I saw Alan standing there, a Cheshire cat grin gilding his face. "Best part of my job," he said, leading us to the nursery.

I peered through the scratched Plexiglas picture window. My palms were sweaty and my heart beat fast as I watched a pink-uniformed nurse walk among the rows of babies on the other side. In her matching pink cushioned-soled shoes, she walked slowly up, then slowly down perfectly straight rows of newborns lying side-by-side in little see-through plastic bassinets. Taped to the side of each one was a last name written in bold letters.

Her steps seemed to take forever. The procedure felt like a surreal game of slow-motion musical chairs. Where and when is she going to stop? Nobody knows. But when she does, we'll have a son. No pushing, no moaning. She finally paused next to a bassinet. Squinting, I could just make out the letters "O-b-e," Kira's last name. The music stopped. She leaned over to pick up the tiny swaddled baby inside, then held him up, directing his pink face towards the window so we could see him.

All hell broke loose on our side of the Plexiglas.

We were all crying when the nurse came out to us. She walked straight to me and placed the baby in my outstretched arms. I leaned over to kiss his warm forehead, then looked up and smiled at Robin and Barbara. I had just noticed the unbelievably thick shock of long, reddish-blond hair on his tiny head.

"This is my baby," I squealed, in a voice I hardly recognized, roughly two octaves above normal. Robin was busy taking pictures while I smothered Baby Boy Obe in wet kisses. "Isn't he the most beautiful thing you've ever seen? And look what he's wearing. Where did the sweet little blue outfit come from?" I looked towards the nurse.

"The volunteer ladies," she replied. "They have a 'thing' for the adopted ones. They always knit little going-home sweaters, booties and hats." Her explanation sent me into even deeper sobbing, complete with snorts each time I came up for air.

"You've got a feisty one there," the nurse said as I handed the baby to Robin. "And I know feisty. I'm Irish."

A beaming Robin took his blue-sweatered son into his arms, gushing almost as wetly. Then on to Barbara, who tucked a fluffy white bear she called Teddy gently into the folds of his tightly wrapped flannel blanket.

"Your first friend," she told him, sweetly.

People say you can feel the moment the soul leaves the body of someone who has just died. Though I have been at the deathbed of people I love, I could not say this had been true for me. I could say, though, that the moment my son was placed in my arms and I held him to my heart, a little bit of his soul entered mine.

If I loved the Island before, I adored it even more on the day we brought Michael home from the hospital.

We took the noon ferry. As the horn sounded to signal our arrival on the Island side, I gathered up the diaper bag we bought at Storkland, then walked down the boat's gangplank with Michael in my arms. Robin was steps behind, proudly pushing the big, elegant navy blue and steel English pram we borrowed from Ellie for the occasion.

A crowd was waiting for us. Dozens of neighbours were clapping, yelling and cheering, welcoming our new family home.

In the centre of the crowd stood a bunch of goofy-looking

musicians, members of the Island's homegrown, cacophonous marching band. They were wearing homemade costumes of rags and lace, feathers and beads that looked like cast-offs from Mardi Gras '54. They came complete with tuba, drums, trumpets and tambourines and called themselves The Arhythmics. Entry into their ranks required nothing more than good intentions and a well-tuned heart.

Grahame, sometime tuba player, more regularly TV's *Guerilla Gardener*, yelled out "Hit it folks." On cue, a chorus of voices and instruments belted out "Happy Birthday" to welcome our baby as the community's newest member.

Robin was speechless. I was not. I was crying and waving, pointing, hugging and screaming. I worked my way through the crowd like a campaigning politician, pointing at everyone and making whatever physical contact I could while yelling out their names. "Oh, look, Robin, little Lizzie and Hanne too," I said, pointing at the children. They were standing with red and white helium balloons drifting upwards from the colourful ribbons their parents had fastened to their wrists.

As it was a sunny spring day in May, I had dressed that morning in a pastel floral skirt and lacey white blouse for the occasion, assuming that's what you wore in spring, out for a stroll, showing off your new baby in your English pram. From the docks, we walked along the path by the lagoon, past the freshly painted community clubhouse surrounded by aging black willows. Everyone took turns pushing and cooing at Michael. He remained content under the blankets, still asleep in his soft blue hospital outfit.

We marched onward, artfully dodging the ubiquitous green guano from the Canada geese gobbling grass along the knoll leading to a string of sailboats moored in the lagoon, and winding our way past the old fire hall and playground. We were almost home, all that was left was to cross the wooden bridge to take us from Ward's Island to Algonquin.

I paused momentarily when we reached the flattened crest of

the bridge. It was my favourite spot, where I marked changes in the seasons during the thirteen years I had lived on the Island. Even with Robin nudging me on, I stopped, looking west along the lagoon, hoping to see the tufted crewcut of my favourite bird, the kingfisher, and then down the bridge at the enormous pink-bloomed weigela in front of my friend Barbara's house.

"Keep moving," Robin called out, noticing my descent into never-never land. "Only a little way more."

We would be home when we spotted the tree house in the cottonwood in our front yard. The graying hand-built structure was a replica of a traditional South African elephant lookout, built to scale by the South African architect who lived with his family in the house before us.

We arrived. The Arythmics noisily marched us past the apricot-coloured tulips, up our fieldstone pathway — all with great glee, silliness and a wee bit of pretend pomp. We weaved along until we reached the front porch.

We were greeted there by a huge hand-lettered and festooned poster board. It must have been hung on our front door while we were at the hospital collecting our son. I couldn't read it through my tears, so I asked Robin to read it aloud.

"Welcome Home Michael Asher Rosenbaum Christmas," he said. "We love you."

In Michael's room that afternoon, the air smelled perfumed with the burning scent of sweet molasses wafting through the window from the nearby Redpath Sugar plant on the city's waterfront. Looking out from the window to the cotton-woods in the distance, I had my first glimpse of the migrating white-throated sparrows on their brief spring stopover.

Robin was now standing at the bedroom door. "You looked a million miles away," he said. "A peaceful million miles away, so I let you be."

Pressing my warmed cheek next to Michael's, I smiled at my

lovely husband and murmured, "Nice, huh?"
"Glorious," he said.

Everything was perfect. It was a gorgeous, sunny spring day. I was home, rocking my newborn to sleep in my arms, running my fingers through his thick bush of hair.

At last, my pine rocking chair and I were exactly where we were meant to be, at home, in Michael's bedroom with the sun streaming through the antique lace curtains I hung just before leaving for the hospital.

For seventeen years, since my first days in Canada, that chair had followed me in and out of more living spaces than I cared to remember. It rocked me happily through a myriad of boyfriends and consoled me through just as many heartbreaks. In addition to its scratches, it had earned a satiny smooth patina.

I moved my hand off its arms to run my fingers across Michael's peaceful, silken face. "How can it get any better than this?" I thought, as Robin walked into the room.

He was beaming at the sight of us. This was one happy man. He too had waited forever for this proverbial moment of marital bliss. I was thirty-nine, Robin, forty-three. This precious first child of ours, lying asleep in my arms, was already beloved.

The afternoon sun continued to pour through the lace. It made me woozy as it created shadows on the farmyard *trompe l'oeil* Robin had painted on the wall next to Michael's crib.

"I'll first paint a window, then a scene you'd see through it from a farmhouse," he announced several days before, while sketching details on graph paper. "Wouldn't it be nice for the baby to look out on rolling hills and a perpetual blue sky? I can throw in a barn, a few cows, sheep, grass..."

Robin had so many plans and dreams for his son. They were going to build a crystal radio set together and make volcanoes erupt from test tubes. He would teach him to make a raft out of 2x4s, fly a kite and throw a perfect pitch over home plate. Finally, someone to watch Formula One racing with!

I hadn't yet allowed myself similar reveries ... except perhaps for one. I saw Michael standing on the *bimah* at his *bar mitzvah*, my father at his side.

"Everyone get a glass," I said that night to the crowd gathered around our pine table at the homecoming party for Michael. The happy sound of corks popping and bottles overflowing added a festive sort of joy as we raised our glasses.

"Okay. A toast," I said, not having any idea what I was about to say, but rattling on anyway. "I'll try to do it without crying, but don't expect it..." Everyone laughed; they knew me too well. I took a breath. "May this lovely, peaceful Island," I said at last, "the one our lucky child has come to at birth — may this Island forever bring him, as long as he needs or wants it, the same delight, refuge, inspiration and shelter from life's storms as it has brought me, his mother, and Robin, his father. To Michael. To Robin. To the Island. To us all."

After the last guest left the homecoming celebration, Robin lowered Michael into the small, handmade pine cradle next to our bed, on loan from a neighbour. We placed layers of soft flannel blankets on the bottom to cushion Michael's bony little body. Carved underneath, on the bottom of the cradle were the names and birthdates of babies before him who had spent their first days cradled there. Sometime during the afternoon Robin had etched the next line in the cradle's history. Michael Asher Rosenbaum Christmas, May 20, 1987.

Robin let me choose Michael's first and middle names. In the *Ashkenaz* tradition, I named him after deceased people I wanted to honour, using their first initials. Michael was named after an aunt and my mother's father. I chose Asher to honour Alberta Evans, a woman who worked for our family when I was a child, a second and beloved mother to me.

While Robin and I liked the sound of both names, their Hebrew meanings had great significance too. Michael meant "he who resembles God." Along with Gabriel and Raphael, Michael was mentioned in early Judaic texts as an archangel. Asher meant "blessed."

After the long day of celebration, I crawled under the covers next to Robin. I was exhausted, but sleep would not come.

"My eyes keep popping around my sockets," I said to Robin, then laughed. "They've got *shpilkes*," a Yiddish term for the jittery feeling, akin to "ants in your pants." I again tried to sleep. I wanted to put aside, for a few hours at least, a turbulent undertow attached to my joy.

"What a day it must have been for Michael too," I said, ignoring the signal Robin was giving by shoving his head under the pillow.

It troubled me to think how wrenching those last few days must have been for Michael. He'd been pulled away from the familiar sounds, movements, fluids, smells, touch and warmth of his birth mother's body. He'd just begun to adapt to the nursery, then after seven days, was whipped away from that. Somewhere, somehow, this had to affect this sweet young thing's nervous system. Whether or not it could be measured, it had to have hit hard. How could it not? Even if the world's top neurological experts told me otherwise, I knew in my heart. This wee little body and its complex collection of neurons, pathways, synapses and soul could not be completely unscathed from not one startling jolt, but two.

To counteract my thoughts, I said to Robin, "Let's list all of the nice things our little Michael experienced his first day with us."

The tired new papa grunted into the pillow.

"I guess I'm on my own then," I said loudly.

"Okay, this will be the last thing I talk about tonight, I promise. But think about it. In one day, our little fella felt heat from the sun, heard Canada geese squawk, shared germs with twenty people dying to hold him, listened to Glen Gould play Bach's

Goldberg Variations, watched hockey in his dad's arms..."
"And," Robin muttered from his pillow, "heard his mommy sing 'Kumbaya.' Now go to sleep."

Maybe Michael had *shpilkes*, too, during the night. He couldn't settle for long. Except for brief moments of sleep, he thrashed around in his little cradle. We had no idea why. Even after frequent feedings and diaper changes, the poor thing continued to holler and wouldn't fall asleep. We wrapped him tightly in blankets, which calmed him for a while. So did holding him close to our bodies, caressing and making soothing noises. These moments never lasted long, though. He startled to the slightest movement, sound or change in light around him.

Robin and I took turns staying up with him. One morning, I got out of bed after a total of two hours sleep. I felt sleep-deprived and anxious, partially because of a short but vivid dream I had. In it, Robin and I were frantically running up and down a long, linoleum-covered corridor of a big, two-storey institutional-looking building that I remembered from my childhood. It was called The Home. We were opening doors as we ran from room to room, searching for something. When we didn't find it, we slammed the door behind us and rushed into the next room. At the end of the corridor, we lay down and cried. We never found what we were looking for — a child.

The Home was a drab, gloomy-looking brick building near Winship, my elementary school in Detroit. I was never sure then what The Home was, only that many of the kids who went to Winship lived there. It was shrouded in mystery.

I found out in my teens that The Home was an orphanage. In my memory, kids who lived there wore frayed clothes, had drippy noses, didn't do well in school, and were always in trouble. I believed they ate only cold porridge and mashed potatoes with canned gravy and peas, morning, noon and night.

I went to Winship for nine years but never once visited The Home. I never asked my parents why kids lived there. Nor did any teachers address the obvious question. Why were so many kids at our school not living with their parents?

It wasn't hard to understand why my dream that morning felt so haunting. If our Michael had been born in the 1950s like those other kids, he would have been one of the orphans. And what if parents looking for a child never chose him? Both Robin and I were already thinking Michael was frail, so I shuddered to think of him living in an orphanage, being raised without parents to give him extra doses of care. And I shuddered at the disdain he would have met from the likes of my friends and me.

Another building next to the main structure was a Home for Unwed Mothers. Many of the children at school were probably born in this building, shifted to the other where they would wait for the big dream — adoption — so they could move into a family to live happily ever afterwards.

I graduated Grade 8 with a handful of Home Kids still amongst us, dozens coming up behind. I didn't know then that if you weren't adopted into a family by the time you hit an age with double digits, chances were you never would be.

There were more children to adopt during my youth than families for them to go to. Thus, orphanages. A social shift in the early 1970s changed all that, with the introduction of birth control pills and sex education in the schools, and more readily available and safer abortions. Promotion of safe sex and use of condoms had impact as well. All these factors, along with a relatively more accepting attitude towards single motherhood, meant babies to adopt were fewer. That's why when Robin and I were ready to adopt, Alan said, "You have to find your own."

Unlike the ending of my dream, Robin and I did. But our dream didn't come true exactly like we thought it had.

We kept Michael next to us at night. Because he never took more than a few ounces of milk at any one time, we feared missing his repeated squeals for a top-up if we moved him downstairs. Despite strategies offered by friends, family and parenting gurus on how to train Michael to drink more, and therefore sleep more, we weren't successful; he was crying every few hours. After warming his formula, we fed him in the bedroom, tucked him back in the cradle and rolled over for a one- or two-hour trip into dreamland.

When people asked "How's Michael?" we usually said "A little unsettled." It seemed kinder than "fussy" or "agitated." But agitated was more like it. If he wasn't performing a serpentine full-body squirm, he was flailing his arms and legs in the air, as if swimming freeform in ether. His little razor-sharp nails often swiped at his face, scratching it when contact was made.

To make him feel more grounded, we swaddled him with soft flannel blankets wrapped tightly around his body, arms and legs tucked inside. The gentle pressure against his skin and feeling of containment definitely made him more settled, and we hoped comfortable.

Repeated visits to the pediatrician ended with "He's doing fine. It looks like his digestive system may be underdeveloped and giving him a bit of trouble, but he'll grow out of it. Just relax." I liked our pediatrician a lot, but relax? How could we relax with a crying, fidgeting, fussy baby we didn't know how to comfort?

Despite reassurances, this was a common conversation between Robin and me: Do all babies cry this much? Dunno. Do all babies squirm this much? Dunno. Are we doing something wrong? Probably.

Michael was so tiny and seemed so frail, we thought the pine cradle, small as it was, might still be too big. We switched him to a woven reed basket we bought. It was the same model Cecil B. DeMille used in *The Ten Commandments,* when he directed Miriam to put her brother Moses in it before sending him down river. It was also the one my friend Ellie used as her laundry basket.

Michael did seem a bit more settled in the narrower space — perhaps the confines made him feel safer. We experimented with something even smaller during naptime one day while visiting friends in the city. We placed Michael in a small dresser drawer we padded with soft blankets, to see if he would stop thrashing if he wasn't swaddled. To our astonishment, he fell asleep immediately. It wasn't convenient to use a dresser drawer at home, so we layered in extra blankets in his basket to make him snug-as-a-bug-in-a-rug, as my father used to say when he bundled me up at bedtime.

Michael, like a crate-trained pup, was more secure in small, tight spaces. Perhaps it helped him feel less adrift in the forces of nature he was born into. Though he was a full-term baby at five pounds thirteen ounces, he was acting more like a preemie.

"I'm wondering if his body isn't ready to be outside Kira's womb," I said one morning after wrapping Michael in blankets. "Maybe there's too much for him to take in. Think of all the sounds, smells, touch, light and movement coming his way. They may just be too stimulating."

It was silly to think I would miss Michael's nighttime calls if he were downstairs in his own bedroom. Even though I didn't have the leg-up provided by a new mother's hormones, I wasn't about to miss my baby's cry. Our tiny child had a remarkable ability to let both Robin and me know he needed us. Like a hospital intern, I was always on call. Red Alert was the default position my sympathetic nervous system was starting to call home. I was lucky the CBC gave Robin four weeks of paternity leave to stay with me. Our worlds were being rocked upside down by this needy little guy.

Feeding time with Michael was a blessedly peaceful time, one of the few. I had invented a way, I hoped, to compensate for Michael being deprived of a nice warm breast to suck on.

Whenever I fed him, I sat in our oversized, cushy green leather chair with my legs tucked under. I held Michael tightly against my chest so he could feel my heartbeat. I dropped my head down until our foreheads touched, and gently pressed my cheek against his. One of my irrepressibly curly locks would usually brush against his skin as my warm breath drifted over him. Not the same as a breast, but pretty cozy, I thought. How could it not be good for him?

My favourite feedings were in the wee hours of the morning when I would get up, wrap myself in a chenille bathrobe, and bring Michael downstairs. We'd sit on the rocking chair in the living room in front of the French windows, and wait. From our front-row seat, we'd watch a fiery red and orange sun rise above the waters of Lake Ontario. I felt soothed by the calm and quiet from the stillness in the world at that time of day, I was sure Michael could feel it too.

I always took heart watching him suck enthusiastically as dawn pushed aside the night. Michael wasn't the only soul being nourished in those moments.

I was thrilled when my parents visited a few weeks after Michael was home. My dad had become so frail, I worried that flying from Florida, followed by the *shlep* to the Island would be too hard for him. When I registered concern, his only words were, "Nothing could keep me away."

We first thought my parents should come immediately after we brought Michael home, for his *bris*, the ritual Jewish circumcision that usually takes place when the male child is eight days old. I knew my dad would want to hold his grandson in his arms during the ceremony. But we brought Michael home when seven days old, so of course we couldn't have the ceremony on day eight. We originally assumed it would be shortly after, and planned my parents' trip accordingly.

The pediatrician told us not to do it. He thought Michael's health was too fragile to have the circumcision right away, and he couldn't predict when he'd be ready. "When he puts a little more meat on his body," he said, "we'll know." Instead of waiting for who knew when, my parents came when Michael was two weeks old. I knew they wouldn't be back for the *bris*.

I never worried that my parents would love Michael less because he was adopted. My sister Sharon had an adopted child, and my parents' love for her was never in question. When I told them I couldn't get pregnant, they didn't betray any disappointment in their voice or push us to try longer. They appeared to accept what we told them and asked to be posted every step of the way along the adoption route. I was lucky. And enormously grateful. This scenario is not always *de rigueur* in families with adopted kids. There's no passing on of the grandparents' genetic line.

"I bet my dad will do nothing but *kvel* the whole time he's here," I said to Robin before my parents arrived. And that's pretty much what he did, *kvel*. In Leo Rosten's *Joys of Yiddish*, the book I somehow managed to hang onto since my father gave it to me when I was a teenager, the word means to take great pride and pleasure; a peculiarly Jewish joy most often associated with the accomplishments of one's children. My father was doing just that, experiencing a peculiarly Jewish joy.

From the plush green leather easy chair we set up for him in the living room, my dad *kveled* non-stop. He couldn't stop smiling, and the twinkle in his eye which had noticeably vanished after the Detroit riots had miraculously returned, if only temporarily. Everything delighted my dad. Of course, his delight delighted me. Bringing him joy remained high on my life's to-do list, in part, as payback for the years of the "care packages" he had sent me in Washington.

But in recent years, bringing my dad pleasure was like asking Job to buck up. Yet there he was in my home, *kveling* as he watched his baby daughter be a mother, taking enormous pleasure as I bustled around the house, fearlessly performing high-wire acts like warming bottles, changing diapers, doing laundry, rocking Michael.

The biggest thrill of all for me was watching my dad *kvel* at his new grandson. My dad's heart was full when Michael was in his arms, so much so that one day I watched as tears sailed down his cheeks. It wasn't because of anything Michael did, how he looked or how he acted, though. He just loved Michael for being.

I was pleased that my mother seemed excited about seeing Michael too. She told me how much she was looking forward to the visit. But I prepared myself emotionally. My mother was critical of her daughters, and I worried I'd be giving her fodder with my inability to keep Michael content and settled. I was already beating myself up, I didn't need another punch.

"Don't get yourself worked up in advance," Robin said, trying to ease my worries. "Your mother has her own way of showing love." He was fond of her, but saw how tough she could be on me. "And sometimes you have to ignore what she says."

As it turned out, my mother said very little, positive or negative. I kept waiting for her to criticize me, especially because Michael was his usual fussy self, but she didn't. She was pleasant and pretty much stayed out of everyone's way — mine, Robin's and even Michael's. She offered little advice and looked on from what seemed to be the sidelines. I had to ask her if she wanted to hold Michael or give him a bottle. She answered yes to both.

What stood out noticeably was how stiff my mother was around Michael, as if she didn't know what to do. When she was holding him, she extended her arms out, a short distance from her body, as if she was holding a broken egg she didn't want to ooze on her clothes. It made her look like someone who had never held a baby before and was afraid it might bite if it came too close. She never made goofy sounds or faces at Michael. She didn't run her fingers through his hair, smell his wonderful baby scent or caress his skin. No spontaneity, no sweet nothings. "It makes me wonder what she was like with my sisters and me," I said to Robin, who was also a little shocked at how ill-at-ease my mother seemed. "It's not like she's new to this. She raised three daughters."

I wasn't mad at my mother's disconnect, but I *was* chilled. It was scary to think how cold she might have been with the three of us girls when we were young. It may explain why her criticisms during our childhood were so stinging. We weren't sure there was love behind them.

After they had left Toronto and headed home to Florida, I continued to ruminate about my mother. For the first time in years, I began to think about her own mother, my grandmother, and the disturbing news I had learned about her. Perhaps, it had something to do with how my own mother was with her children. Possibly she hadn't learned how to mother.

I was ten when I learned my grandmother was living in a mental hospital, too young to feel compassion for the shame and sadness my mother must have been living with. Instead, I was only furious about the secret, and swore that I would never ever keep secrets or lies from the people I loved.

How wrong I continued to be.

6.
Michael's First Year:
One *Mohel,* Seven Doctors
Toronto Island, 1991

WE RECEIVED THE GO-AHEAD for a *bris* when Michael was one month old. He hadn't grown or put on weight, but was definitely sturdier.

As a surgical practice, circumcision had come in and out of fashion for the general North American population, but for most Jews, circumcision wasn't a fashion or subject of debate. You just did it. A *bris,* performed by a trained practitioner, *mohel,* was considered more than a simple medical procedure. It was a honored historical commitment to the faith. Blessings were said and prayers recited as the child took his place among peers as a member of the Jewish community. It was a happy occasion and an important milestone in the first days of the Jewish life cycle.

I knew all the medical pros and cons. I was aware of ethical concerns about putting a child though an involuntary surgical procedure and even listened to one person hector me about possible long-term psychological consequences. Nothing made me budge. Jewish males have been circumcised for thousands of years. I never heard one complain about it.

When the time finally came, most of my Jewish friends were shocked by my determination to go ahead with the circumcision. The non-Jewish ones remained relatively mum, probably trying to show open-minded tolerance towards another culture's tradition. But I knew they were secretly asking how an otherwise intelligent, seemingly progressive friend would subject her son to a Byzantine ritual of debatable medical merit.

I warded off comments as best I could, suggesting good-heartedly that if anyone had a problem with my son's *bris*, they should take up the cause of female genital mutilation in sub-Saharan Africa, instead.

Even Robin found my commitment to a *bris* a bit surprising, considering Jewish life in my childhood home was more cultural and culinary than religious. My childhood rabbi called us Chopped Liver Jews. "You think all you have to do is eat a little chopped liver, go to *shule* on *Yom Kippur* and you can call yourselves Jews?" he asked. Well, we were wrong. It wasn't good enough to keep the religion alive, he told us. The warning signs were already there in the 1950s. Intermarriage was looming.

So it was strange that my culturally Jewish home became the breeding ground for my lifelong love of tradition and ritual. My parents went to *shule* on *Rosh Hashana* and *Yom Kippur* only. We celebrated Jewish holidays by eating *latkes* or *matzo brei*. Yet for me, Judaism was poetry, drama, inspiration and comfort. I loved Bible stories of sibling rivalry, jealousy and heartbreak; the Hollywood-style spectacle of an arbitrarily cruel and vengeful god smiting whole armies in retribution. I cried when the cantor at my *shule* wailed ancient melodic lamentations during *Kol Nidre* on *Yom Kippur*; I daydreamed to love poetry in the *Song of Songs* and took comfort in "forever is mercy built," a line from King David's Psalm 89.

I began going to synagogue on my own on Saturday mornings as a young teenager, but was already hooked on *Shabbat* by the time I was eight. I was invited to my friend Beverly's house for Friday night dinner, and watched in awe as her mother lit Shabbat candles and sang the blessings. She explained that females are given the role of lighting candles as part of their duty to bring light into their family's heart — and home. What on earth could possibly be more beautiful than that, I thought. In the first flicker of the flame, I felt engulfed in the warmest, coziest, most peaceful glow imaginable. It momentarily separated me from all that was mundane. Mystery, magic and mythology trumped matter for me. It left me longing for more.

As well as being a religious ceremony, a *bris* was a celebration, and Jewish celebrations of course mean family, friends and food. And for a *bris*, food meant "trays," as in "So you'll order in a few trays," as my mother would say. It meant platters upon platters of fresh bagels, lox, cream cheese, sliced tomatoes, cucumber and onions, cheeses, creamed herring, tuna salad, egg salad and loaves of rye bread, *challah* and pumpernickel. To follow, cinnamon-crusted *rugelach*, a little sponge cake and a few nice cookies so you shouldn't go hungry.

But getting trays to the Island would be as easy as bringing over a *mohel*. Impossible.

I called my friend Ellie for help.

"Just have the *bris* here," she said, offering her city home.

"I'll owe you big time, forever, for this one."

"I know. That's why I'm doing it."

I was thrilled my sister Barbara and family came from Detroit for the *bris*, but disappointed that my parents, particularly my father, couldn't make it. I had always imagined my *tallit*-draped father there, his deep blue eyes moving from twinkling to tear-soaked as he held my son in his arms and recited blessings with the *mohel*. Yes, it was from my father that I inherited my sloppy sentiments and tender heart. But his arrival was not to be.

After welcoming the guests and *mohel* to Ellie and Bob's, I ducked for cover in the kitchen. It was the traditional hideaway of a long line of chicken-shit Jewish mothers like me who didn't want to be anywhere near their baby while the surgical cutting *they*, including me, had specifically asked for took place in another room. In this case, Ellie and Bob's dining room.

I was told that with Robin by his side, my nephew Steve donned his *bar mitzvah tallit* and held Michael in his arms while the *mohel* dipped a white linen cloth into syrupy sweet red Manischewitz wine. He then placed it in Michael's mouth to take the sting from the brief surgery. Manischewitz the anesthetic, as it were.

Meanwhile, I was in the kitchen surrounded by a bevy of females. I squealed when I heard Michael wail from the incision. When done, I joined the men and held Michael. My son was officially circumcised, named and welcomed into his new community. And the trays! They were to die for, though the fabulous raisin-studded *rugelach* were wolfed down long before I even got a taste. Divine retribution for not being at my son's side, no doubt.

Later that evening, back at home, my sister asked if she could speak to me alone.

"I was wondering," she started, in a near whisper. "Do you think maybe Michael could be going through withdrawal or something?"

My mind was blank. I was incapable of saying anything.

She continued. "You know the way he cries so much, jerks his body and thrashes around. Maybe he's so agitated and sensitive because he's going through cold turkey or the DTs. Maybe his birth mother was taking drugs or drank when she was pregnant."

She was right. Michael had not yet stopped his long bouts of crying, and frequently seemed uncomfortable in his skin. Yet I could feel the back of my neck heating up from what my sister was saying. She had tapped into every adopting parent's worst fear. We are all scared out of our minds that something might be wrong with our children because of the genetic stew and nine-month gestation period that we have no control over.

I didn't know what to say or do. My sister would never say anything that would hurt me unless she thought it vitally important. Nevertheless, I was devastated. She had planted seeds that couldn't be unsowed. She couldn't take it back. The harm was done. My post-*bris* euphoric bubble had been burst.

Pandora's box of worry was now open.

"Sure, Michael's having a rough go," I said, dismissively, "but Kira said she didn't do drugs or drink much during the pregnancy. Plus, the doctors at the hospital ran all sorts of tests on him and said he's fine."

We went and joined Robin. The issue wasn't mentioned again.

As part of my routine with Michael, I took long daily walks through the community. Whichever route, I made a point of starting my walk past one particular neighbour's house. Jean had been a pediatric nurse at the Hospital for Sick Children for many years. If she was out puttering, I'd stop for a chat. Her warm smile and calm presence made me think of a fluffy white pillow I wanted to sink my head into.

I always asked Jean for advice about Michael. No matter what the question, her answer was the same: "A nighttime sherry for mum."

On Michael's first birthday, I found Jean outside, pruning her forsythia. She was her usual warm self, though noticeably earnest. She walked over and put her hand on my shoulder.

"Linda, I want to congratulate both you and Robin. The power of your love is extraordinary. You've done a beautiful job with Michael. That little guy really had me worried. It's a miracle Michael made it through his first year."

I burst into tears and clasped Jean in an unexpected bear hug. Then my brain clicked in. Had she thought Michael as vulnerable as I too thought? What made her think so? Why hadn't she said anything? Were Michael's doctors secretly thinking the same?

I could barely speak. "Really?" was all that came out. I had never let on to anyone, not even to Robin. I too thought it a miracle Michael was alive.

Jean said she was aware Michael wasn't growing and hadn't put on much weight the whole year. She had other concerns too, but thought it too early to say anything. She could see we were doing okay day-by-day and didn't want to worry us. Encouragement was what we needed. She believed the most important thing during the first year was to maintain the bond we had with Michael, and build on our attachment to him.

"I was keeping a watchful eye, though. Don't think for a second I was ignoring you."

I took her painfully sobering thoughts as affirming, almost comforting, in a strange way. It *had* been a terribly rough year with Michael. Maybe his difficulties *really weren't* of our making. Close friends relentlessly reassured us, suggesting Michael's particular temperament and tiny, undersized little body were the source of his problems, not our parenting. But I was still hearing Island scuttlebutt, all with the same theme. Not enough tough love. We had to be stricter about feedings and sleep, let Michael cry until he wore himself out, if necessary, and ignore steady demands for milk and comfort. He had to find out who was in charge.

Were they right? Two parenting bestsellers counselled parents to get feeding and sleeping routines set early on, *no matter what it took*. But would they have given me the same advice if they knew Michael? Or could he be an exception? The only book I related to during this time was *The Difficult Child,* about children who had particularly sensitive temperaments. I was selfishly and secretly pleased that the book had a market beyond our family.

My own instincts were telling me that the parenting books weren't about Michael. I felt he was different, a vulnerable soul who needed nurturing and compassion above all else. Yet I continually questioned myself. Perhaps I was being weak-willed and defensive. Perhaps I *was* insufficiently firm with the little guy. If so, I wasn't doing anyone a favour, not me or him.

Jean's words that morning were bittersweet, making me seriously question if there was something really wrong with Michael. It was still a thought I was willing to take only so far — just far enough to think *if there is something wrong with Michael, we could find out what it is and fix it.*

Nothing was pointing in any clear direction, though. A neo-natal specialist we took Michael to when he was three months old suggested he might have attention deficit disorder. It was too early to tell for sure, he said.

Fortunately, soon after we brought Michael home, a friend introduced me to the words "easy" and "difficult," replacements for "good" and "bad," the common terms of the day when talking about babies. Like me, Mary bristled when someone asked if her daughter was being a "good baby." How do you answer that question if you've got a kid who cries and fusses? Do you say, "No, she's a 'bad' baby?" And what about a sick baby? Also bad? How, pray tell, could a baby be bad? Our hearts broke for our babies. We're going to tell people they're being bad?

It's a good thing I learned these new terms. It gave me an answer to use when my mother phoned from Florida each week asking if Michael was being a good baby. I could respond without making my teeth clench and body tighten. I could say, "No, Ma, he's being difficult."

As Michael got older, we seemed to be acquiring a new medical specialist every week for his growing number of physical problems. At six months, enter the dermatologist. Michael had a constant urge to pick at his skin and nothing we did could stop him. When I couldn't stand watching him anymore, I asked our pediatrician for a referral. Michael was never without a bleeding sore or a scab somewhere on his little white body. He even began to scratch any sore, loose skin or scab that Robin or I might have that he could feel when we were holding him.

We kept his nails clipped and hands away from his face to minimize damage. We often gloved him, but it agitated him so much we had to take them off except at night. His picking was so compulsive we worried what might happen if Michael came down with chickenpox or measles.

The dermatologist asked Robin and me a few questions, then barely glancing at Michael's sores, provided the following useless information: "You've got yourself a picker," she said matter-of-factly. "Some people are pickers, some aren't. This little one is. Nothing you can do about it."

When I looked at her quizzically, she added, "You probably know some adults like him. People who love to pick. They're everywhere." Clearly, we were on our own.

Then to the eye specialist. The corners of Michael's eyes had been crusty and oozing for months. The pediatrician initially thought it might be a cold virus and suggested we wait it out. Eventually, a specialist performed surgery to open Michael's tear ducts. Problem solved.

Michael had continual bouts with ear infections, one after the other. Neither antibiotics nor herbal remedies nor warmed oil helped keep them from coming. Then an ear specialist conducted a small operation to insert tubes for drainage, stopping the marauding bacteria in his Eustachian tubes dead in their tracks. When the tubes fell out, a second operation.

Two ailments down, new ones kept cropping up with horrifying regularity. A few nights before his first birthday, Michael's breathing suddenly became laboured. We took the next boat to the city and an ambulance to emergency at the Hospital for Sick Children. They gave him oxygen, said they thought it was asthma but suggested we wait and see. A year later, same thing. He couldn't get enough air in his lungs to breathe. We were so frightened watching him strain, we called the on-Island firemen. They rushed to our house and gave Michael oxygen, which improved his breathing temporarily, then drove us to the ferry docks where a police boat was waiting. With incredible speed, they ferried us across the bay to an ambulance waiting city side. Then off to SickKids again for a full-fledged diagnosis of asthma.

Our pediatrician referred us to a cardiologist for a thorough review of the heart murmur Michael was born with. Though he pronounced the condition mild, he recommended that Michael always and forever be administered prophylactic antibiotics before undergoing any surgery, even dental, to avoid possible infection and damage to his heart.

When Michael was eight months, an endocrinologist assessed his growth — or more accurately, non-growth. "It will be important to follow closely his development in coming years," he said, "since Michael isn't yet growing or putting on weight." Providing minor relief to our fears, he thought Michael would soon start developing.

The rest of his diagnosis was less reassuring. "Unfortunately, I don't think he will ever make up the lost growth from his first year. But I'm predicting that if he continues to get good care, he will grow at a normal pace hereafter." If later tests found Michael lacked sufficient growth hormones, they could administer them then. "Until then, just wait."

Besides feeling sorry for my little boy and tired of days filled with doctors' appointments, hospitals and visits to our local pharmacy, I felt continually blessed by the Canadian medical system and taxpayer. We didn't once pay extra for the medical care Michael received. We had no waits. The care was superb. Before he was one year old, Michael had seen seven specialists: a cardiologist, pediatrician, ear, nose and throat specialist, neo-natologist, dermatologist, respirologist and endocrinologist.

I often thought what this would have cost if we lived in the United States. We would be bankrupt. As it was, we were only emotionally overdrawn.

And it was only the beginning.

7.

Sarah, the Jewish Christmas Miracle

Toronto Island, 1989

DESPITE ALL OUR PROBLEMS, I loved being a mother, loved Michael, loved Robin and being a family. So much so, by the time Michael was two, Robin and I began talking seriously about a second baby. We were as shocked as everyone else.

Although I had gone back to work full-time when Michael was one, it soon became clear that I would need to work part-time if I was going to be Michael's mother. It had also become evident that my career wouldn't be going anywhere, and our family income, dependent on my salary as much as Robin's, would be drastically cut. I had to make compromises because of Michael, and work was the biggest. We were lucky Robin had a solid job at the CBC. But now that I was working part-time, I could take care of two babies.

It was one of those sunny, crisp, blue-skied autumn days in late September that made me think I loved fall as much as I did spring. It was a non-office day and I was at home looking after an active, two-and-a-half-year-old Michael and, at the same time, working alongside the once-a-week cleaning woman we hired to bring a modicum of order into our home.

Let's just say there was a lot of busyness going on. Maria had finished washing the kitchen's wood floor and had just turned on the noisy vacuum cleaner in the living room when the phone rang. Both noises startled Michael so he began to cry. I picked him up in my arms, took my shoes off, jumped across the wet kitchen floor and hopped onto the kitchen table — all with Michael still attached to my hip.

I picked up the phone and offered a distracted "Hello."

"Hi, I'm calling about the ad in the newspaper," said the young woman on the other end.

"Ad?" I thought to myself. What ad? Were we selling the fridge? The washing machine? The car? I continued to pause and said nothing. I had no idea what ad she was talking about.

"I'm sorry," I finally said, "we didn't place any…" but before I could finish the sentence I was thunderstruck.

"Oh, my god, THE AD! I had no idea it went into the paper."

"Yeah, it's in this morning's *Sun*," she said, to her credit, laughing sweetly at my new mildly hysterical tone.

She was waiting for me to talk, but in the last five seconds I had realized that this phone call could change my entire life. It began to sink in that I had to pull myself together immediately and act like a totally mature, responsible human being. Even though I was standing on a kitchen table.

"Would you mind holding on for just a minute?" I beckoned to Maria who turned off the vacuum cleaner so I could hand Michael over to her, and then I hopped down from the table. Who cared about the floor anymore?

"Sorry, I was a bit shocked by your call," I said. "We sent in the ad to the paper ages ago. They said it would take months before it would actually go in."

Adoption ads had to be approved by the government to make sure they didn't say or imply that money would exchange hands in return for a baby. So, there we were! The newspaper had received approval and had put the ad in today's paper! Just a little thing they forgot to tell us when they ran it! Keep it together, Linda! Just be yourself.

"You must be pregnant," I said.

"Yes, six months." I quickly did the math. It was early September. Nine take away six. Three more months to go. A late November baby. Three months away. Yikes.

"Would you like to tell me a little about yourself? Or," I

speedily added, "would you like me to tell you about myself?"
It had to be as tough at her end as it was at mine.

"Things haven't been going well with my boyfriend," she
said, "and I decided it would be best to give the baby up for
adoption. I didn't know how to go about it, so when I looked
in the classifieds this morning and saw your ad, I thought it
was a miracle."

The miracle ad, which read: "Pregnant? Couple looking to
adopt newborn. Can provide loving, caring home. Call."

"I'm glad you called," I said.

I liked Denise right away. I was touched by the honest, straight-
talk about her life. What stood out most was her heartfelt
desire to do what was best for her soon-to-be-born child. She
was bright and tough, and had strong survivor instincts. Like
other people I had known, she could have used a few breaks.

Later, she told me she'd felt comfortable talking to me. I
wasn't judging or putting her through an inquisition, two things
she was so worried about before the call, she almost didn't.

What was there to judge? How life dealt different hands?
How fate sent me one way, her another?

Denise's heritage was mostly French Canadian and partly
Métis. Born into a working-class family, she'd dropped out of
school before Grade Twelve. She was twenty-three and in an
unstable relationship with the father of the child.

I told her about my background, so very different from hers.
I was happily married with one child and came from a close-
knit family I was in constant touch with. "This might sound
idyllic," I said, "but my life has been far from storybook." It
was just that by the time I hit forty-one, the age I was when
she and I first spoke, a lot of basics had come together.

We chatted away like two motherly souls, both moved that
the finger of fate was bringing us together. Was it possible to
give each other what we longed for? For Robin and me that
meant another child. For her, a loving home for her child and

a family she could maintain contact with after the child was born. We talked and laughed and cried. No specifics had yet been mentioned.

I knew Denise would soon want to know what kind of people Robin and I were, and, therefore, what kind of home her child would be brought up in. Up until the call, I hadn't given a thought to how I would make us look good. Soon Denise would start asking questions. How would I answer?

I decided to be completely honest right from the get-go. It sounds strange that I *decided* to be honest, but the world of adoption is trickier than most people realize.

First off, babies just aren't there to be had. I had one chance, and knew I was lucky to get that. If I wanted her baby, I had one chance to convince her that she *wanted to give me her child, the most important thing in the whole world to her.* I needed to make the most out of every second.

It's a seller's market in adoption land. We had to look good, because there were a lot of other families to compare us with. Though I *knew* we would provide a wonderful, loving home for the child, what if Denise had different values, a different religion or worldview? What if she wanted all kinds of things for a kid we were convinced had nothing to do with a good and loving home? And, of course, what if I didn't like her and didn't want her baby? A lot to figure out.

Denise and I had been talking for ten minutes and had already established some warmth. The questions we each had for the other were going to come soon. I was already thinking through four areas that had popped into my mind where my family might not look ideal.

The first was religion. From what Denise told me about her background, I knew she was Christian. How would she feel about her child being raised Jewish? I knew religion could be a thorny issue. It wasn't exactly like the whole world loved Jews. What did I know about the way she was raised, whether she'd known Jewish people in her life, or how open a person she really was? Besides, why would she necessarily want to put her child into a minority religion, culture or race when the child could lead a much easier life in the majority religion, culture or race?

The second was family income. Though Robin and I lived comfortably and had few material wants, we were far from flush. I was working part-time, Robin's job was steady, but we didn't have cash to spare. I had read that birth moms often look for homes where children have financial opportunities they hadn't had. Who could blame them? Denise had had to struggle hard for her next dollar. All other things being equal, why wouldn't she want a family for her child who could provide more "things" than Robin and I could.

The third area of concern was age. I was forty-one and Robin, forty-six. We were both young at heart, ready for our next child, and were, in our opinion, just the right age to have another child. But would Denise agree? All things being equal, if you were comparing us to other potential parents, would you want "old-timers" like us to parent *your* child?

The fourth was Michael. We already knew he was "different." We still didn't know what that meant exactly, but we were beginning to put a few things together. Even at two and a half, he hardly stopped moving, twisting or being what seemed agitated. He never stuck with anything he was playing with. He constantly went from one thing to another. He didn't make eye contact with people, and he didn't like to be touched except by Robin and me. He was playful and delightful in many ways, but he was more than just a "handful." He only seemed to do what he wanted to do. Might Denise think this was because we were lousy parents? If she felt something was "wrong" with Michael, was he the brother she wanted for her child?

So wouldn't you try, at least a little, to make your family sound like the Partridge Family? Wouldn't you want your prospective birth mother to think everything in your life was coming up roses in as many departments as possible?

NOT EXACTLY AS PLANNED

No, I decided I wouldn't. I couldn't. I was all for painting a pretty picture, and a pretty picture was exactly what I believed our family to be. With all the flaws and difficulties in our lives related to Michael, Robin and I remained devoted to family. Our home was a good place to be. I would tell the truth about everything and explain, as best I could.

Then it happened.

"What religion are you?" Denise asked.

"I don't know if you have met many Jewish people in your life, but I am Jewish. Robin is not." I could have left it there, but wanted to be clear. I needed to give her an idea of who I really was beyond the labels.

"My religion is important to me and we are raising Michael Jewish. We would hope to raise your child Jewish too. Though I am not highly observant," I added, worrying she was already picturing men in black coats with big fur hats dancing on tables. "I think it's important to raise children with some religion. Who knows what they'll decide to do when they're adults? But I think it's a good way to teach values and give a strong moral foundation and rootedness to a family."

She paused and thought. "I'm fine with that. How old are you?"

I gave the numbers. "Robin and I waited a long time to have a family. We're what you call 'mature' parents. Both of us had a lot of living, learning and growing up to do. Also, it took me a long time, a lot longer than most people, to find the right man."

Like two girlfriends at a pyjama party, we started talking openly about "finding the right man," and about making mistakes along the way. "Do you have any other children?"

I told her about Michael, our love for him, our concern for him. I let her know we were dedicated to our family and would be as loving to her child as we were to Michael.

She was happy to know her child would have a sibling. She was sympathetic about our difficulties with Michael, but his problems did not confound her. I was beginning to see that Denise travelled life without a script or any sense of grand entitlement. We both knew that life held no promises or guarantees. You try to make good things happen, and give all you've got to the rest. Fortunately for us, Denise said she could tell that what Robin and I had was a lot of love to give.

We couldn't believe our luck in finding one another. We had a long way to go in the bureaucratic adoption process before this materialized into anything other than talk, but we both knew we wanted to move forward — together.

Denise was clear that she wanted an "open" adoption. Though she didn't plan on meeting any time soon, she wanted to maintain telephone contact. She wanted to know how the baby was, to hear my voice again. She wanted to call when she needed to, and she would like it to be the same for us.

This would be a completely different form of adoption than we had with Michael's birth mother, but both Robin and I were open to this arrangement. More than open. The idea that we could make Denise happy the way she could make us happy was a dream.

Still, I was scared. What if I gave her the contact info for the adoption counsellor to work out the adoption details and she never called him? What if we never heard from her again? On her part, she had to be worried that we would change our minds and she'd be back to square one, looking for another miracle.

I knew enough not to get too excited. It wasn't easy in Canada and the United States to find a second, let alone a first newborn baby to adopt. We had been counselled not to get our hopes up, even if things started to look good. There were so many steps and stages, something could easily go wrong. A natural wariness is smart in the adoption world. Strange and heartbreaking stories about adoptions that never get finalized because birth mothers change their minds are not hard to come by.

In fact, many adoption counsellors recommend that if you put an ad in the paper to find a baby to adopt, as we had, not to give out your own phone number. Instead, have friends or family accept the calls first. They should test the callers to see if they are bogus or real. Only when sure that (1) there is a real baby being born, (2) the birth mother might honestly be interested in giving her child to you, and (3) there was no possibility of being asked for money, were they to give out your home number.

If being cautious meant handing the phone to other people if someone called, I wasn't willing to do it. I couldn't put the chance of a lifetime into someone else's hands. It wasn't that I feared someone else couldn't do it *my* way. I needed to hear the sound of the woman's voice at the other end the first time she called. I knew it would tell me something.

As it turned out, Denise did call Alan, the adoption counsellor. She met with him several times at his office, filled out forms, talked about her life and plans for her baby, and about the form of adoption she preferred — open. He answered questions, gave advice and actually hired her to work in his office when he learned how badly in need of money she was.

Two days after they first met, Robin and I went to Alan's office to fill out the bazillion forms required for the adoption, same as we did for Kira's baby. Alan confirmed what I thought about Denise — life had been tough, she had a strong character, clearly wanted her child to have a life she could not yet provide. She did not think it fair to keep the baby to give her the love *she* needed — she had to find that elsewhere. She wanted her child to have a good home, and that home was ours.

Eureka! Alan felt this would all unfold as it should. He sensed Denise could be trusted and that she would respect necessary boundaries after the baby was born. An open form of adoption, in which we stayed in contact with one another, could work really well. And best of all, Alan spoke to the boyfriend and got him to come in and sign the necessary papers.

In the weeks that followed, Denise and I talked often on the phone. Her positive feelings about the adoption never wavered, and she worked out all the final details with Alan. He would go to the hospital with her for the delivery and spend time with her there until she felt ready to leave and go home.

It was time to break the news to our two-and-a-half-year-old Michael. We had been reading baby books about adoption to him since he was an infant, so the concept wasn't new, but having a sibling was.

"Michael, you know how Mommy and Daddy adopted you when you were born?" I asked. "Well, we're going to adopt another baby. You're going to have a little brother or sister."

"No baby."

"You know how Zorah has a new baby sister named Maeve? And how Noah has a new sister, Suzanne? Well, you're going to have a new baby, too."

"No baby."

Right. No baby.

"Well, Michael, your little pals love having a baby and we hope you will too."

He was pretty clear on the matter. He just needed a little time to get used to the idea, we thought. How could he know what it all meant until he actually saw some little creature taking residence in his house? We were plying him with as much attention as possible to minimize jealousy, but who knew what would happen when he actually saw his mom holding another baby that she didn't hand back to someone else?

Early in November, several weeks before Denise's due date, Robin was sent to Stuttgart, Germany, to produce a documentary about the then developing European Market. On November ninth, his executive producer called from the Toronto office. "Take your crew and go immediately to Berlin," he said. "The Wall's come down." After covering Berlin, Robin was then asked to continue the European Market story in Prague. It was mid-November by then.

"It's getting dicey," Robin said, on the phone to me from Germany. "If I go to Prague, it'll be hard to extricate myself if I have to." I agreed. He told his boss the extension was a no go. "I've got to get back," he said. "My wife and I may be having a baby any minute." He said the producer just laughed, warmly.

Three days after his return, Denise called. "The doctors say they miscalculated my due date. They now think it's mid-December." Aargh.

More waiting. November came and went. Chanukah came and went. Christmas was fast approaching. We were nervous, excited and anxious. We continued on with our lives as best we could, even making plans with our neighbours Penny and Peter for a Christmas Day feast at their house. We never assumed we'd actually go.

It was below zero Fahrenheit outside and the ground was covered with an overlay of black ice topped with crusty snow. Robin and I were listening to "O Holy Night" as we sipped rum-soaked eggnog, made mashed potatoes and baked pies for Christmas Day dinner at our friends, Penny and Peter's home. The phone rang. It was Alan. The time, four o'clock in the afternoon.

"Denise has gone into labour. She is now at the hospital but nothing much seems to be happening. I'll keep you informed."

I could tell he was about to sign off. "Not so fast. You mean I just sit around and pretend I'm not having a baby anytime soon?" The oddity of rolling out a piecrust while I was about to become a mother again didn't escape me. Nor did the dreadful feeling of powerlessness and disconnect I had over something so enormous in my life. Not once in the last nine months had anyone given me a knowing smile or patted my belly.

Alan made abrupt noises about this always being the toughest time for adoptive parents, then hung up. Not knowing what was happening, or when, Robin and I just kept on mashing and rolling. I also hummed quietly to myself, which reminded me of the annoying nervous habit my dad developed after the riots.

At 6:00, we packed a wooden toboggan to transport Michael, food, presents, drink and amusements over to Penny and Peter's. I dressed Michael in his snowsuit, then myself in an orange down vest, puffy lime green parka, black toque and beat-up brown suede mukluks. The finishing touch to my dashing outfit was a red-and-black-checkered wool scarf wrapped around my neck and face so only my eyes would be exposed to the brutal weather outdoors. Robin wore similar stylishly layered attire for the ten-minute walk along the boardwalk overlooking the lake, through the blustery cold.

Icy waves crashed over the sea wall, making it slippery to walk but perfect for pulling the heavy toboggan. Freezing sprays of water splashed onto our faces. As we reached Penny and Peter's, we slid across beautiful sheets of perfectly smooth black ice covering the beach in front of their home.

"We can't ruin everyone else's Christmas by being too pre-occupied with ourselves," I said to Robin just before we went inside. "We'll just tell them Denise is in labour and then forget all about it, okay?"

"Sure, just forget about it," Robin said in an undeniably mocking tone.

Before we even had our jackets off, I blurted out our news. Penny quickly uncorked a bottle of bubbly for a toast, the one and only for that moment. "To Denise," we all said, in unison.

Against our protestations, our friends proceeded to indulge us by tossing around baby-naming possibilities, should the child be born before midnight. "Mary Christmas," I said, citing the most obvious. Being one day too late to play with the name Eve, we soon exhausted the options and moved onto more Christmas-related themes. I was truly enjoying the celebrations and really tried to forget I was "in the waiting room" while Denise was in labour, but no matter how beautiful Peter and Penny's tree was, how golden the turkey and ambrosial the perfume of sage stuffing, I was antsy and only half there.

After dinner we played Monopoly with Alison and Kate, Penny and Peter's children. When Michael showed obvious signs of becoming overtired, we tried reading to him, snuggling, making new constructions with his Lego, but our luck had run out. He was restless, cranky and creating a squawk. We were lucky he had remained in good spirits for as many hours as he had.

"We should think about going," Robin said.

"Okay, but I'm calling Alan first. I can't wait any longer."

He was in the hospital room with Denise. "She's just now dilating," he said. "Her labour is really slow. It's not looking good for a Christmas baby."

Disappointed, Robin and I repacked the toboggan, dressed Michael and prepared ourselves for the arctic walk home. Heading towards the door, I stated the proverbial, "Now that we're leaving, Alan will probably call." As if the gods were listening, the phone actually rang. It was Alan. The time: 11:07 p.m.

"It's a girl. Both she and Denise are doing beautifully."

I yelled out an ecstatic "Oh my god," then rushed to Robin. We hugged and kissed and with eyes bulging, stared at each other, laughing.

Penny poured another round and we clinked our second toast of the evening. Besides Denise, we now had another person to celebrate. Our newborn daughter.

"To serendipity. To order. To life," I said. "*L'chaim.*"

"I truly see this baby as a Christmas miracle," Denise told me on the phone the next day.

"That is for sure," I said. But exactly how great a miracle, Denise did not know. Nor could I tell her.

Even though we had all decided on an open adoption and would remain in contact by phone or letter after the baby was born, Alan had advised us not to disclose our last name or address to Denise. It was a precaution against unplanned visits to see the baby, now or in the future. "It's standard practice, even with an open adoption," he told us. "It's better for everybody to have a built-in boundary like this. You can always make changes with the arrangement if that's what you both want. But until you know one another better, precautions are sensible."

We trusted Alan. Holding identifying information back, for the present at least, made sense. These were still early times in our relationship with Denise. But "holding back" meant keeping secrets and, in this light, the idea weighed on me. It took away the equanimity in our relationship with Denise. Until *and if* our daughter decided to meet Denise in the future and the final details came out, she wouldn't know the Christmas baby she had just given birth to would have the last name of Christmas. I was keeping from her just how much of a Christmas miracle her child really was.

We gave our daughter the name Sarah as her first name, honouring my grandfather Samuel. Ellen became her middle name, to honour my mother's mother — the grandmother-un-beknownst-to-me from Eloise, Esther. I felt this was my opportunity to ensure the spirit of my grandmother, whoever that was, was not left forgotten.

Robin and I were on pins and needles waiting to hear when we could bring Sarah home. Other than speaking to Denise the morning after she gave birth, Alan had told us not call. It was Denise's time, and we should respect it. So until she left the hospital and handed the baby to Alan, Sarah remained like a desert mirage, still out of reach.

We waited for three days. "This might be the day," Alan told us, calling in the morning on Day 4 from the hospital. "Denise has gone home, and remains comfortable with her decision. It's looking like the hospital will give permission for you to take Sarah home today. And by the way, the nurses say she's a gorgeous, quiet little baby. Sleeps, wakes, hardly makes a peep."

"Is it horrible for me to say we wouldn't mind a quiet one this time around?" I asked. He assured me not.

I asked Michael if he'd like to go with us to the hospital to see the new baby. Stupid question.

"No baby."

Of course my friend Barbara would be going with us to pick Sarah up, this time along with her daughter Suzanne, born just one month before Sarah. We decided to take Michael, "no baby" or not.

Later in the afternoon of Day 4, Alan called. "You can come get her." Robin, Michael, Barbara, Suzanne and I bundled up, caught a ferry, packed into our aging Honda station wagon and drove to North York General Hospital, in the suburbs. It was the worst, blizzardy, snowy day of the year — even colder than Christmas Day. It didn't matter. We were thrilled to have permission from the hospital to take Sarah home the same day we were to meet her.

The hospital's social worker met us at the front door and took us to the nursery where Alan was waiting for us. Within minutes, a nurse brought out the bundled baby, and I burst into tears the second I saw her.

"She is the most beautiful, pink, sweet, perfect child I have ever seen," I said. Robin and Barbara both laughed, probably because I had said virtually the same thing when I saw Michael. They become equally tearful, nevertheless.

Michael just wanted to ride the elevator again.

The nurse handed Sarah to me and I immediately pressed her against my heart. I then ran my hand across her warm fuzzy head. "It feels so different than Michael's," I said, thinking back to the thick bush of long strawberry blond hair he came into the world with.

We took Sarah to a room to get her ready for home, where we changed her into a warm outfit, kissed her, swooned over her, held her and took what seemed like a thousand pictures.

Michael played with the wooden train his new sister "brought" with her.

Leaving the nursery area, the head nurse came out from her office and approached us.

"I have two adopted children of my own," she said. "I made sure your daughter got all kinds of extra cuddles and rocks in the rocking chair while she was in there." Her kindness was like the blue-knitted outfit Michael came home in that volunteers made for the adopted children. The gesture sent me into another motherly torrent of tears.

We zipped Sarah into a down sleeping bag, wrapped her with wool blankets and took her out to the car after saying good-byes to Alan and hospital staff. She slept like an angel all the way down to the ferry docks.

The weather was so miserable, we didn't think for a second anyone would be waiting for us on the Island as they had done when we brought Michael home. But there were our neighbours, admittedly in smaller numbers, waiting for us at the docks, balloons, band and all. Trading in summer costumes for down parkas, boots and toques, they cheered as we walked off the ferry.

Ten-year-old Lizzie came up to Michael and handed him a set of wooden train tracks. "It's a consolation prize, Michael," she said. Looking at Robin and me, she added, "Will you explain to him what it means?"

We trudged home through deep snow, pulling Sarah in a big two-wheeled handmade wooden cart packed with sleeping bags and blankets to protect her from the cold. It had been two and a half years since we brought Michael home on a glorious, blue-sky spring day in the impractical English pram. But in my mind, both occasions were bathed in sunshine.

Sarah was a peaceful newborn, content being held, petted, pressed close to our hearts. I carried her around everywhere, hanging from my hip. At home, I'd set her in a baby seat on the dining-room table so she could follow me with her eyes as I dusted, cleaned and puttered around her. Robin tucked her into a Snugli under his down jacket for daytime outings with her and Michael. He looked like a silly puffed-up Michelin Man with Sarah hidden inside his jacket, but she slept the sleep of angels next to his chest. She'd give a few tiny little peeps now and then to make sure we didn't forget she was there, but that was about it. Sarah was easy.

But the waiting wasn't. Robin and I tried hard not to spend too much time thinking about the number of days to go before the adoption became permanent, but each morning began with a countdown like an advent calendar. We had twenty-one days to wait from the first day she was home. Robin and I both tried hard to hide our worry from each other, but our frayed nerves were palpable, tempers short, but only with each other, not the children.

Funny thing, Michael didn't seem too worried about the countdown. When our neighbour Joanna came to visit one day, she said to him, "I hear you have a new baby at home."

Michael responded, "I drop the baby. I step on the baby."

Not a complete surprise. The previous night Robin was in bed with Michael to get him to sleep. Robin swore he heard Michael saying *in his sleep*, "When the bough breaks the cradle will fall ... ha, ha ha." Guess who was in the cradle?

Though we kept our eyes constantly on him, Michael was actually gentle around Sarah, and for the most part ignored her. He retreated as usual into his own world, climbing into small snuggly spaces, banging on pots and pans and constructing things with blocks or Lego. We told ourselves that when Sarah started to smile and became more of a person, he would start coming around. What could she offer at this stage?

My sister Barbara came up from Detroit right after we brought Sarah home, just as she had with Michael. She held and cuddled Sarah, doing night feedings so we could get some sleep. Because of my father's increasing frailty, my parents were no longer travelling, so wouldn't be coming up to see Sarah. I was disappointed, so Robin and I planned a trip to Florida in early spring. We'd then go on to Virginia to show Sarah off to my middle sister, Sharon.

I started to lug Sarah everywhere with me, even into the city. It was easy; she was so good-natured. She became my little pal. She looked around and quietly took *everything* in. She remained a contented baby until she got hungry, which happened often. I fed her, played with her; we smiled back and forth, then she'd go back to sleep. I began to wonder how I ever lived without her? Like Michael, she was under my skin, part of my being. The love affair with Sarah was complete, but of course, had an edge. We hadn't yet reached Day 21.

I woke up thinking: today's the day! All we have to do is get through it and our Sarah will be OURS. I was packing to go out for a walk with the two kids when the phone rang. I expected it to be Alan, but it was Robin, calling from work. From the second he said hello, I could hear alarm in his voice. I'd known him long enough to recognize the tone. It was his I'm-hysterical-in-my-own-composed, English-born-male sort of way.

"Alan just called. Denise is having second thoughts. Issues about whether she wants to go ahead with the adoption. Alan feels that if she is in any way unclear about giving the child up, *he pretty much has to take Sarah away from us. Today.*"

I became unhinged in my own, American-Jewish-Detroit-non-composed-female sort of way.

I called Alan. "Can I talk to her?"

"I don't think it's a good idea. It will escalate everything. We have to be really calm and address her concerns. She has to make the right decision for herself."

His last line nearly killed me. I cared for Denise. I couldn't bear to think of her as unhappy. That was why everything in the adoption had seemed so brilliant from the get-go. Not only were we making *ourselves* happy, but we were making Denise happy too. But if Denise's happiness now meant *my complete and utter unhappiness ... well ...* I just knew I couldn't part with Sarah and want to continue living. It was as simple as that.

"Alan," I pleaded. "Do you know how hard it is to leave something so important like this in someone else's hands?"

"I'm going off now to meet with her," Alan said. "Soon as I know anything, I promise to call."

Robin abandoned the documentary he was working on and came back to the Island. Hours passed. We were numb, barely spoke. Nothing seemed real. We didn't allow ourselves to think the worst. Correction: We didn't talk about the worst. It was all we could think about.

Sarah moved from one set of arms to the other. We never put her down. We walked around a lot, talked to her, sang to her. Fortunately, Michael was at Yolanda's. He would have picked up how crazy we both were.

After several hours, I had had enough. "I have to call Alan," I said.

"He said he would call if he had anything to tell us."

"I can't NOT be part of what's going on."

I called his office and got his sympathetic secretary. "He's out of the office. He'll call you soon as he knows something."

"Will you tell him I called? I just want to hear how it's going, even if there's no final word. It will help me adjust to whatever happens." I knew, in fact, it would. I thanked her profusely, wondering how many times in her working life she had received calls from anxious adoptive mothers like me, desperate to hear an encouraging word.

Another hour passed, then the phone rang. Neither Robin nor I moved. We just looked at one another. Neither of us wanted to get it. Finally, I did. I don't think I even said hello.

"Linda, everything is okay. Denise is clear. She wants to go ahead with the adoption. We had a good talk. She just needed a little support. She is very happy that you and Robin will be raising her baby."

We made it through Day 21. Sarah was ours.

"Thief! Thief!" I yelled.

Michael and I were on a walk in late April, pushing a sleeping Sarah in her stroller. As we reached the Algonquin meadow, I stopped by a grove of dogwoods, lifting my binoculars to the flock of blue jays flying past. I turned to Michael who looked up at me and smiled. He knew not to panic. No bandits in sight.

"Blue jay," he said.

"Good going, Michael. Okay, here's another. 'Cheer! Cheer!'" I burbled into the air.

"Cardinal," he responded, proudly. I gave him a hug.

"I think you're ready for a harder one this time." Unfortunately, it required me to sing.

"O sweet Canada Canada Canada," I trilled.

Michael laughed at me. "White throated sparrow, Mom."

I was delighted that he was having so much fun guessing the name of the bird I was imitating. Perhaps Robin and I had successfully passed along our passion for all things bird during our many walks over the years. Because of Robin's name, I had started Michael on robins when he was a baby.

"Look Michael, there's the first robin we've seen this year. Look how it hops around looking for worms."

I then moved on to other species. "See the bright red and orange patches on the shoulder of the red-winged blackbird?"

"Did you see that kingfisher dive into the water for a fish? Doesn't he look like he has a crewcut? Did you know that's Mommy's favourite bird?"

Still lugging my camera along as I had for the past four years since Michael was a baby, I now also carried my beat-up copy of *Peterson Field Guides to Eastern Birds*. Once we saw a bird, we'd look through the guide together until Michael picked out the bird we had just seen. I'd write Michael's initials and the date next to the bird so we'd have a record of his first sighting.

Peterson Field Guides to Eastern Birds had become one of Michael's favourite bedtime books. Instead of reading a bedtime story, we'd often open up the book and riffle through. Sometimes we'd look for what we thought were the most beautiful birds. Then the ugliest birds, the biggest, smallest or silliest-looking birds. Michael was always proud when he could point to a bird and identify it.

By the time Michael was three, he could name more than twenty birds in the field guide, and by age four, another twenty, including "flingoes." His goal was to see a roadrunner "because they're so funny-looking." He knew kingfishers were "Mommy's favourite bird" and "Daddy's name is the same as the robins." He often asked to listen to tapes of bird songs we bought to help him get to sleep at night. And best of all, he loved to play "baby robin" with me, an activity I invented while watching a mother robin feed worms to her fledglings. As mother robin, I dangled a lifelike multi-coloured gelatinous gummy worm candy from my mouth to baby robin, Michael. Baby robin Michael would then open wide so Mommy could feed baby. It was a real hit.

Michael's ability to identify and name birds from such a young age was astonishing. After one of our walks I said to Robin, "Maybe we should be teaching him how to pick stocks instead of guessing bird calls. You know, something useful."

"You're joking, right?"

"Only a little. Maybe it's possible to make a kid interested in whatever it is you want. If so, maybe we should work on practical stuff. People program their kids all the time with stuff they think will make them smart, talented or rich."

Robin was incredulous. He gave me the look I have learned means "Are you talking about someone else's kid or Michael?"

"We've been lucky with birds," he said. "Don't push it. For whatever reason, Michael is interested in birds. That's why it worked. You know we can't get him to pay attention to anything else we talk about. He loves being outside and he loves birds. Enjoy it."

What made these birding moments so special was that Michael lived in his own dimension most of the time. Though it didn't usually allow Robin, Sarah or me in, I took comfort thinking it was a pleasant place for him to be. When really young, he was always busy, banging away on something, building something, climbing into wastebaskets, drawers or cubby holes in blanket folds or piles of clothes — places where he obviously felt safe and cosy, just like when he was a baby. As he got older, he would retreat into his own (small) bedroom with the door closed, another cocoon of sorts.

Michael usually flitted from one activity to another, but sporadically struck upon something that absorbed him — so much so that you couldn't get his attention without a serious squabble. It was usually when he was building with his hands, oftentimes with blocks or Lego or making origami frogs. Because of his otherwise general frenzy, several people suggested Michael might have ADD, attention deficit disorder. But his keen ability to focus from time to time with such vengeance made us all think that wasn't the case.

Sarah was different. Even when she was small, she was curious, especially about people, knowing how to charm them and make "contact" with them.

At home, she'd contentedly play with her toys, books and stuffed animals. I would check in with little chats, smiles and caresses, but she just seemed happy knowing I was orbiting in her sphere. Little Buddha Girl we called her because of her general sunny, peaceful glow. As she got older, we also called her Sarah Bernhardt, after the great actress. Sarah was all of that too.

Michael wasn't impressed with her theatrics, though. One day just when Sarah began to crawl, she headed straight for our front door. It looked like she was on her way out. Seeing this, Michael responded with great glee: "Look Ma, *it's* leaving." Not "her," "it."

By the time Sarah was four, she was already figuring out how to ingratiate herself into people's hearts. That was the year she publicly affirmed there was something special about her. It happened while we were going to Detroit to visit my sister and family during the Christmas holidays. An immigration officer on the U.S. side of the border between Windsor, Ontario and Detroit, Michigan stopped us.

"Everyone's ID, please," the officer said.

I passed him two adult passports and the children's birth certificates. The officer looked at our passports without comment, then took one look at Sarah's papers and burst out laughing. The next thing we knew his head was inside Robin's open window, straining to see into the back seat. He wanted a better look at Sarah.

"You gotta be kidding," he said. "Your name is Sarah Christmas and you were born on Christmas? Well, you've just made my day. What were the chances of that?" He was shaking his head in bemused amazement.

Sarah knew he was talking about her, and was clearly enjoying the attention, yet we weren't sure she understood exactly what the fuss was about. Then she suddenly chimed in, unprompted, sounding like a wound-up Chatty Cathy doll, and said to the officer, "Yes, my name is Sarah Christmas and I was born on Christmas Day." She delivered her one-liner with such confidence and timing, we all broke into laughter.

The next few years were filled with similar scenarios, especially at Christmastime. By the age of six, she had figured out that she could get even better reactions by adding one more detail when answering questions about herself. She called these details "my coincidences." For example, one day we were in a downtown bank opening up a savings account for Sarah. When the manager scanned the application form I had just filled out, she looked at Sarah with a huge grin on her face and said, "Really, your name is Sarah Christmas and you were born on Christmas Day?"

I waited to hear Sarah's usual pat response, but instead she said, "Yes, I'm Sarah Christmas, I was born on Christmas Day ... and I'm Jewish."

8.
The Secrets and Lies of Adopted Realities
Toronto Island, 1990

I WAS STANDING in front of the bathroom mirror doing a last minute run-through of my after-dinner speech, already dressed in my bridesmaid's gown. "Six years ago to the day," I began, "my husband Robin and I took vows to love one another in good times and bad, just as Lynn and Don did today..." I stopped, as I had on two previous takes.

I yelled for Robin to come upstairs.

"I'm a mess," I said. "I can't avoid talking to her. We're both giving speeches. I'm right after her. And besides, it wouldn't be right to avoid her. She's Don's daughter."

After living together for six years, our friend Lynn was tying the knot with her partner Don at St. Andrew on-the-Lake Anglican Church on the Island. I was truly happy for them. I just wasn't happy for myself. Because guess who was coming for dinner — or should I say wedding? Michael's birth mother.

I had done reasonably well avoiding her up until this day. My scorecard wasn't perfect, though. I had dodged Kira several times during Michael's first two years when she had come to visit her dad on the Island, but recently ran into her as I was getting on the ferry with Michael. Fortunately, only minutes earlier, my friend Barbara had taken him from me because I was having trouble wrangling a crying Michael, six-month-old Sarah and bags of groceries. Preoccupied with my logistical mayhem, I hadn't noticed Kira. But she noticed me.

"Hi, you're Linda, aren't you?" she said, walking up to me. She was small and thin, with short reddish hair. She had a few freckles dotting her face and a very perky, childlike demeanour. "I'm Kira, Don's daughter. We met a few years ago at my dad's."

Barbara, having figured out whom I was talking to, made a hasty beeline with Michael to the other side of the boat.

I was tongue-tied mortified. Mustering hidden thespian skills, I smiled and said. "Sure, I remember you, Kira. Your dad often talks about you. Coming for a visit?"

"Yeah. The Island's a good place to take it easy," she said, bubbly and cheerful. "Did they tell you I'm pregnant?"

A brick just landed on my forehead. Pregnant? Another baby? Number four? You already have three you're not raising. What are you thinking? Oh, right, you're not.

"Congratulations," I said. "How are you feeling?"

"Great, thanks, everything's good."

"Well, good luck. I'm sure we'll see each other again before the baby's born."

Again was in two hours, at Lynn and Don's wedding. I was sick about it. It meant more phony-baloney yakkety-yak. Kira was so charming and friendly, it was disarming. I'll be making sweet talk to someone who doesn't know I'M RAISING HER BABY, now three years old. I'll be keeping a huge, monumental secret while staring right at the person to whom I'm lying, and all the while thinking bad thoughts, wondering why she's having another baby.

Who is this person I'd become? I didn't like this me and wasn't looking forward to hearing each insincere word I was about to sputter within a few hours.

The wedding was beautiful, and so was Lynn, wearing my wedding gown, a nice parallel since we both married on September 14. Hers 1990, mine six years before.

Kira gave a delightful tribute to Lynn and her dad, emphasizing how happy she was that he had found someone special to love. I then gave my speech. After the speeches, Kira came over to my table and tapped me on my shoulder.

"I loved your speech, Linda. You spoke so well. I was really nervous and forgot to say half of the things I planned," she added, giggling nervously. I reassured her that she had done beautifully. She honestly had. There was something so seemingly innocent and charming about Kira, I could almost imagine her sprinkling pixie dust around the room and onto the newlyweds.

"I'm sure your dad was very proud to see you up there," I added. We both stood there, silent, until Kira spoke again.

"I'm really glad you're such a good friend of Lynn's," she said. "She's very special. I guess this means you're now part of *my extended family.*"

Robin, sitting across the table from me, had been watching our interchange with hawk eyes. Hearing Kira's last words, he sprang up and came to the rescue.

He put out his hand out to Kira and said, "We haven't met. I'm Linda's husband, Robin."

With a lovely, warm smile, Kira shook Robin's hand and said, "It's nice to meet you. I guess that means *you're extended family as well.*"

I don't know why it happens, but in moments of great emotion, the most descriptive word I often find to explain how I feel is in Yiddish. Go figure. I don't really speak the language. But in this case, the word that came to mind was *plotz*, the definition being "to be aggravated beyond bearing; to collapse or faint." The word was perfect. I thought I was going to *plotz.*

In my head, I was thinking, "Kira, we're *already* extended family. We're raising your child. And the new baby you're going to deliver will make us even more extended. He or she will have a half-brother, our son, the other son you gave birth to, three years ago. Is this extended family enough for you?"

"That's a lovely thing to say, Kira. Yes, extended family."

Three months after Lynn and Don's wedding, Kira gave birth. She was twenty-six. She and her partner decided to raise the child they named Andrew, now the third blood-related half-sibling my son had floating around in the world.

A few months later, Lynn received a late-night phone call. "We've been told you're Kira's next of kin," the voice said at the other end. "She was wandering around inebriated in a mall, with her son in a stroller. We've picked her up. Come get them." It was the police.

Within a few months, the police called again. Same story. Then another call. Eventually, Children's Aid was brought in to keep tabs on Kira, her drinking and Andrew's well-being. Upgrading Kira and Eddie's parenting skills was high on their agenda. Maybe Kira would have been better able to look after Andrew if he was an easy child, but he wasn't. He was difficult.

Kira and Eddie held tight in their desire to raise Andrew, so by necessity, Lynn and Don were continuously looking out for Andrew's welfare and supporting Kira and Eddie in some form or other. They kept Andrew for days at a time; took him to doctor's appointments, gave financial assistance; acted as role models and were forever troubleshooting.

A little over one year later, and still in the midst of this steady maelstrom, Kira announced that she was pregnant again. Baby #5, same father. I was so sickened, I harboured fantasies of asking the police to pick her up and put her in a cell until the baby was born, to keep her out of trouble. Thoughts of politically incorrect forced sterilization also crossed my mind.

The pregnancy didn't change Kira. She was still running loose with Andrew in tow. Another call came in from Children's Aid. Kira was wandering the streets again with Andrew, drunk — what Lynn referred to as Wandering Under the Influence (WUI).

Children's Aid issued an ultimatum to Don and Lynn: "Come pick Andrew up," they said. "He either lives with you permanently, or we're putting him directly into foster care." By this time, Andrew was sixteen months old.

NOT EXACTLY AS PLANNED

It was not exactly what the professional working couple had in mind for their future. As far as Don was concerned, he was finished with childrearing. In his sixties, and having problems with his health, he felt he deserved to have another life at this late stage. But for Lynn, no question. Planned or not, Andrew was family. He was coming to live with them. Full stop.

One month before the next baby was due, Kira's partner left. Because she had now lost custody of Andrew, and with no father to help her raise the next child, she decided to give up Baby Boy #5. As she had given up Michael.

After Kira gave birth, the medical staff at the hospital checked Baby #5 for possible problems and found him "harm free." The adopting parents picked up their new son. I said to Robin, "I have an idea for a documentary you could make in a few years. It's a little sick, but bear with me. We rent a hall, plan a Thanksgiving meal, invite Kira and her babies' fathers, all of her kids, their respective parents, grandparents, partners and siblings. You just put a camera on a tripod and roll film." I, of course, didn't want to be within five hundred miles of the place.

Andrew's birth didn't initially pose major problems for the Rosenbaum-Christmas household. Kira came to the Island for the odd visit to the grandparents and, as before, we kept our distance. But with Lynn and Don taking custody of Andrew, he was now living just blocks away. Kira was coming often to visit, sometimes planned, sometimes not. Things were starting to get messy.

I knew that most families had secrets in their family histories, some inconsequential, some life-shattering, but do they all have people they *hide* as well as *hide from*?

Maybe keeping secrets and telling lies was inevitable in certain families. I was no longer seeing things like the ten-year-old child I once was, saying, "No Secrets. No Lies" after learning about my grandmother. Perhaps Kira should know we were raising Michael? But if we told her, how could we keep the boys separated? What would we tell Michael? And do we then tell Michael and Andrew that they're brothers?

Maybe secrets and lies do serve a purpose. At least for a while.

When Andrew moved to the Island, we realized immediately it was impossible to keep him apart from Michael and Sarah. Lynn and I were visiting back and forth at each other's houses with the kids. They were at Yolanda's together. Lynn and I took the kids to the beach. Lynn and Andrew would be coming to our next Chanukah party. We'd be invited to their house to decorate their Christmas tree. Immediately upon Andrew's arrival, Lynn was at our door, Andrew in tow, seeking hand-me-downs, company, solace, comfort and parental advice.

On the surface this was fine. Nice for the boys, nice for Sarah. But what were we going to do about the nature of the boys' relationship with one another? It wouldn't be an issue for a while because they were so young when Andrew first arrived, but they were now growing up together. If Andrew knew Michael was his half-brother, wouldn't he start talking to Kira about him as he grew older? Yes, he would. And this would not be a good thing.

None of this was part of the deal we made with Kira. And we wanted to keep that deal. We also didn't want Kira to become part of Michael's life, and certainly not ours. But we hadn't counted on a little boy named Andrew living down the street from us, being part of the deal either.

After much thought and discussion, Lynn and Don and Robin and I decided we shouldn't tell the boys they were brothers. For now.

Soon after Andrew's arrival on their doorstep, Lynn took him to Michael's pediatrician for a full examination. After the physical, the doctor asked Lynn to come into his office.

"Mum drank?" he asked.

"Yes. From what we see now, she seems to be a binge drinker."

"I'm going to refer you to SickKids. I suspect fetal alcohol syndrome (FAS)."

Lynn looked at him blankly. She didn't have a clue what that meant.

9.
Special Needs Son, Special Needs Family
Toronto Island, 1993

R OBIN WAS HOME FROM WORK one morning when the phone rang. "Can you get it?" he asked, "I'm making coffee." "No," I said, "it might be the school. You talk this time. I'm sick of handling everything myself."

It was like every other morning I was home from work. I'd lie in wait, as if a bomb were about to detonate. When it did, in the form of a phone call from Michael's public school principal, my shoulders tightened and I'd feel as if I was about to explode. I dreaded hearing the sound of her voice once again telling me Michael had done something "bad."

When he was six, Michael entered Grade One in the public school system after successfully completing two years of pre-school and one year of kindergarten at the Island's Montessori School. Each morning after Robin dropped Sarah off at Yolanda's on his way to work, I embroiled myself in the usual struggle getting Michael up, washed, dressed and fed. Mission accomplished, I'd get him out the door and we'd walk hand-in-hand to the path at the bottom of the Algonquin bridge, where I'd lie in wait until the school bus picked him up for the one-mile ride to the Island Public School. I'd come home, get back into bed, stuff my head under a pillow and wait for the phone to ring. More often than not, it did. The complaints went like this:

Michael threw stones in the playground during recess and lunch hour.

He hit some kids and a teacher.

He keeps fidgeting and won't sit still when asked.

He walks around the classroom.

He kicked two kids after they teased him.

He doesn't follow instructions, and willfully disobeys the teacher.

He doesn't move from one classroom activity when asked.

He won't get involved in group activities.

He's more interested in "parallel" play than actively playing with the other children.

I was going to meeting after meeting to discuss these issues with Michael's teacher and the principal. They called and asked *me* what to do about the problems. "How should I know?" I wanted to say, "You're asking me? You're the professionals," but I didn't. The best I could do was to describe the successful strategies Michael's Montessori teachers had used during the three years he was there:

Don't make Michael work in groups. He is a loner and can at best "parallel play."

Don't let him "just play" or be left on his own during recess in the playground. He needs structure and programmed activities.

Have him clean blackboards or put books in bookshelves...

Repeat instructions. He doesn't understand them the first time he hears them.

If an instruction is multi-stepped, have him do one thing and come back for a reminder of what the next step is. He doesn't remember steps that follow.

Give Michael advance notice and repeat warnings before he has to move from one activity to another. He gets stuck and needs time for transitions.

Give him a small ball, play dough or clay to play with in his hands at all times. It controls his fidgetiness and helps him concentrate.

Let him get up and walk around every fifteen minutes or so.

Reach out and connect with him. Have him sit close to the front. Make eye contact with him. He wants to please.

And, most importantly, find creative ways to demonstrate to the entire class how each of them is "different" in some way, and that it's okay to be different. Teach tolerance, appreciation of diversity. No bullying or teasing allowed.

To underscore the last point, I pleaded to Michael's teacher. "Please don't make Michael the example of a 'bad' kid to his classmates. It isn't right to say, 'If you act like Michael, I'll make you sit outside with him.'"

I had asked the Montessori teachers if it would be too difficult in a large classroom to do what they were suggesting? "I can't imagine they'll have time with so many other kids."

They didn't think so. "All kids are different," they said. "Once you figure out what a child needs, it makes it easier for the teacher, not more difficult. There was nothing difficult or time-consuming about what we did with Michael."

Unfortunately, that's not the way they saw it at Michael's new school. I provided Michael's new teacher with a copy of the Montessori strategies, but the teacher didn't feel she'd have time to implement them. Actually, she soon forgot I'd ever given them to her, and reminders during meetings never twigged any response.

One change that *would* have taken time *and* school policy was to address teasing. When it happened, Michael responded like a caged animal, fighting back for his life. I doubted the school would be successful in getting Michael to change his reaction to bullying, so a well-thought-out plan to tackle the broader issue was needed. I was optimistic, presuming that if Michael wasn't bullied, he'd just keep to himself, exactly where he wanted to be.

It wasn't looking good for Michael. His young teacher was inexperienced, over her head and too proud to admit it. The principal meant well but didn't call upon other professionals for guidance. I tried to be understanding. The teacher had the needs of thirty kids to look after. Michael was difficult. Teachers were overworked.

But my anger was building. Since the school didn't know how to deal with Michael, why didn't they get help? Why couldn't they say: "Michael has problems and we don't have the resources or training to deal with them. We're not clear what the problems are, so let's find out." Why should this be so hard?

Instead, they let him fail day after day in the classroom. He was behind in his school work, had problems with his teacher, didn't know what to do during recess and lunch, and was still teased by classmates, whom I suspected liked seeing Michael's highly volatile, dramatic responses. In turn, he was scolded, caught in a cycle beyond his control, continually bullied, punished and isolated. He was failing at everything he did. And the principal was calling *me* for answers? What was I supposed to tell her? I felt like I was being interrogated by the secret police. They wouldn't believe I had already told them everything I knew. The only thing left to say was, "There are people more knowledgeable than I am."

Michael's continuing failures made him fight going to school every morning. I dreaded waking up to a new day. After cajoling, manipulating, bribing and threatening, we were generally able to get him off to school. But after he left the house, I lived in fear that the telephone would ring, the principal at the other end saying: "Trouble again."

Three months after he began school, the principal ordered the school board's psychologist to do an assessment of Michael. She spent several hours with him over two days, then wrote her report: Michael had severe behavioural problems. He is aggressive, unable to control himself, lacking in social skills. Did we need her to tell us that?

I had started to read about difficult students like Michael and possible conditions at the root of their behaviour. The psychologist's report had no reference to possible causes of his problems or recommendations for remedial actions to address them. Both Robin and I thought she was one more young and inexperienced person in over her head who didn't have the good grace to say, "Let's get help for Michael." I refused to accept her simplistic finding that Michael was "bad." He remained, as ever, difficult.

After I railed at him to get the phone, Robin put down the coffee and picked up the receiver.

"Can I speak with Linda, please?" Robin put his hand over the receiver, and whispered, "It's the principal. Here…" he said passing the phone on to me.

I was furious. Why hadn't he said, "It's Robin, Michael's dad, can I help you? I'm up-to-date on what's been going on." But he didn't. He didn't want to talk to the principal any more than I did. But someone had to. Why did I have to always intercept, wheel, deal, bargain and cajole? I was getting sick of it — and him.

"I'm really sorry Linda," the principal said. "You've read the report. After discussion with the psychologist and Michael's teacher, we've decided it's best for Michael that he not return to school this semester."

I was struck by her clever phrasing "it's best for Michael…"

"Are you telling me you're kicking him out of school?" I asked. "Expelling him? Wouldn't getting proper help be better for Michael?"

It was November. A new semester wouldn't begin until January. I felt like a total failure. I hadn't been able to stop the train wreck. Robin and I thought full-time school for Michael might be good for both him and us. We were looking forward to the structure, discipline, socialization and stimulation Michael would get. Obviously, it turned out to be the wrong structure, wrong discipline and wrong stimulation.

The principal paused before answering. She didn't like the way I had rephrased her comments and used the words "expel" and "kicked out."

"We'd like you to attend an IPRC, an Identification, Placement and Review Committee meeting in the new year so the school board can decide whether to place Michael in a special needs class in a different school next year."

Because the meeting wasn't scheduled for several months, Michael had to stay home every day. That's when I learned that expelling children from school was more of a punishment for parents than children. *He* didn't care if he stayed home from school. I had returned again to work part-time after Sarah was born, so being home with Michael posed the first problem, solved once again by our Yolanda. Though she already had a full complement of kids in her daycare, she willingly took Michael along with Sarah on my work days. Robin and I weren't the only ones with a soft spot for him.

But I was worn thin on the days I was home with Michael and Sarah. I tried to keep Michael busy and out of mischief from the second he awoke until Robin came home, but it wasn't easy. He lived fast and furiously. Fortunately, he still loved making major constructions out of his Lego that kept him occupied and in one place long enough for me to get some housework done. Otherwise, he was busy every second, curious about everything he could get his hands on and touching everything in his sight.

After a few weeks at home, Michael began losing interest in things that once brought him pleasure, even his beloved Lego. Not even my exhortation "Let's go kingfisher hunting along the lagoon" rallied him. Something was going on inside of Michael and it wasn't good. Not surprising. What was there to feel good about?

During this time, I was often desperately overcompensating to ensure that Michael didn't keep me from giving a much less demanding Sarah her due. I only partially succeeded, though. I had to keep my eye on him constantly. Fortunately, Sarah had an inner life that soothed her, and she was very connected to the outside world, either through play or people.

Michael's weren't the only spirits flagging. I felt terrible that

I didn't know what to do to help my busy son be more relaxed in his own skin. I was so used to fixing things, making things better for the people I loved. Why not my son? He was already six and still, no answers. Was it possible I might never have any?

It was progressively harder and harder to do things like clean the house or do laundry. I became depressed. The cumulative worry was catching up with me. I could barely drag myself out of bed in the morning. Taking care of Sarah and Michael was my only reason for getting up.

Besides being occupied by my teetering mental health, I had to prepare for the IPRC meeting. Since my experience with the school system had been less than idyllic, I couldn't leave anything to "experts." If Michael might be considered "special needs," I needed to know what those needs were and ways to get help for him. "Special needs," according to the school board, was categorized in two ways, as having a "Behavioural Disability" or as having a "Learning Disability." There were classes for each.

I never heard the public school teacher or principal mention the possibility that Michael might have a learning disability, and berated myself for not knowing to ask that he be tested. But since he hadn't been, how would we know if he had a disability or not, and if so, which one?

I called the special education consultant at the school board to ask whose reports, tests and observations the decision would be based on. The consultant's response: "The committee has its own autonomy, so there's no set protocol for their decision-making." He did however tell us that we were welcome to make a presentation at the IPRC. "You can raise your questions then."

I started reading voraciously about kids with special needs, repeatedly hearing that most kids with learning disabilities *have* behavioural problems, and kids with behavioural problems usually *have* learning disabilities. They get in trouble because they can't learn like the other kids; they fail in the classroom, feel stupid and develop confidence problems; they "act out" because of their frustration and unhappiness. I repeatedly read, to my surprise, that it's typical to have social disabilities along with learning disabilities too.

I assumed members of the IPRC committee were reading the same literature. There was no reason for me to believe that, however. Since our experience with educational professionals in the school system had been so unimpressive, Robin and I decided it was time to get Michael tested for everything and anything. Though our pediatrician had previously felt Michael was nothing more than a highly energetic boy who was small for his age, our recent concerns encouraged him to give us a referral. Michael's differences were beginning to impede his life. And ours. If there was something actually wrong with him, it was time to find out.

Our pediatrician referred us for testing at the Child Development Clinic at Toronto's Hospital for Sick Children. Unfortunately, the appointment was one week *after* the IPRC meeting.

On the day of the IPRC meeting, Robin and I, along with Kathleen, Michael's previous Montessori principal, walked into the dimly lit corridor of a 1950s-built elementary school and up the stairs to the second floor. As we entered the conference room, a thin woman in a dark-grey suit motioned for us to take a seat.

We sat facing a long table occupied by six people looking like bone-tired members of a jury who had just delivered a guilty verdict to their previous guest. The woman introduced herself as the chairwoman of the IPRC. No one else gave their name, smiled or said hello. Robin and I looked at each other and telegraphed to each other "What the fuck did we just walk into?"

"We've had a look at Michael's files and have made our decision," the woman said. I was dumbfounded. We had spent hours preparing our presentations. What was going on? I felt compelled to say something before she went any further. There was no time to confer with Robin or Kathleen.

"Excuse me," I said, "but we've each prepared a presentation for the panel. We were told we would have the opportunity to speak before you made your decision."

The chair looked at the other panel members, several of whom gave her minimalist nods. "All right then," she said, not sounding pleased.

Kathleen spoke about various accommodations made at Montessori for Michael, how easy they were to make, how little time they consumed. "He was so creative and fun, he inadvertently became a leader," she added. "We just had to be careful what he was leading the other kids into," she concluded, with a good-natured chuckle, "but all in all, he was a real asset."

Kathleen spoke so assuredly, it buoyed my spirits. Robin and I then talked about Michael's strengths, our concerns that he may have an undiagnosed learning disability and our desire to get proper help for him.

There was silence when we finished. No one on the panel blinked, spoke or asked a question. Eventually, a voice broke the silence. "Thank you, Linda and Robin. Thank you Kathleen," said the chairwoman, barely moving a muscle on her severe face, eerily reminiscent of an imperious Queen Elizabeth delivering her yearly Christmas message.

"As I mentioned before you spoke, we have made our decision about Michael's placement. An opening has come up in a behavioural class in this district. Our funding formula dictates that the classroom has to be filled, so Michael will be labelled behavioural."

She was clear. The sheer inappropriateness of their placement, our willingness to take Michael to a school in another district or to wait for an opening in a learning disability class had no bearing on their decision.

I clenched my hands. "Is there anything further I can say

or do to convince you that Michael belongs in LD?" I asked.

"To get him labelled LD, you would have to attend an IPRC next year and make a case to get the label changed on his official record," she advised.

What happened to this year? "Even if a learning disabilities class comes up next week, we can't put Michael in it?"

"Correct. He wouldn't be eligible."

"Can we appeal your decision?" I asked.

"Yes, there is an appeal procedure," the chair said, noticeably stiffening into her chair. "I can explain the process after our meeting." Her mild display of displeasure — the first crack in her well-fitted armour — fuelled my resolve.

"I understand you've made your final decision," I continued, attempting to sound conciliatory. "However, we're not really clear that you have taken all the relevant factors in Michael's case into your decision-making. We're likely to appeal. So may I suggest something?" I paused, then continued. "I'd like you to consider a dual designation for Michael. Instead of labelling him 'behavioural,' label him 'behavioural/learning disabilities.'"

They could put Michael into the behavioural class for now, but we'd have the opportunity to get him into LD if space came up. "It would spare us all the cost of an appeal or another time-consuming IPRC meeting."

Until that moment, committee members had appeared so utterly bored, I wondered if the proceedings had overlapped with morning naptime. But they were now rotating their heads, scanning from left to right, like owls waking in the night. The lay of the land had changed.

"Yes, all right," she said. "The committee can do that. We have dual designations."

I wanted to scream, "Oh, you can do that, can you? You uncaring cows. Why didn't one of you let me know I had the right to appeal? Why didn't one of you suggest a dual designation?" It was a pure fluke that I came up with the term. I had no idea if such a thing even existed. I wanted to ask, "What will happen to the next poor fool who sits in front of you?" Instead, I said, "Thank you. So Michael will be designated LD/Behavioral." It was a victory, of sorts. We should just get the hell out of there.

Robin, Kathleen and I rushed out of the school. It wasn't long before we came to the same realizations. Michael's needs had not been on the committee's agenda. It wouldn't be the last time this happened. If Michael was to get what he needed in his life, it would be up to Robin and me to get it for him. This was likely just the beginning.

"It's ironic," I said, as we walked to the street. "In the sixties, I was fighting for other people's sons — the demonstrations, picketing, sit-ins, marches. We were all desperately trying to stop the war in Vietnam and bring our troops home to safety. Well, look how times change. I don't have to fight for other people's sons anymore," I continued, "I have to fight for my own."

The first cracks in our marriage had begun to show. The differences in Robin's and my temperaments started to dramatically clash, exactly where once they complemented each other. The cups of tea Robin once brought to me in bed each morning had long ago stopped.

We found a counsellor at the Hincks-Dellcrest Treatment Centre, a children's mental health facility that worked with families of "at-risk" youth. In theory, we were going to get help raising Michael, but in all honesty, we were there just as much to save our marriage. The therapist at the Hincks wasn't surprised. She had seen it all before with parents of kids with special needs. She wanted us first to explore our family backgrounds.

"I come from a culture where family members were highly involved in each other's lives," I explained. "Even though there were secrets, as I brutally learned, on a day-to-day level we shared feelings, hashed things out, gave opinions. Lots and lots of talk. It was often messy and unpleasant, but part of being family."

"I was initially attracted to Linda's straightforwardness," Robin explained. "I knew she wasn't beating around any bush, manipulating me or hiding anything. She said what she thought, even if it was unpleasant. It made life easier for me. My mother wasn't like that." Robin was never sure what she was really saying. "There always seemed to be an underlying message, something she wasn't telling me." The dishonesty left him unsure and confused. "I never had to second-guess Linda. It was refreshing."

Well, that lasted only so long. As problems crept up and we began to disagree on how to treat Michael, Robin wasn't so sure he liked my straight talk anymore. "It's hardly refreshing sometimes to know what Linda is thinking."

Where I once found Robin's measured, reticent manner to be steady and calming, I was now seeing it as indifference. "I know Robin is sad about Michael," I said to the therapist, "but his way of dealing with it is to escape. He closes off and clams up." To ease his suffering, he was distracting himself with any electronic device within reach, be it radio, TV, computer, camera or video. Not surprisingly, the more I wanted to commune or confront, the more he ratcheted up his firewall. "I get angrier and Robin further retreats."

In our early years of parenting Michael, Robin and I talked about problems as they unfolded. Should he sleep next to us to make him feel more secure? Do you think the bright lights are making him anxious? Is it okay to feed him on demand? When he was crying and unsettled, we'd try to find solutions together and soothe one another. We shared a determined belief that we could make a difference in his life by how we raised him, no different than other parents.

As years crept along, though, we began talking less and less about anything important. We were overloaded with problems, and too often, we differed on what might be the right way to handle them. To avoid a steady stream of arguments, we stopped talking. Parents often differ, but with a disabled child the stakes feel higher. We continually wanted to "correct" or teach or model. We thought we had the power "to fix." Every move counted.

Robin thought I was too firm and tough on Michael. I thought he was weak and non-directive. Too flexible, not flexible enough. Too unaware, too involved. Ultimately, too much anger.

We clashed on whether Michael should do assigned homework or whether we should just stop harping about it in the interest of peace. We disagreed on how to make him do chores and what to do when he didn't. We battled on strategies to get him to brush his teeth, wash or change clothes. We differed on what the consequences ought to be if he broke or smashed things. Should we punish him when he didn't do things we asked of him or accept that he was damaged and ask less of him?

From reading parenting self-help books, I even began to wonder if Michael needed a more militaristic type of father to get him in shape — a strict routine, discipline and no buts about it — rather than gentle, laid-back Robin. But Michael's pediatrician tried to reassure me that the "fit" with Michael was perfect. "Robin's temperament is just right for parenting a difficult, contrary child," he said. "Someone else would have walked out years ago or taken the strap to Michael. They would have been at war with each other. It would be tempting to use physical punishment with Michael, but it would be the worst thing for him."

Still, every day there was something. I would get angry if I didn't think Robin was "following through" when trying to get Michael to wash his hands and change underwear. Robin hated me being on top of him, thinking he was taking the easy way out. He thought I was anxious and overbearing. I hated being the one always negotiating with the school, camps, doctors, hospital, social services. He thought I was better at it so it was just natural I'd want to do it. Natural, my ass.

The therapist went easy. "Most marriages aren't ever tested the way yours is on a daily basis. That's why we see so much divorce here. People think family hardships bring people together. It happens, but it's unusual. People go through things so differently that they usually wind up suffering alone, get angry and eventually split up."

The therapist directed her next remarks to me. "Linda, you have such a verbal facility, you can run circles around Robin. It's hard for him to take it all in, and it can be very intimidating. You may sound like you know what you're talking about and come across completely sure of yourself, but I'm not sure that's always the case. Your approach can have the effect of shutting Robin down. It's not what you want, I know." She was right on every count.

The therapist was clear with one other important message, meant for both of us. While strong parenting was essential for Michael, it didn't necessarily matter whether we were doing things my way or Robin's way. "Maybe there isn't always a right or wrong way with him. Maybe one approach doesn't produce results appreciably different from another."

Right. My way didn't get Michael to brush his teeth. Robin's didn't either. My way didn't get Michael to make his bed or put dishes in the sink. Robin's either. You'd think, then, we'd let up on each other. But we didn't. There remained a little part of us that thought if we only did the right thing, we would help Michael develop. We both had such hope for him. We continued "to believe."

We were nowhere near thinking that there might be problems that had no answers. Michael seemed so capable on the surface, so we were forever wondering if his resistance to doing things, or being contrary to instruction, was because he didn't *want to do* something or because he *couldn't*. All of his teachers told us the sky was the limit for him because he seemed so smart. "He just has to try harder." They believed laziness and lack of motivation were holding him back. Therefore, I refused to stop pushing, cajoling, encouraging and teaching.

But I also wondered if Michael was more damaged than was apparent. I wondered if there really is such a thing as laziness? Or is there some hidden, undefined pathology that robs people of motivation, ambition and desire to succeed? I still wonder.

Over time, Robin and I grew tired and cranky from the worry and the arguing about all of this, and somewhere along the way we lost the ability to comfort one another. We each started hiding in our own bed of sorrow. Eventually, with the help of our counsellor, we began to understand that the way we parented Michael, whether my way or Robin's, was going to have little effect on Michael.

"Of more importance to both his well-being and Sarah's is to have parents who don't argue in front of them." It was probably even more important for Sarah who was so much more attuned than Michael to people's moods and relationships. Several times I had to console her after Robin and I had a fight, assuring her it wasn't because she had done something wrong.

The counsellor was clear. "You and Robin need to rally to your children's needs with unity. It's more important than anything else you say or do." We knew we were hurting the children as well as ourselves, but still, we didn't always have whatever it took to completely jettison the anger.

Fortunately, when Robin and I travelled, our problems seemed to vanish as soon as we hit the road, so we tried to get away often. Travel was the key to remembering what it was we loved about being together. It was a magical elixir to our troubled marriage. Undoubtedly, one of our trips' positive attributes was the pact we made before we left: we wouldn't talk about the children. It was always hard the first leg of a trip, but got remarkably easier as we hiked the Bruce Trail, rambled through England's Cotswolds or ate our way through a Tuscan hilltown. We still called home daily, but never talked much about the kids afterward.

Michael had worked his way through all the babysitters on the Island, so we were always on the lookout for some strong, level-headed young or older adult to stay with the kids during our absences. Someone looking for a challenge. Our version of a "handyman's special."

My life had become more preoccupied by my children than I ever dreamed it would be, or wished it were. I had always wanted a family, but never expected it would so define me or have such an enormous impact on the way I lived. Fortunately, I had what I referred to as my "saving graces," things that brought me pleasure and joy, and most of the time, they did. My saving graces, which included my friends, were essential, the much-needed counterpoint to periodic meltdowns I didn't have the power to avoid. I never experienced panic attacks as severe as the time after the ill-fated airplane voyage, but there were periods when I couldn't cope: everything seemed overwhelming; making dinner, paying bills, doing laundry, wrapping a birthday present.

It was never perfectly clear when or why these dark days appeared. It once happened when things were particularly bad at school for Michael. Another time it happened when he was in an aggressive, destructive period and I never knew when he would erupt next. Other times when I fell apart, nothing seemed all that different in my life except my perspective.

The depressions were relatively short, though always frightening. Perhaps it was one of the characteristics of the illness, but when in it, I was always afraid I might never come out. The thought only served to frighten me more. Fortunately, Robin was always comforting and optimistic during these periods. Equally fortunate, medication worked.

The most important saving grace I had was my garden, a source of wonderment, frustration and comfort in my life. According to friends knowledgeable about such matters, my garden had equally been a source of therapy for me, especially during times of great despair over Michael. I reluctantly agreed. I did notice how deeply satisfying it was making nasty weeds, slugs and other dark forces of nature succumb to my brutish will.

Writer Dominique Browning, an avid gardener, asked the question in one of her essays, "What really goes on when we give in to the compulsion to garden?" and answered, "Digging in the ground helps to fill the holes inside." It was doing just that.

Out of necessity, and possibly wisdom, we turned our backyard over to Michael when he was young. His energy was so physical and oftentimes destructive, he needed somewhere to dig, kick, punch, stomp, swing, slice, bang, slash, cut, chop and slice. We did live close to meadows, stretches of open land and playgrounds — however, not ours to do with as we pleased. This was a hard concept for Michael to embrace. We had to repeatedly say:

"No, you can't chop down trees to make a raft."

"No, you can't dig underground tunnels and turn open flats of land into lakes."

"No, you can't throw sticks and stones and dirt anywhere you please."

Then one day we had an idea.

"Here's the backyard, Michael. Take it, it's yours. Go to it."

And he did go to it, rendering it useless for anyone but him. For over ten years, we never went outside our back door.

That left me the front yard, and after years of work, it began to offer a welcoming face to the world, and to me.

10.
Six Years In: A Diagnosis
Toronto, 1993

ONE WEEK AFTER THE MEETING with the school board, Robin and I trudged off to The Hospital for Sick Children, Michael in tow. We were told that a child psychiatrist would collect background information about Michael at this meeting, followed by neurological tests a week later.

A tall man in a white lab coat met us in the waiting room. He introduced himself to Robin and me, and explained that he was a teaching fellow working under the clinic's director. I was a little uncomfortable because he hadn't introduced himself to Michael. Perhaps I had made a mistake by bringing him. The doctor assured me otherwise and led us to his office.

Without yet making eye contact or any other form of connection with Michael, he opened a file containing blank sheets of paper. He grabbed a pen, and began the questioning.

"Tell me when problems with Michael began to surface?" he asked. "When did you start to notice he was different?"

Robin and I looked at each other but said nothing. A little confused about what was happening, we just stared at the doctor, as if we hadn't heard his question.

"Perhaps it might be easier for you to tell me what makes Michael so difficult."

My stomach was churning. I could see the doctor getting frustrated by our silence, but he pursued his line of questioning. "How does Michael differ from other children his age?"

Neither Robin nor I were about to answer. They were fair questions, all of which deserved answering. But we were not going to rhyme off a list of Michael's problems in front of him. We were there to get help for Michael, not make him feel bad about himself. What were we supposed to say, "He was trouble from the day we brought him home?"

The doctor put down his pen and looked at us as if we were idiots, but carried on with his line of questioning. Both Robin and I remained tongue-tied.

"Tell me about the problems Michael's birth mother had."

I'd had enough. Michael's birth mother had plenty of problems, but nothing Michael needed to learn about in a doctor's office, if ever. It took me too long, but I eventually mustered the nerve to say, "Could I speak to you outside?"

The doctor and I got up and walked into the hallway. I shut the door behind me.

"I'm sorry to sound rude," I said, noting that I was saying "sorry to sound rude" more and more before I said something, usually rude. "But I think your questions are inappropriate to discuss in front of Michael." I was on a roll that I wouldn't be stopping anytime soon.

"He doesn't know the sordid details of his birth mother's life, and you're asking us these questions before even saying hello to Michael or explaining who you are?" I wasn't sure what to say next, so ended with "I don't want to go on with the interview."

I thought the doctor's eyes might pop out in front of me.

I excused myself, went back into the office and told Robin and Michael to pack up. "We're leaving," I said, and from my tone, they knew not to ask why.

I put in a call the next morning to the director of the Child Development Clinic to explain my actions during the previous day's fiasco. I started with my usual apology. "I'm really sorry to be making trouble, but…" Though furious with yesterday's doctor, I made sure not to rant and be dismissed as a lunatic. I took a deep breath and calmly explained what I felt the problems were with the previous day's interview. I let the director know I hoped I hadn't done anything to stand in the way of Michael's getting proper care. "We need the clinic's expertise."

The wonderful Dr. Wendy Roberts listened, sympathetically. She understood my point of view. She would be pleased to take on Michael herself as his doctor.

Robin and I took Michael back the following week. Dr. Roberts and several members of her staff spent a day interviewing Michael, reviewing his medical and growth charts, testing his cognitive and neurological abilities, measuring social interactions and developmental milestones. Robin and I were on hold emotionally. On the one hand, we were scared to think there might be something seriously wrong with Michael. On the other, if there was something wrong, we could fix it. Right?

We still had self-doubts about our parenting, but among the many gifts our Sarah had given us was the belief that maybe we were not so bad after all. Everything seemed to come so naturally for her, and therefore for us. If we hadn't had Sarah to retest our parenting, Robin and I would have felt even guiltier than we did, assuming we were the central cause of Michael's difficulties. Many friends had tried to reassure us with the phrase "It's not you," but that only helped a bit. It didn't compete with the cold stares we had to endure in public places when Michael was wailing, or comments from strangers about his need for "more discipline." All added to our self-doubt and chipped away at our strength.

The following week, we returned to Dr. Roberts's office. Greeting us in the waiting room as before, she smiled warmly, offered a firm hand, and led us to her office. "I have the results from last week's tests on Michael," she told us. "I'm sure the wait was difficult."

She was right. It was difficult, but it wasn't only the week that had been hard. In some ways, we had been waiting for this moment since Michael was born in 1987. It was now

1993. During that wait, there were times I actually hoped one of Michael's doctors would find something wrong so we could get on with the business of fixing it. More selfishly, I thought a diagnosis could expiate the never-ending stream of guilt and shame Robin and I were drowning in from Michael's problems, and our inability to make them go away. Of course I felt shame having these thoughts. What kind of mother wishes for doctors to find something wrong with her child?

I watched as Dr. Roberts rummaged through a rumpled stack of papers on her desk. I tried to read her face. She was giving nothing away.

"After discussion with my staff," she began, "we've settled on a diagnosis." The fluids in my stomach took a nosedive.

She continued riffling through her piles, eventually pulling out two photocopied sheets of canary yellow paper. Without saying a word, she handed a copy to both Robin and me. A hand drawn outline of a child's face was sketched on the page. Features, including eyes, nose, ears, and mouth were filled in and had handwritten labels attached to them.

Robin and I looked up from our sheets and stared at each other. I was the first to break the silence. "It looks exactly like Michael," I said flatly, as if shell-shocked.

"The resemblance is uncanny," Robin added. "It's eerie."

"The drawing is used as a teaching aid at medical schools," Dr. Roberts said, "to train budding pediatricians."

I looked at the drawing again, and for the first time noted the small letters printed on top. The sheet was titled *Common Facial Features of Fetal Alcohol Syndrome.* I looked at Robin, also studying the drawing, and noticed a slight smile forming on his lips. I understood. He must have just read the title too. It was the smile that comes upon discovery of something excitingly new, beautiful, profound, or so wrenchingly awful you can't deal with the feelings it brings.

"Oh my god," he said in a subdued voice, eyes still glued to the paper.

There was no room for disbelief or protest. Flat midface, short nose, indistinct philtrum (the area above the upper lip), thin upper lip, minor ear abnormalities, low nasal bridge. Check. Check. Check.

All I could think was "Kira had been drinking with Michael too." The liar. Why hadn't we put all this together earlier?

Even though Michael's half-brother Andrew had been diagnosed with fetal alcohol effects (now known as "alcohol-related neurodevelopmental disorder" — ARND), considered a lesser form of the syndrome, our pediatrician never suggested the same might be true for Michael. In retrospect, I wasn't sure why. Whatever the reason, we must have engaged in a strong case of denial on our own part. When Lynn talked about Andrew's diagnosis, why hadn't we questioned whether Michael should be checked too? But because of Andrew, I had done a bit of reading about the syndrome. Enough to understand that the diagnosis Dr. Roberts just gave us meant our son was brain-damaged.

If we had been in denial, we were no longer. A part of our Michael's brain was destroyed while in Kira's womb. He was damaged in a way that said, if you looked at the statistics of the time, our son would quit school, would never be able to hold a job, and would live on the streets or worse. We had the next ten or fifteen years, at best, to see if we could change the prognosis.

Tears streamed down my face. Robin, knowing me well, had come prepared. He reached into his pocket and handed me a tissue.

Dr. Roberts finally spoke. "You'll recognize Michael when I tell you that the earliest characteristics of FAS during infancy include trembling and irritability. The child may cry a lot, act agitated. As the child gets older, he may 'flit' from one thing to another; have short attention spans; be prone to temper tantrums and non-compliance; is easily distracted; often hyperfocuses and doesn't respond well to changes, particularly when required to move from one activity to another." The list went on.

"But Michael's birth mother said she didn't drink during her pregnancy," I said, noting how little conviction I had in my voice.

"If at all possible, I suggest you go back and check with her again. Unfortunately, we've seen this before. The drinking history she gave you is incorrect." Dr. Roberts left no room for doubt. After seeing the line drawing, we knew she was right. Yes, Kira had lied.

Dr. Roberts explained that fetal alcohol disorders vary and are manifested in different ways, depending on when the mother drank and what areas of the fetus's brain were affected. Tests showed Michael's brain damage manifested as attention-deficit hyperactivity disorder (ADHD), possible oppositional disorder, and severe learning disabilities. His relentless skin picking was possibly some form of obsessive-compulsive disorder, or perhaps a Tourette's syndrome type tic.

"I know you won't be surprised to hear that Michael has some autistic characteristics too," she continued. "They showed up in his interactions with other children, but aren't significant enough to be labelled Asperger's syndrome, the type of autism he is considered closest to. But that explains his tendency to parallel play rather than interact directly with other children."

Dr. Wendy Roberts was a pioneer in the field of FAS and was devoting her career to families with children like Michael. She was one of the few pediatric specialists in Canada who could diagnosis the syndrome, unnamed and absent in the medical literature until 1973. That explained why Michael had been to so many doctors during his short lifetime, yet none of them even hinted at the possibility of FAS. Nobody knew anything about it. The problems associated with drinking during pregnancy eventually became common knowledge, but very few medical professionals had ever heard of fetal alcohol syndrome at the time of Michael's birth in 1987.

To Dr. Roberts's great disappointment, the syndrome had been studied minimally since first named, though interest was starting to gain momentum. She was disappointed that more attention, money and research had been directed to crack babies. Despite the mythology and sensationalized media hype surrounding these newborns, evidence was showing that crack was much less harmful *in utero* than alcohol.

"The toxic effects of alcohol are devastating to the fetus," Dr. Roberts added. "I personally don't think there is any safe limit, though the jury is still out on the issue."

"What does all of this mean for us, Dr. Roberts? What can we expect, what should we do?" I asked.

"Unfortunately, there's little research to tell us what the future holds for Michael. Recent findings are based on children diagnosed in their teens," she said. "It means they hadn't been diagnosed early enough for caregivers to make significant interventions in their lives." She was trying to soften the blows of the dismal futures predicted in the literature. It wasn't hard to see the effect her words were having on us. Robin was slouched in his chair, his eyes moist. I was unusually quiet, unable to dam a torrent of tears.

"If early interventions had been made," she continued, "the children might have fared better." The majority of those studied led lives as predicted. They had dropped out of school, were living on the streets, unemployed or on welfare and were repeatedly in and out of jail by the time they hit twenty.

"The part of their brain that affects impulse control is damaged," she continued. "So is their ability to learn from their mistakes or understand cause and effect as we do. They may feel remorseful after doing something wrong, but it doesn't mean they will have the impulse control not to do the same thing again. That may explain why they're in and out of the prison system."

"I don't want you to be too upset from all this literature," she added, seeing our distress. "Michael is only six. With early diagnosis and intervention, he has a better chance than those kids for success in life." She suggested we make an appointment for the following week to discuss the possible use of meds to help with some of Michael's symptoms.

"You two have already done a wonderful job with Michael. Most kids with FAS can't bear to be touched and many don't bond with their parents. The fact that he is so warm and connected with you is a testament to your love and hard work. He's lucky to have you."

Hearing the kindness in her words, desperately welcomed and needed, my sobs deepened. Tears of sorrow. Tears of relief — a diagnosis telling us something was *physically* wrong with Michael relieved some of the guilt. And tears of rage — at Kira, the world, the gods, the Fates, everything and everybody — except Michael.

In my gut, I had believed something was wrong with Michael, no matter what doctors said. Now, I no longer had to pretend everything was fine. I wouldn't have to make excuses for Michael, Robin or myself. We no longer had to listen to someone telling us Michael was bad. We didn't have to live with the confusion of ambiguity. We could take action, move forward. We could help Michael and turn the tide of expected events.

"I feel hopeful," I said to Dr. Roberts, with remarkable energy, then looked over to Robin. He was still slouching in his chair, bleary-eyed. I sensed it would be best to keep my momentary optimism to myself. Who knew how long it would last. Probably not very.

We met with Dr. Roberts the following week. I could tell when we walked into her office that she wasn't her usually cheerful self. The contrast in her manner was obvious. I asked if something was wrong.

At first she hemmed and hawed. Doctors don't bare their souls to patients. I gently prodded, though, and eventually she told us she had just met with parents of another child with

FAS, now ten. She had been working with the family for several years. At this morning's meeting the parents told Dr. Roberts that they could no longer care for their child. The demands were too great and home life untenable. They were "sending" their child away to live elsewhere and were looking for some permanent option for his care.

Dr. Roberts was devastated by the news. "I thought the family was doing extremely well," she said. "I understood how difficult it can be at home, but I can't imagine this child's future without his parents. I wish there were something I could do."

I was appalled by the story. Never for a second, not even in my worst moments with Michael, could I imagine sending him away.

"I'll never do that," I said quietly, under my breath. I had no idea what it really meant to send your child away. I just knew I'd never do it. "Never."

Dr. Roberts talked about some drug options for Michael, the first being Clonidine. She thought it might help reduce Michael's aggression in the schoolyard, so that if he were teased or bullied, his response wouldn't be so strong.

Though the drug was developed to combat hypertension, studies had shown an unexpected side effect, to calm aggressive tendencies. Dr. Roberts had had some success using it with several children and found side effects to be minimal. Because Michael was still being bullied at his new school, we were willing to consider this option.

Unfortunately, Dr. Roberts had no suggestions about Michael's skin picking habit that hadn't stopped since he was a baby. He still had open sores, and now scars on his body.

She then recommended the amphetamine Ritalin for Michael's ADD (interchangeably called ADHD, the H referring to hyperactivity). We knew, as did Dr. Roberts, that many of the symptoms interfering with Michael's functioning had to do with his attention span and restlessness. Therefore,

Dr. Roberts suggested he go through a three-part controlled study to determine if Ritalin would work for him, and if so, at what dose.

We were game. We had tried many things over the years to help Michael calm down, pay attention, stop fidgeting, have more control, be less volatile and impulsive. All with little if any success.

One of the things we did early on was to cut out sugar. Everyone from my mother and my hairdresser *knew* that cutting out sugar would calm Michael down. I read about cutting out sugar. I heard stories from mothers telling me that it would work. Why? Because *their* kids got out of control at birthday parties after eating just one slice of cake!

So we tried it. We cut out all sugars for a few days. We noticed no effect. No one believed it. So we cut out all sugars for weeks. Still, no effect. We tried for months. *Nada.*

Following other advice, we then cut out wheat. Then dairy. Still no reaction. My mother suggested we give fish oils. One of the teachers at Michael's school knew a woman who treated children "like him" with a liquid vitamin B supplement she sold. The woman had seen miracles with the supplement. "Why not try it?"

"How can it hurt?" I said. It didn't. Nor did it help.

I felt let down every time someone promised a miracle cure. We tried them all. I was hopeful, probably gullible. But why shouldn't I try everything and anything for Michael so long as I didn't believe it to be harmful. I needed to become thicker-skinned, though, because of the failure rate. Contrary to other people's hype and good intentions, they didn't know Michael's body. I also discovered that some people love to talk about things they know nothing about. And, though I didn't entertain the thought for long, I sometimes thought there might never be a "cure" for Michael.

I told Dr. Roberts about our experiments with food, and the roller-coaster rides these new routines put us through each time. She understood, but was careful not to say anything negative about the practices of other professionals. She did say that research at SickKids had not shown that cutting out sugar, wheat or dairy helped their patients.

"But some patients are extremely sensitive to Red Dye #2," she said. "It makes them hyper manic."

She recommended we pay attention to any foods that might contain red food colouring. "See if it makes a difference."

We left it at that. Michael seldom ate foods that had red dyes in them, we thought. We became extra careful about checking labels, though, and soon discovered items we would never have expected to contain Red Dye #2, including candies and hot dogs. We learned that the hard way. Michael went absolutely batty at a baseball game.

We were more than ready for the three weeks of drug testing. Each week, six-year-old Michael would be given either a dose of Ritalin at one of two different levels, or a placebo. We wouldn't know whether he was being given the Ritalin or placebo. If it was Ritalin, we wouldn't know which dose. Michael wouldn't know either. Nor would Michael's teacher, who would be spending the most hours with him every day. Not even the social worker from SickKids would know, though she was the one overseeing the study and interviewing Michael each week about how he was feeling and functioning.

Only the *pharmacist* would know what Michael was being given each week.

At the end of each week, Robin and I, his teacher and the SickKids social worker were asked to fill out forms to evaluate Michael's behaviour, moods, and ability to concentrate, learn and interact with peers and family. The information would then be assessed to see which week he functioned best.

When the results were tabulated we would know whether the placebo or the drug and at what dose was helping Michael.

Ritalin stayed in the system roughly four hours. That meant

Robin or I or his teacher would be required to administer a pill to Michael every four hours until dinnertime. We explained all this to Michael. Our six-year-old son was willing to comply. Funny, we thought. He didn't usually agree to anything.

I couldn't wait to start.

Week one began. We noticed a difference in Michael twenty minutes after giving him the first pill. It took twenty minutes for Ritalin to take effect. He was calmer, though far from calm. Didn't fidget as much, though still fidgeted. He could pay attention better, but still didn't *really* pay attention. He could follow instructions better, but still needed help. There was a marked change in him. A good change.

"No way this could be a placebo," I said to Robin.

I was dying to call his teacher to hear what she had to say. I forced myself to hold back, though. I was not supposed to contact her during the study.

Michael gladly took the pills the rest of the week. He told us he felt quite good.

"Did you notice a difference in anything?"

"Yeah, I think so."

"How?"

"I don't know."

Week one ended and we all handed in our forms.

Week two started. Twenty minutes after administering what we were again sure was Ritalin but at a higher dose, we noticed another marked improvement in Michael. He was calmer, though not calm. His fidgeting had remarkably lessened. He paid way more attention to us when we spoke and actually seemed able to understand what we were saying. He still had trouble following any multi-step instructions, but was doing better.

We went on with this for a few more days, remarking how enormous the difference was in Michael. I still hadn't called the teacher. I was so sure about the results that I was even more determined to talk to her than I was the first week. I wanted to know if things were as markedly improved at school as they were at home.

I had realized over the years that only Michael's teachers or camp counsellors understood what life was like with Michael. They understood him better than anyone else we worked with, including the psychiatrists, social workers or doctors handing out advice. The teachers actually spent time with him. They had the same knocks, ups and downs and frustrations we did. The other professionals were all smart and well-intentioned when providing advice on how to parent Michael. Unfortunately, it was usually theoretical. Or if "proven," it had been proven on kids different from our son. Michael's teachers, however, spent all day with him. They weren't talking theory. Their input and knowledge was of tremendous help to us at home.

But as much as I wanted to talk to Michael's teacher, I held back the second week, too. However, I did ask Michael once again: "Do you notice any difference this week from the drug?"

"Yeah, I think so."

"Do you have any idea how it makes a difference?"

"Yeah."

"How?"

"Now there's a tunnel between my teacher and me."

"I'm not sure what you mean, Michael."

"We're connected."

I was blown away. Michael had described in his own words the profound affect the pill was having on him. There was a tunnel now. He was able to connect with his teacher. He had never been able to connect with anybody, really.

"Anything else?"

"Yeah, they make my ears pop."

Ears pop? This confused me. How could Ritalin make his ears pop? Then I realized. His ears had popped "open." He could hear.

Hallelujah, encore.

The third week started. Nothing. We waited longer. Still nothing. Michael was back to the same old, same old. It was disturbing to see him go back to negative, self-destructive behaviour. Things had gone so much better at home with him for the past two weeks. We had almost forgotten how bad it had been before.

I called Dr. Roberts. "I know the third week isn't up, but I'd like to talk to you about the study results."

I told her I was positive the first week was a low dose of Ritalin. The second week a higher dose and the third week, which we were still in, a placebo. "Will you tell me if I'm right? Can we stop the placebo and put our energies into working out what's best for Michael now?"

I told her about the "tunnel" between him and his teacher. She was speechless.

"Yes," she told me. "You are right about the pills. And Michael's teacher noticed exactly the same type of changes as you and Robin did. The Ritalin is clearly working."

Dr. Roberts agreed to stop the study. We soon met to talk about dosage, potential side effects and long-term effects. She prescribed week two's dosage. It would be ten mg four times a day, every four waking hours. We were asked to watch him closely. We had to jot down everything that might be relevant in terms of his mood, spirit, side effects and/or his concentration.

One thing we did notice was the uneven effect of the drug. We could see it slowly "taking effect." We would then see it "working," then "wearing off." We could *really* see the wearing off period. It was in marked contrast to his behaviour while the drug was working fully. The wearing off period usually started roughly two and a half hours after he had taken the drug. With other children it was roughly three and a half to four hours before the drug wore off. Therefore, most kids were on four-hour schedules. We reported this to Dr. Roberts. She explained that Michael's metabolism must be faster than most other children's. She changed the dosage to one pill every three hours rather than four.

Dr. Roberts warned us that she hoped the only obvious side effect from Ritalin would be loss of appetite. His appetite would come back after the pills wore off each evening. Not a good thing for our small Michael. He had never been a good eater so his eating would most likely get worse. Still, we thought he should try the Ritalin. Robin made Michael a three-egg cheddar cheese omelet for breakfast every morning before Michael's first pill of the day kicked in. Then we fed him "make-up" food after the pills wore off.

While on the pills, Michael barely and rarely put a bite in his mouth at regular lunch and dinner times. Around 8:00 at night, he made up for it. That's when he would start eating his favourite foods, pretty much all protein or dairy. They included beef, fish, chicken, huge hunks of cheese, milk, ham and tuna sandwiches. Bagels, cream cheese and lox were a major hit, as were mashed potatoes. Even after the pills wore off he didn't eat a huge amount of anything, but it always felt good to see him eat then. Seldom, however, could we get him to eat fruits, vegetables or grains, though this was no different than before he began the Ritalin.

Robin and I had to weigh another possible side effect of the drug: growth retardation. Michael was already small for his age because he had grown so little during his first year. An endocrinologist we had been referred to had already told us that, at his present growth rate, he would be lucky to reach the short end of "normal" height range as an adult. He even predicted Michael would, at best, be five-foot-four. We certainly couldn't mess up his chances for that. Dr. Roberts understood and said she would monitor his height closely to see how he was progressing. We could stop the drugs at any time if she felt it was interfering with his growth. With her reassurances, we decided to go ahead with the meds.

It isn't easy to put your kid on a drug. Particularly when you know he has to take it daily, until who-knows-when. I, more than Robin, was brought up in a very anti-prescription-drug home, so it was tougher on me than on him. I felt I was sentencing Michael to life on bad drugs. The positive effects of the meds were too clear — on Michael and on us. It would be cruel to deny Michael that.

We gave Michael his meds at 7:00 a.m., 11:00 a.m., 2:00 p.m. and 5:00 p.m. every day.

"Do you realize," I asked Robin, "that this is the first time we've found something that actually *helps* Michael." I would have liked to think it had been love, devotion and good parenting that did it, but it wasn't.

It was the meds.

My mother had been mailing clippings to me ever since I left home at eighteen. Her choice of articles had been eclectic over the years, having included recipes for *mandel* bread, salmon loaf and, most recently, glowing reviews for the Cabbage Soup Diet. More often than not, the articles had been targeted for self-improvement. Most came from the *Ladies' Home Journal*, *Family Circle* and *Better Homes and Gardens*, but newspapers were also represented, with clippings from the *Detroit News*, *Jewish News* and now the *St. Petersburg Times*. I'd received articles on how to fold sweaters neatly, swallow multiple vitamins at one go, dress appropriately for a job interview, keep whites white and choose the best Jewish Sunday school for your kids.

Having recently told my mother about our decision to give Michael Ritalin, I wasn't surprised to see a letter from her in the mail the following week. I knew a clipping would be inside. She knew, rightly, that her opinion might carry more weight with me if it came from someone else's mouth. The clipping was going to tell me something negative about Ritalin. My mother hated prescription medications.

I had thought twice about telling her about the Ritalin but

went ahead anyway. I was a grown-up, right? I didn't need to hide things from my mother anymore just because she might not like them. But I must not have been completely sure about this since I opened the letter and unfolded the clipping with caution. "Use of Ritalin in Children Overprescribed" read the headline. I wasn't happy.

My mother hadn't exactly been overly helpful or encouraging since Michael and Sarah were born, so I probably over-reacted to something I thought was undermining my parenting. Rather than laughing at the clipping and taking a "there she goes again" attitude, I wanted to rip it into shreds, throw the pieces on the floor and scream the headline into oblivion.

It seemed the whole world (which now included my mother) was appalled about the number of kids taking Ritalin. They were pissing on doctors for prescribing it, pissing on multinational corporations for making it and pissing on parents for giving it to their children.

When I looked at the extraordinarily high number of Ritalin prescriptions in both Canada and the United States, my hunch too was that Ritalin was being overprescribed. Drug companies spent billions of dollars to convince everyone that attention deficit disorder is a disorder rather than the symptoms of normally active, oftentimes creative children (usually boys) who need more exercise and less sugar to keep their behaviour in check.

Of course a certain amount of distractibility, messiness and acting out were all part of being a "normal child." But a sloppy room, messy school binder, occasional tantrum and short attention span weren't the reasons doctors were prescribing Ritalin for Michael. If his diagnosis of ADHD and script for Ritalin were based on a little distraction or abundance of energy, I'd toss the pills straight out the window. What parent *wants* to give a child medication every day? Not me, and my mother knew this. She also knew that without the Ritalin, her grandson could barely stay still long enough to dress himself, stand up and sing "O Canada" every morning at school, or look anyone in the eye. But with the medication and a devoted teacher, he eventually learned to read, print his name and string a few numbers together.

Unfortunately, many children like Michael with ADHD had serious behavioural problems, showed extreme disorganization in everything they did, were hyperactive, had learning disabilities, impulsivity or aggressive behaviour, inappropriate social interactions and oppositional personalities. Individually, one or two such problems might not be serious. But taken together, those traits could seriously interfere with a child's ability to make friends, learn how to read and write, tie his shoes, find his way to the corner store or develop loving relationships with his family.

These children might need Ritalin. Like Michael. So I begged my dear mother as well as friends who didn't like prescription drugs, "Why can't you just be happy for those of us who have actually found something to help our suffering children?"

Instead of a clipping, why couldn't my mother have wired me a bouquet of roses or sent a gift certificate for a back massage?

11.
Facing Family Secrets
Toronto Island, 1993

I SPOKE TO LYNN AND DON IMMEDIATELY after Michael's diagnosis. We were furious that Kira had lied about her drinking. We wanted them to tell her about Michael's diagnosis and find out the real story. No bullshit this time.

But that wasn't all we needed to talk about.

The mood was tense when Robin and I walked into Lynn and Don's house. It reminded me of the day Lynn came to our house to tell us Kira was pregnant. No room for small talk.

The second we were all seated in their living room, I blurted it out, "Didn't *you* know Kira was drinking? Why didn't *you* tell us? Were you hiding it?"

Both Lynn and Don looked stunned. It took a while before Lynn spoke. Like mine, her face was bright red. "We knew Kira was drinking during her pregnancy *with Andrew*," Lynn said, "but we didn't know it was an issue until the doctor diagnosed him with FAE (fetal alcohol effects). We actually didn't know about her drinking with Michael. Even if we did know she drank, though, we had never heard of FAE or FAS."

Neither had anyone else, including us.

Lynn wasn't being cagey. Knowing Kira drank and knowing it was a problem were two different things in those days. That's why Lynn didn't understand what Andrew's doctor meant when he told her he suspected Andrew might have FAS. Few people, not even doctors, had ever heard of fetal alcohol syndrome in 1987, the year Michael was born. The general public had no idea of the harm alcohol could cause.

It might appear self-evident, but it wasn't.

It was like cigarette smoking. Hard to believe, but doctors smoked when I was growing up; some doctors even told patients to smoke for relaxation. People smoked in restaurants, airplanes, elevators and movie theatres. Cigarette companies sponsored children's cartoon programs on TV. No one dreamed of asking someone to go outside to smoke.

People didn't worry about cigarettes until the U.S. Surgeon General issued his health warning in 1964: Smoking Causes Cancer. It was a revelation to the public. Same thing with alcohol. The first time FAS came up in the "literature" was when an article was published in *The Lancet* medical journal in 1973. Little showed up elsewhere in the next twenty years.

We were in the thick of the AIDS epidemic when Michael was born, and that's what everybody was worrying about. Not alcohol. They checked Michael for HIV and other problems at the hospital when they pronounced him healthy, ready to go. Who knows if they even thought about problems from alcohol or would even have known what to look for if they had.

"I did wonder if you had thought about Michael having FAS when Andrew was diagnosed," Lynn said, "but your pediatrician never brought it up with you. I was hardly an expert myself. In light of all the other problems you were facing with Michael, I thought you didn't need my non-expert opinion. I didn't want to be the one to raise the prospect of a lifelong issue."

Right, right, right.

We left asking ourselves the Mother of all Questions. If we had known Kira was drinking during the pregnancy, would it have made any difference?

"Probably not," I said to Robin. I would have been more worried about crack.

Robin agreed. "I honestly don't remember ever reading anything about alcohol during pregnancy. People we knew were careful about drinking, assuming it couldn't be good for a baby.

But no one had a clue what the actual harm would be, if any."

Lynn met with Kira. Lynn told her the couple raising her son had been to SickKids, and he had been diagnosed with fetal alcohol syndrome. Kira knew what it was because Lynn had already told her about Andrew. "The parents need to know your drinking history during the pregnancy."

Lynn was surprised how frank Kira was. "Yes," she said, "I did drink." She didn't remember when or how much. "It wasn't steady, though. I'd binge sometimes."

She admitted to a long history with alcohol as a binge drinker, starting when she was thirteen, but "I hid it," she said. Lynn said that Kira "didn't seem comfortable giving it a name," but "we can assume she's a secret alcoholic from what she says." Supposedly Kira squirmed when Lynn told her Michael had been diagnosed with FAS. "I could tell she didn't feel good about it. But she never asked questions or showed interest in knowing more."

"Not much different than when we told her about Andrew," Lynn continued. "She never accepted that Andrew had FAE. Her only response was 'But he's so smart.' She glossed over it with Michael too."

I didn't have a clue what Kira was really feeling, but there had to be *some* shame or guilt. If not, why did she lie to the adoption counsellor? Clearly, Kira didn't want him or the prospective adoptive parents to think she was drinking. She knew it sounded better to say, "I'm drinking lots of milk" than "Yeah, I just downed a mickey of vodka."

Like the rest of us, Kira probably didn't know enough about the actual dangers of alcohol. Nevertheless, she still knew it would be best for *her* if she kept her drinking a secret. Why else would she lie to the adoption counsellor if not to protect herself from possible disdain?

So was she just like my mother, and even myself, protecting ourselves from what might happen if our secrets came out of the deep? Maybe. But unlike what I now felt for both my mother and myself, I had little, if any compassion for Kira. The costs of some secrets are too high.

When we told people Michael's diagnosis, I could see they were rethinking their perceptions of the past six years. Everyone, of course, first told us how sorry they were. No one knew anything specifically about FAS, so we spent a lot of time doing FAS101, then shared our determination to turn the dire prognosis around. They were sure we would.

Many people, in their wisdom, asked if we were sorry we had adopted Michael. I was taken aback. Neither Robin nor I ever expressed regret or remorse. Michael had been our beloved lost soul since the day we brought him home. He didn't change with the diagnosis. We already knew who he was. We now had a name to help explain it. Sometimes people or things come into our lives unexpectedly, whether through birth, adoption or other fortunes of fate. It then becomes our job to love them.

As before, Michael was both difficult *and* lovable. Even during the relatively nightmarish period after he was kicked out of school, he retained many of his appealingly quirky ways. Each night when he was six, he asked for six pieces of cheese — his favourite food. On his seventh birthday, he asked for seven. The night before the birthday he told me, "Six was a good year, Mom." I was pleased to hear it, but shocked. He had been through so much. Then he farted and said, "That's my last fart as a six-year-old."

Part of the reason he could say "Six was a good year" was because of the change in his schooling. After that miserable Placement and Review fiasco, we had managed to get Michael into a learning disabilities (LD) class. The teacher at his new school rescued him from behavioural when she saw the much larger boys in the class repeatedly threatening him in the playground.

The teacher was one more jewel in our lives, in addition to Dr. Roberts. Mrs. G., as she was called, was tough and demanded strict routine in her classroom. She was also kind and encouraging to her students, all trying desperately to learn how to read, add and subtract.

I was so grateful to Mrs. G. that I volunteered in her classroom every Wednesday, bringing my little pal Sarah with me. On each visit, I was amazed at how patiently Mrs. G. went over and over the same words with students, trying to teach them to read. I would be bald from pulling my hair out if I had had her job. D-o-g, dog. C-a-t, cat. H-o-u-s-e, house. Over and over and over and over.

I honestly couldn't understand how the kids couldn't get it. With all the repetition, explanation and time Mrs. G. spent on the sounds of each letter and the collective sounds they made together as a word, why didn't it click in? But Mrs. G. knew "it" would come at some point and was hanging in willingly until it did. I constantly questioned how she had so much devotion and patience, and knew it had to come from a deep place.

Slowly but surely, Michael started learning to read and write under her guidance. One day he came home proudly, wanting to show me he had learned how to print his first and last name. He took the pencil and paper I handed him and sat down at the kitchen table. It was taking time, and I could see how painstaking the task was. Finally, he handed the sheet of paper to me and said, "Look, Mum."

Michael had printed his name mirror-image backward, starting from the right hand side of the page moving to the left, each letter backward. I couldn't have done it if I tried. It helped me to have more compassion for the underlying neurology of learning disabilities and to better understand what Mrs. G. was working with in her classroom. She had a lot of brain pathways to unscramble.

Michael's spirits were picking up day by day in Mrs. G.'s class. One day he came home and announced, "I want to be a biologist." His fascination and interest in the natural physical world was back in operation, so for his seventh birthday, my friend Sybil gave him his first pair of binoculars, bright red. My sister Barbara sent him his own *Peterson Field Guides to Eastern Birds*. He started going out with me again to bird watch, and now with his own field guide. Each bird we spotted, he'd find in the book and ask me how to write the date beside it. "So I can remember when I saw it," he said proudly.

Michael's love for small, cozy spaces did not abate, even as he grew. He started calling himself a bald eagle and at night would pile up household sleeping bags to make a nest to sleep in. He would crawl into the middle then curl up and close his eyes. One night, just as he was dozing off, Robin said to him, "Mommy and Daddy thought we might be raising an ornithologist. Instead, we're raising a bird." Michael laughed and laughed.

When Michael wasn't a bald eagle, he was Fluffy the Cat who went around meowing and cuddling. He lapped up his milk and juice from bowls. He loved the attention Fluffy got. Sarah loved playing Fluffy with him. She was a dog, giving Fluffy rides on her back.

Michael had begun to improve his eye contact with people when he started on the Ritalin. He began to say hello and goodbye as long as they said it to him first. He told Robin and me about twenty times a day "I love you, Mom" and "I love you, Dad." It made us melt because the statements were unsolicited and he always seemed to say it at an appropriately warm moment. We had a saying in our family, "I love you with all my heart." At some point Michael began to say "I love you with all my toes" or "I love you with all my teeth." That, too, made us melt.

Michael still could not handle much commotion or energy around him. Nor people. At his seventh birthday party at our house, he wandered off, unbeknownst to us and walked over to an elderly neighbour's house for respite. The next year, we kept the numbers down, but realized halfway through the party that we hadn't seen Michael since the party games began. We looked around and found him upstairs in our bedroom, door closed, under our covers, putting together his Lego pieces, as far away from the hoopla as he could get.

Even on days when only Robin, Sarah and I were home, he would go into his room and create fantasy worlds with animals, books, space Lego and Construx. He would play for hours by himself. When he was with other children his age, he could at best "parallel" play alongside his peers rather than interact directly with them. No conversation. He stayed with parallel play long beyond the age when other children had grown out of the stage. I found it hard watching them pass him by, one by one.

The only child Michael seemed to have some affinity for was Andrew. In many ways, they were like two peas in a pod. Peas with electrically charged nerve endings. The true Energizer Bunnies. They didn't know they shared genes, but they sure knew they both enjoyed creating havoc. Both of them remained fearless, even on the ADD meds they were both taking. They were always crashing into furniture, banging anything that made a loud sound if clashed together, running away when called for meals and making messes everywhere, indoors and out. They brought out the worst in each other, no doubt about it.

Not that Michael was that much better on his own. He always pretended not to hear us when we said, "Don't go further than the rope swing," "Keep your helmet on when you ride your bike," or "Put down that hatchet." Wash up? Brush teeth? Change clothes? Put away toys? Come to the table? Forget it. I was devastated the day he whacked away the lower limbs on the Japanese maple sitting right outside our front door, using a homemade sword he had carved out from a tree branch. While my eyes were on something else, he knocked them off. One by one.

Michael did not do anything he didn't want to. He was determined and stubborn. He whined, squealed or had tantrums to get his way. He was constantly testing our boundaries. We often broke our resolve to get Michael to do the routine activities of daily living, like getting himself dressed in the morning. His unholy squawk each morning wore us down.

Both Robin and I continually thanked Mother Nature, God, the biological imperative or whoever was in charge for providing Michael with a cuddly, adorable, sweet side along with this other, less adorable side. I don't know what we would have done without it.

Fortunately, he still loved snuggling. When I read to him on the sofa, he burrowed into my side and tucked himself under my arm. Other times, he jumped up on our laps and settled in. If Robin was lying down with him in bed, Michael made sure as many of his body parts as possible had contact with Robin. If I was sitting up in bed watching television, he'd hop up, plunk himself down between my legs, lie back on my tummy and make himself at home. He loved the physical contact, something considered very unusual for children with FAS. We loved the physical contact with him too. It played a huge role in sustaining our love. We worried, though, what would be. One day soon, we assumed, his enjoyment of physical contact with his parents was going to end. How would we connect, then?

I took comfort knowing how much Robin loved the kids. Lesser men would have walked. In fact, Dr. Roberts told us that more than 80 percent of families with special needs children end in divorce. So it heartened me that Robin remained the proudest of papas to Sarah and Michael. He loved taking them to the Island tadpole pond and showing them off at work. He'd make them breakfast each morning, usually cheese omelets, or soft-boiled eggs with toast "soldiers." As Robin liked to sew, every year he made the children's Halloween costumes. His best was the year he turned our blond, blue-eyed Michael into a black-mustachioed carnival strongman, complete with homemade bar bells and furry, mock-leopard loincloth.

We received little support from any social service after Michael's diagnosis. Nobody knew anything about FAS. Dr. Roberts was still with us, but she wasn't a behavioural therapist or social worker. She didn't know any better than we did what to do with Michael's behaviour. I was in tears one morning over the phone with her. I could hear how helpless she felt listening to my pleas. But the truth was that she didn't know how to get him to brush his teeth, do homework, say please and thank you or stop running around like a maniac. Diagnosis and meds only do so much.

Lynn and I perked up one day when a social worker from SickKids called. "There's a support group for parents of kids with FAS. Give it a try."

Thinking it would be good to talk with parents who had similar kids, we toddled off to a meeting in a nearby church basement cityside.

We all sat on folding chairs in a circle. The group leader asked us to go around the room, one by one, giving updates about our children and, in our case, a brief introduction.

Lynn and I kicked each other after hearing the first three presenters. We both knew it was time to get the hell out. Of course we couldn't, so we continued to listen as one by one, depressed parents of much-older children told nightmarish stories about promiscuity, jail sentences, school dropouts, unwanted babies, children beating parents. All their kids had been diagnosed in their late teens.

It was my turn. I was conscious of how our situation was different than theirs, and I didn't want to come off too Pollyannish. "Of course we were devastated when Michael was diagnosed," I said, after giving a brief backgrounder on Michael and our experience at SickKids. "We're feeling relatively optimistic about the future, though. Or at least we're trying to. Since

Michael was diagnosed at a young age, we have a lot of years to try and turn things around. With luck and a lot of support, we hope we can help Michael stay in school and develop skills to help him later in life. We have time on our side."

Those who spoke thought I was naïve. "Yeah, we used to think like that too." "You really think you can change them?" "Come back again in a few years, and let's see what you think then." A support group? They resented our early diagnosis. If they had had it, perhaps they could have had time to turn things around. But they didn't have it. There was no turning around.

I was the last person they needed to hear speak. They were the last people I needed, too. Lynn and I never returned. I couldn't find much help elsewhere. Down syndrome and autism had made it onto the world's social service radar, to some degree. Not yet fetal alcohol syndrome.

Michael continued to do well in his LD classes. After two years with Mrs. G. and then another equally fine teacher, we were devastated to learn this would soon come to an end. Michael and his classmates were to be integrated into large mainstream classes with only one resource teacher to provide support. Recent elections had brought in a Conservative premier who slashed school budgets. No more special education classes in our area. Integration was the new buzzword.

While some parents of special needs children liked the idea of having their children integrate into mainstream classes, I knew it would be a disaster for Michael. He got lost in a crowd. He needed one-to-one attention from his teachers. He needed constant repetition to learn. He got bullied by "regular" kids. He needed special ed.

Robin and I met with his teachers to talk about next steps. If we could afford it, Michael should be in a private school with special education classes, they said. I had inherited a little money from my grandparents many years before. Now was the time to use it. After much research and on-site visits, we finally found a private school for Michael we could afford. In addition to school, other costs were adding up. We were lucky, though. Michael's prescription drug expenses, close to $300 a month, were covered by Robin's extended insurance plan with the CBC. But there were special needs summer camps, tutors, Michael's weekly therapy with a psychologist, respite workers if Robin and I went away, family counselling sessions, costly psycho-educational tests.

Money was becoming an additional stress on the marriage. We didn't need one more.

It was a summer sunset, Friday night. Sarah had set the dining-room table beautifully with the damask tablecloth and Birds of Paradise china I inherited from my mother. The braided *challah* we had baked that morning sat in the centre of the table next to the silver *Kiddush* cup holding preposterously sweet Manischewitz wine. We were lighting candles to usher in the Sabbath.

Sarah held my hand as we lit the candles and sang blessings. In the warm glow of our candlelight, we went around the table, one by one, giving thanks for whatever it was we wanted to give thanks for that week. My usual weekly gratitude "for family and friends" was considered routinely boring, as in "There Mum goes again."

Michael took the prize for originality that particular night: "I give thanks for the light inside the refrigerator." None of us could top that. After each of us had our turn, it was time to eat, having been tortured long enough by the perfume of brisket waiting in the oven.

I was as close to heaven as I was going to get — in this life, anyway. I loved our Friday night *Shabbats*. I felt they helped to bring a consciousness of the sacred into our everyday life. My children were learning to be thankful for the bread on their table, remembering loved ones who had passed away, and for one night, separating themselves from all that was worldly.

Celebrating *Shabbat* with my family was my childhood dream come true. I wasn't for a second deluding myself, though. I was doing *Shabbat* as much for myself as I was for them. It was having children that gave me the opportunity to bring *Shabbat* back into my life after turning my back on it. All did not glitter on the silver Rosenbaum-Christmas *Kiddush* cup, however. Yes, we had been lighting candles on Friday nights for years. But no, it wasn't always weekly. And when it did occur, it wasn't exactly a romantic scene from *Fiddler on the Roof*.

On that particular Friday night, Robin was wrestling with a rambunctious seven-year-old Michael, whose sole interest was blowing out the *Shabbat* candles, getting out of his chair and going back to his room. After much coaxing and bribing, I had succeeded in getting Michael to the table, but like so many other *Shabbats*, the chaos came at a price. On this night, we managed to get him to stay until the brisket and roast potatoes were served, but once he began kicking and pushing his plate and cutlery around the table, we gave up and let him leave.

Robin had always encouraged me to do *Shabbat*, but it was often out of sync with our secular lives. If I mistakenly made other plans on Friday nights, I felt ashamed, guilty, angry, sad. I questioned the wisdom of marrying a non-Jew. I questioned my parenting. And I questioned my chosen, off-the-Jewish-grid life. I wrestled with all of these, but more often that not, ended up accepting the choices I had made.

When I told Robin I wanted to raise the children Jewish, it meant I wanted us to celebrate Jewish holidays, including the Sabbath, and build a layer of Jewish principles and ethics into the moral foundations we passed on. I hoped that sending the children to Sunday school would teach them relevant lessons from the Torah; religious and ancient world history; and the meanings of Jewish traditions, ritual and prayer. It would be my job to teach them to appreciate Klezmer music, Billy Crystal's jokes, brisket and gefilte fish.

Though I did my best, I faced multiple barriers running a Jewish home. The Island was not a hotbed of Jewish cultural activities that the kids and I could participate in. Nor could we send the kids to a *shule* around the corner. Any place we went for Sunday school would involve a boat trip into the city and a long drive uptown.

Also, I needed a Jewish Sunday school where my blond blue-eyed adopted children whose surname was Christmas would be welcomed and made to feel comfortable. I also wanted to make sure Robin wouldn't be perceived as a misfit because he wasn't Jewish. Although some synagogues in the Toronto area had opened their doors to couples in mixed marriages, they were not great in number.

My first try for the schooling was at the Jewish Community Centre at Spadina and Bloor in downtown Toronto. Michael was eight and Sarah six. It had a progressive, non-Orthodox Sunday school. It was close-by, only half an hour by car or subway once off the ferry. Anyone in the community could send their children there, and both kids had already success-fully gone to the JCC for summer and Christmas break camps. This boded well.

I made an appointment. I wouldn't dream of enrolling Michael without first speaking to the director about him. He would not be their everyday Sunday school student and I had to see if they were willing to take him. If so, could they accommodate some of his needs?

My hopes were high as I walked up the steps of the JCC building. Based on the three years Michael had been at the Montessori school and in his new learning disabilities class, I thought that maybe he could function in a JCC classroom too. For all his problems, Michael had his strengths. We were hoping the JCC staff could build on them as the folks at Montessori had and the way his new teacher was doing.

"Do you think you can take him?" I asked the director after giving her the background. "Robin and I have seen that with the right teachers and environment, Michael does learn and benefits greatly from it."

She didn't hesitate. "Yes, we'll give it a try," she said. I was in tears, happily so. "I'm going to set up a meeting with Michael's teacher and her assistant so you can explain what might be useful for them to know." Brilliant.

I then let the director know both kids would be enrolled as Rosenbaum-Christmases. I would like to say she barely blinked. But how could she not blink when she had to enter the word Christ in the heading under *Name of student.* "We have other children from mixed marriages," she said, "but your children will be the first Christmases."

We both laughed nervously. My entry as a mother of the little Christmases into Jewish institutions had begun.

Michael and Sarah Rosenbaum-Christmas stayed for several years at the JCC. Sarah just rolled along successfully from one class to another. All of Michael's teachers did their best to accommodate him, which mainly meant they allowed him to stare out the window and do his own thing.

At the end of his third year at the school, Michael's teacher mentioned a Special Ed Jewish Sunday school that she knew of in the city. Michael was now eleven.

That summer, I met Dr. Zeev Greenberg, the school principal of Tikvah Hayim, the special needs Sunday school at Beth Tikvah synagogue, located in the northern end of the city, when I enrolled Michael. Beth Tikvah in Hebrew means "House of Hope." *Tikvah Hayim* means "Life's Hope." For me, for Michael and the family, it provided both.

Dr. Greenberg was a former Israeli living in Toronto with his family and teaching at the Ontario Institute for Studies in Education. His Jewish Sunday school took every kind of special needs kid you could name. Kids with autism, Tourette's syndrome, obsessive-compulsive disorder (OCD), and pervasive development disorder (PDD), learning disabilities, Asperger's syndrome and hyperactivity issues. He would now take Michael, a kid with fetal alcohol syndrome.

Dr. Greenberg and his merry band of teachers — including a music therapist, otherwise known as an accordion player, and a clutch of male volunteers from the synagogue's men's group — did everything in their power for these kids. They wanted to make sure they came happily to Sunday school, learned, had a good time and felt good about themselves. What they did was called a good deed, a *mitzvah*.

The place started to pull on my heart strings the moment we arrived each Sunday morning to drop Michael off. Or, I should say, pulled on Robin's heartstrings. For the most part, he *shlepped* Michael in the car up Bathurst St. each week. I continued to transport Sarah to and from the downtown JCC classes by streetcar from the docks. The school suited her well, though going there forced her to learn the term "schedule conflict" at an exceptionally early age. As we walked to the boat each Sunday morning, Sarah watched longingly as her Island buddies headed off to the soccer field for their weekly game.

Every Sunday, Michael rushed out of class, smiling, happy to see us. The teachers were cheery, finding something nice to say. Dr. Greenberg talked to us too, understanding our desperation. He told us what Michael did, not what he didn't do. And he never forgot to call out to Michael as we were leaving, "I'm looking forward to seeing you next Sunday, Michael."

Because of Dr. Greenberg's positive attitude and optimism, I opened my heart to the idea that Michael could become a *bar mitzvah* at thirteen, only two years away. It was a long shot, but I thought we should consider taking a run at it. It was a bold notion, one that met with worry and disbelief from pretty much everyone I mentioned it to, including Robin. "It may be too much to ask of Michael." I had to ask myself if it was a selfish dream. Was I setting my kid up for failure?

Maybe. Preparing to become a *bar mitzvah* involved hard work, study, cooperation and dedication. Michael had not yet shown interest in any of these. At the time of the *bar mitzvah* ceremony, Michael would have to stand in front of an entire congregation, read and sing Hebrew from the Torah in an ancient melody. After the ceremony, there was generally a social event of some kind to celebrate the child's accomplishment. Michael was not much of a social creature, so we naturally wouldn't plan anything big or overwhelming, but friends and family would *insist* on celebrating his accomplishment. Would Michael even *go* to a party?

An even more important questions was, "Am I completely nuts?" Possibly. We still struggled at home to get Michael to brush his teeth, flush the toilet and bathe. Or was this an inspired idea based on faith, hope and love for Michael? I mulled this over for months. After many conversations with Dr. Greenberg, I decided that Michael could accomplish something that would bring him pride, satisfaction and, perhaps, spiritual nourishment. We had no clue whether I was right or wrong.

Theoretically, the logical thing would be to ask Michael if he felt capable or was interested in any of this. But we didn't. He would automatically say "No." Michael said "No" to everything we asked him to do. It didn't matter whether it was something he honestly wanted to say no to or not. Dr. Roberts called this "oppositionally wired." His default position when something was asked of him was to say no. Full stop. He was often sorry afterward.

"You must know adults like that," Dr. Roberts said. "They say no to everything."

With Dr. Greenberg at our side, we decided to go ahead with the *bar mitzvah* idea without Michael's consent or agreement.

We eventually said to him, "You, Mommy and Daddy are going to work with Dr. Greenberg so you can become a *bar mitzvah* in two years."

He knew what a *bar mitzvah* was, and had been to several. Before we explained what specifically was required of him, Michael looked at us and said, "If it involves me doing any work, forget it."

We pretended not to hear.

I was standing in the dining room, cleaning up from our Sunday breakfast. I had almost finished clearing the table when a ratty old tennis ball came soaring through the air from the living room, bouncing with loud thuds in front of me. Along with nine scattered lemons, my beautiful hand-painted china fruit bowl now lay in a dozen pieces. Robin and I had recently spent days scouring antique stores until I found it — the perfect centrepiece for our dining-room table.

I wanted to kill Michael and Andrew. Their hands were covering their mouths, but it didn't successfully muffle the sound. They were giggling uproariously. Though they may have felt a modicum of shame, the boys thought the minor debacle was very, very funny.

Michael and Andrew had become inseparable sidekicks. Andrew was virtually the only child Michael related to other than Sarah. Their attraction to one another, usually based on what would kindly be referred to as kinetic hoodlum energy, was uncanny. They each displayed a remarkable overdose of energy and lack of judgment, whether it was vigorously waving sledgehammers and pickaxes found in nearby sheds or slashing live branches off trees in full sight of environmentally rigorous neighbours.

Not only did the boys act alike, they looked alike. Though Andrew had brown hair and Michael remained blond, they both were wiry, small, very pale and had flat features. It wouldn't be hard to figure out they were brothers if you were looking.

It bothered me terribly that the boys had become so close, yet remained totally in the dark about their blood relationship. We were hiding a part of their identity from them — who they were and their place in the universe. Still, it remained just too complicated to tell them.

The main reason, of course, was Kira. She was even more of a concern now than when the kids were little. Andrew was older, now into double digits, he could talk, had opinions, asked questions. If Andrew knew that Michael was his brother, he had the capacity to talk to his mum about it. He was spending more and more time at Kira's since she had entered into a new relationship, so it wouldn't be a stretch for Andrew to say, "Let's have Michael over for dinner." Or, more to the point, "Why did you keep me but not him?"

Whatever the question or conversation would really be, it would mean that the jig was up. Kira would now know that Robin and I were raising her son. That was not part of the deal we made with her, but Andrew was not part of the deal either.

Because he *was* now part of the deal, we had to watch out more than ever. Robin and I remained steadfast. We had to keep the secret going for as long as possible.

When Michael was twelve and Andrew ten, we knew we couldn't put off the inevitable any longer.

Neighbours were getting suspicious. "It's remarkable how much Andrew and Michael look alike. Are they related?" several asked. It meant others must be thinking the same but not asking. I went first to the Island's daycare worker, Yolanda. I had always felt guilty not telling her about the boys because she was so much part of their lives, having taken care of both when they were small.

"It's been hard keeping this from you, Yolanda, but we did it to protect the boys."

She laughed. "I knew it the second I laid eyes on Andrew," she said. "They were just too much alike, the way they looked and how they acted. It was obvious. I knew you wanted to keep it secret."

I was dumbstruck. "Do you think other people on the Island put it together, too?"

"I know they have."

That was all I needed to hear. Better the boys learn from us than on the boat one morning from some neighbour they barely knew.

We were all clueless as to how to go about it. We knew the boys would be furious with us for hiding their kinship, so wanted to do everything we could to make it easier on both them and us. We knew full well though, that they couldn't possibly understand the intricacies of adoption disclosures or the peculiarity of their particular situation. Sure, we adults had all been playing it all by ear, desperately trying to do the right thing. Who among us knew for sure what that was?

We sensed the time had come. The four of us met at our house to work out details. It became evident that we had only questions. Tell them together or separately? What do we say when the boys ask why we didn't tell them earlier? How do we deal with their anger? How do we avoid saying anything disparaging about Kira? How do we explain to Michael why Kira kept Andrew but gave him away? And, what about Sarah, who also had a close relationship with Andrew? Since Michael's her brother, does that mean Andrew was her brother, too? Guess so.

And the biggest question of all: How do we then tell Kira?

Straight to a counsellor who specializes in adoption issues we did go. After several sessions, we had a plan, steadfastly maintained, until the appointed day.

We would break the news to each boy in the confines of his own home at a coordinated hour. We'd gather Michael and Sarah together and tell them at the same time. I'd spill the beans here; Lynn would do the talking there. We all synchronized watches. Lynn and I repeatedly rehearsed our scripts.

Robin and I were anxious on the appointed day. We were counselled to just give the basics, without too much commentary. Let them absorb it and ask questions as they arose.

Robin asked the kids to come join us on the living-room couch. I lit a fire and made peanut butter cookies to entice. There was a good chance they wouldn't want to come to what was suspiciously looking like a meeting. Once they sat down, I spat it out as fast as I could.

"We have something important to tell you. You know Andrew's mother, Kira? Well, she's your birth mother, Michael. She gave birth to you, too. That means Andrew's your half-brother." Complete silence. Both kids just stared at us, expecting more to come.

"You mean we're brothers?" Michael said, eventually. His eyes were becoming glassy with tears.

"Yes, brothers. Kira is your mum and Andrew's mum." Michael began grinning from ear to ear, though still with tears.

"Why didn't you tell us before?" he asked.

"We thought it best to wait until you were older."

"That means Andrew's my brother, too?" said Sarah.

"Yes, he's your brother, too."

They both wanted to know. "Does Andrew know?"

"Lynn and Don are telling him right now."

"I want to talk to Andrew," Michael said.

"Before you call him, Michael, I want you to know there aren't any more secrets. This was the only one. I promise you."

Both he and Sarah seemed thrilled and shocked at the news. Michael was also furious.

He called Andrew, then rushed over to his house, slamming the front door behind him, harder than ever. I tried talking to him again before he ran out, but he refused to listen. What could I have really said, anyway? Was there really any way to explain our good intentions or the generally accepted rules of confidentiality about adoption to a twelve-year-old? Children raised by adoptive parents seldom have anything to do with their birth parents' other children. Usually, each doesn't know the other exists. Our situation was so very different from that of other families.

Andrew was equally furious with Lynn and Don. For weeks after the announcement, the boys completely avoided us. Michael wouldn't come to the table for meals, and stopped making eye contact. Michael and Andrew were together every moment when not in school. They'd hide in each other's bedrooms, slamming the door, one time so hard the doorjamb came loose. They plotted how Michael was going to meet Kira. They were obnoxious, rude, turned the heavy metal music up full throttle, and defied everything we asked of them. A hole appeared in Michael's bedroom wall. They whittled homemade spears and knives. It was pure "us and them," David and Goliath. We were the bad guys. They were blood brothers. And they made sure everyone knew. Lots of neighbours began asking questions of us.

Andrew hurled horrible invectives at Lynn besides the usual "I hate you." She was the prototype evil stepmother, and we had become tainted partners-in-crime. Michael saw his angelic birth mother as victim of an evil plot that we, led by ringleader Lynn, were perpetrating on her. Photographs of a smiling, pixie-like Kira began appearing in Michael's bedroom, some stuck prominently on his bulletin board. The framed family picture with a smiling Robin, Sarah and me had been taken down.

Fortunately, Sarah didn't feel as betrayed. It was a great comfort. Yet Michael's and Andrew's rejection was eating me up. Would the boys ever forgive us? Could they make up for lost time? What had the secret taken from them? Had we caused lasting harm? Did we really betray them or protect them? Should we have dealt with it earlier on? Did these young boys lose something forever, like trust in adults, specifically, us?

Somehow, we managed to get the boys to come along to see a counsellor who specialized in "adoption talk" with kids. She was superb. Michael didn't say much in the sessions. He

yawned a lot, something he often does when people talk about
their feelings. Andrew spun in circles on his chair most of the
time. Slowly, after months of sessions, their anger began to
subside. They at least heard some explanation of why we kept
the secret. Nevertheless, we had to respect, and live through,
the boys' hurt, anger and sadness, all still there. The sadness
belonged to Michael, particularly. Andrew got to be with his
mother. Michael didn't.

During their invective-hurling periods, we made sure not
to share unnecessarily sordid information about Kira. It was
tempting, though. Kira and her partner Kenny continued to
fabricate stories about the horrible Lynn, passed on to Michael
via Andrew. Understandably, the boys became increasingly
aligned with Kira in the war she was waging against Lynn
and Don for "taking Andrew away" and "making me drink."

It came as no surprise when Michael announced, "I want to
meet Kira." It was hurting Michael to hear Andrew announce
when they were playing together, "I'm leaving to go to my
mum's." It was Michael's mum now, too.

We understood Michael's desire. At the heart of it, Michael
could not understand why Kira chose to give him up at birth,
but not Andrew.

But Robin and I weren't completely sure they should meet —
at least not yet. Among other things, we were afraid she might
promise things or make plans, as she did with Andrew, that
she was not able to keep. One thing we were sure of though.
If and when they met, we wouldn't consider allowing them in
a room without us.

With so many concerns, we would wait as long as we possibly
could before bringing Michael and Kira together. We prayed
that time would dampen the flames of Michael's present desire.

Soon after we told the boys, Lynn and Don told Kira that
Michael was our son. She was pleasantly shocked. "Cool," she
said. No obvious burning desire on her part for a "reunion."

We were temporarily in luck.

12.
Lost and Found
Florida, 1997 / Toronto, 1999

WE WERE VISITING MY PARENTS in Florida as we did every year. Because we often travelled during Christmas break, we were there on Sarah's seventh birthday, December 25th. As usual, when we arrived at their apartment, my mother greeted us at the front door. I knew she was thrilled to see us, but when she reached out to hug each of us, she seemed awkward. As I had first noticed when Michael was born, my mother didn't know how to show physical affection.

After Sarah's birthday party, resplendent with the garish blue and white frosted birthday cake she begged for every year from the local Publix supermarket, Sarah and Michael were sprawled on the carpet in front of us, building a spaceship with Lego. For some reason, Sarah looked up and spontaneously said to my mother, "I love you, Grandma." She then got up, ran over to my mother and gave her a great big hug.

I watched, spellbound. The reaction on my mother's face when Sarah said this to her was one of pure joy. She sparkled. My mother put every ounce of her body into it, hugging her solidly back. While still in their embrace, I heard my mother say, "I ... love you too ... Sarah." She almost stuttered getting it out, but she did it. She said, "I love you."

Sarah had unlocked my mother, and with it, my heart. I could feel a lifelong anger towards my mother deflate, like air slowly let out of a balloon.

There was something so stirring about the stunned look on my mother's face during those moments, I asked myself: Was it possible that no one, perhaps other than my father, had ever said "I love you" to my mother?

I had no memory of her ever saying it to me, or of me saying it to her. Perhaps she had never learned to say the words or even knew that this was something you said to your children. Was it possible that her mother had never said it to her? I still knew little about my grandmother or how long she had been mentally ill, but yes, it was possible. You don't forget how to hug and kiss and dote and coo. Perhaps she never learned how. As children, my sisters and I couldn't understand this on a cognitive level, but we were utterly and painfully aware on an emotional one.

A few days after we returned home from Florida, I was speaking to my mother during our weekly Sunday phone call. I was about to end the conversation when I heard my mother say, "Linda ... I ... love you."

Within a heartbeat, I shot back "I love you too, Mom." There was a long silent pause, then we said goodbye. I hung up and went straight to the kitchen where Robin was dicing vegetables. Seeing that I was sobbing, he asked "What's wrong?" with a look of panic on his face. "Nothing," I said. "You won't believe what just happened."

My mother died a few years later, in 1999, at the age of eighty-seven. Michael was twelve, Sarah ten. I was lucky she had lived long enough for me to make amends with her before her death. I needed to, wanted to and worked hard to make it happen. It wasn't easy. She continued to criticize me to the end. As it was for my sisters, the barrage of criticism had chipped away at my confidence, and it had been a long haul building it back. I was well into my forties before I began to accept that yes, I *was* sensitive, something my mother criticized me for as a child. Probably *too* sensitive, as she said, but perhaps that wasn't altogether a bad thing. But you couldn't have told me that any earlier.

After the experience on Sarah's birthday, I was able to forgive my mother for the lifetime of criticism and coldness. She and I had several good years together before she died. I focused on what I thought her *intentions* were as a mother, and decided they were undeniably good. I had no doubt when I looked at her in this way: my mother loved me, she always had.

I sat by the side of her bed, holding her hand in mine when she died. I wouldn't let go until a nurse patted me on the shoulder and said, "It's time."

My dad died three years before my mother. I desperately wanted him to hold on longer so he could be with us if Michael became a *bar mitzvah*. It was probably a good thing he went before my mother, though. He wouldn't have known how to take care of himself without her, and none of his children lived in the same city as he did.

My love for my father had always been so strong that I didn't know how I was going to live in a world without him someday. For so much of my life, I felt like he was the only person who truly knew who I was and could understand me. I always needed to know he was there, somewhere, and took comfort that he was.

As we both aged, things shifted, as they do. I eventually had Robin and the children in my life — the family I had so badly wanted, ever since childhood. Though my love for my father was everlasting, Robin, Sarah and Michael were added to the list of beloveds I couldn't imagine living without.

Growing up made me see my father less idealistically, but more likely, the riots in Detroit thirty years before did actually change him. While my heart felt pity for his sadness and loss, I couldn't stand his ensuing bitterness. For a long time, I fought him when he muttered something misanthropic. He couldn't possibly mean it. Then one day I stopped. He did mean what he said.

His pessimism frightened me. I had always been so much like

him. I became fearful that life's travails might turn me sour too. It would have been easy to follow my father's lead. I had had my share of sorrows, but something in my temperament kept me afloat. I clung to the words I said to my friend Sybil about the Detroit riots. It's not what happens to you in your life; it's how you play it.

My mother was dutiful and cared for my father to the end. My sister Barbara and I were with him when he died, keeping vigil, though as I've heard happening with other people, my father waited to pass for the one brief moment when we left the room. I knew he was ready. Even I, his beloved baby, could no longer bring him comfort.

I mourned solidly, saying *Kaddish* in the mornings. It took a full year of grieving for my father before I believed I *could* live without him.

After my mother's death, I continued to wonder about the effect her own mother's life must have had on her. I decided it was time to learn more about my grandmother's history, the Eloise Mental Hospital and perhaps about my own mother.

"Would you like me to see if any court records exist? I might be able to help," Steve offered.

I was shocked by the question. "My grandmother's records? I've never given them any thought," I answered.

A few days before this phone conversation, I had been rummaging around on the Internet, looking for information about the hospital where my grandmother had lived. While rummaging, I happened on a website about Eloise that also included a discussion forum where people talked about their own relatives who had lived there.

On the site's discussion group, a man named Steve Luxenberg had shared a few comments. He seemed informed, thoughtful and helpful. I went to other Eloise sites. Steve Luxenberg's name popped up again and again. I soon realized Steve had recently written a book, *Annie's Ghosts: A Journey into a Family Secret,* an exploration of his own family's secret about an aunt, who, like my grandmother, had also been hidden away in Eloise.

Steve was an editor with the *Washington Post*, an ex-Detroiter, born in 1952, Jewish. He went to Henry Ford High School. Henry Ford High School? That's where I went, too. Our paths must have crossed. He was only one year behind me.

I then found Steve's blog, along with his email address. Considering we had so many common threads, I decided to drop him a quick note. As a former Henry Fordite, perhaps he'd be interested in knowing I had a hidden relative in Eloise, too, since I assumed we were the only ones. I emailed Steve, doubting I'd hear back.

Within hours, I received a remarkably generous note. He told me we weren't alone; there were hundreds of people looking for information about hidden relatives. Steve suggested we speak on the phone the following day.

That's when he said, "If you're interested in finding out more about your grandmother, it's possible you might find something in court records." That was a big *if* though. Most of the hospital records from Eloise had been destroyed after the hospital closed down in 1984. The records Steve was referring to would only exist if my grandmother was committed through a court proceeding.

"I have to think about it," I said.

I was sitting with Sarah at our dining-room table. We were "negotiating," the word we used to describe arguing about homework. Finally, after enough prodding from me, Sarah agreed to let me help her with math, a subject she was having trouble with. Sarah showed me a story problem from her Grade 8 textbook, *Math That Matters*. I was dumbstruck. The story really did matter.

We had to analyze statistics on a spreadsheet relating to the variation in calorie consumption of rich and poor populations in Brazil, India and Cuba. It led to an interesting conversation about the distribution of wealth, including food, among different social classes. Sarah seemed to honestly care about the issues, and I couldn't be more thrilled that *Math That Matters* mattered to her.

"Oh, Sarah. I forgot. A letter came today from Denise. It's addressed to Daddy and me but of course it's for you too, so I waited to open it. I figured you'd want to."

It was a letter we had been waiting for. Every December, we sent Sarah's birth mother new pictures of Sarah. We always tried to arrange for the photographs to arrive in Denise's hands in time for Christmas, the anniversary day she gave birth to Sarah.

In the last two years, Sarah had asked Denise to send pictures of *herself* as well. And now, for the first time, Sarah asked Denise to send her a picture of her *birth father* too. We had never seen a picture of him.

Denise had had no contact with the birth father for the last eleven years. Therefore, she didn't have a recent photograph. She would, however, look for an old picture of Mike to send to us. She would also look for a photo of Dylan, Sarah's full-blood brother. Dylan was born to Denise and Mike one year after Sarah was born. After Denise and Mike split, Dylan went to live with his father.

For some reason, both Denise at her end, and I at ours, were late sending pictures that year. Christmas came and went. Neither of us received anything. A few days after Christmas, Denise gave me a call.

For the past thirteen years, since Sarah was born, Denise and I had stayed faithfully in contact. At least once a month we spoke on the phone. It was a remarkable relationship considering that we still had never met. It was all the more remarkable considering how difficult it was to manage the relationship with Kira, who we theoretically weren't having contact with.

During the conversation with Denise that day, we both bemoaned our mutual slothfulness and promised to mail our photos.

I handed Sarah the envelope. She began to open it and looked very excited at first. Then, she slapped the letter down on the table next to the math book. She pretended to be calm and we went back to the math. I could tell something was brewing. It was still math, after all.

"I'm too nervous to open it," she said.

"It's okay, darling, we'll open it together. It'll be fine."

She slowly opened the envelope and pulled out a store-bought card, photographs and a handwritten note inside. She put the photographs face down on the table and read the card. "It's so beautiful, Mama," she said to me. She then read Denise's handwritten note.

Hello all,
Sorry these weren't sent earlier but it has been crazy here. I hope you all enjoyed your Christmas.
Please tell Sarah I hope she enjoys these pictures and tell her I love her. I think of you all every day and you will always remain in my thoughts, dreams and prayers.
Love, Denise

Sarah then took the photographs into her hands and held them so we could look together. The first picture was of a twenty-something, solid-looking T-shirt-and-jeaned man with fairly long, dirty-blond hair. He was lying back on a big, plaid recliner. He was holding a baby face-down on his chest. He was looking away from the camera. His eyes appeared to be riveted on something in the distance.

Both Sarah and I started to laugh at the same time.

"What do you think he's looking at?" I asked Sarah. I had already formed my own opinion.

"TV, of course," she said. "Probably a hockey game." We were both laughing because Sarah, much to my horror, *loved* watching television. She especially loved watching hockey games, a game she herself played.

Suddenly Sarah burst into heavy sobs. The revelation of seeing what her birth father looked like hit like one of her pucks. The square face. The dirty blond hair. The blue eyes and narrow lips, the strong chin and solid build. It was all her. And, as we were now seeing, all him.

"I can't believe he doesn't want to know anything about me, Mom," she blurted through her sobs. "Or who I am, or what I look like. Anything. He probably never even thinks about me." She put her head down on the table to cover her face.

"I'm sorry, Mama, I'm sorry." She continued to apologize and cry.

I asked what she was sorry for. Crying, in that situation had to be the most normal, natural and healthiest reaction anyone could possibly have. It was a picture of her birth father and brother for god's sake. Nevertheless, why was she saying "Sorry"?

Then I realized Sarah might possibly be saying it because she didn't want ME to feel bad. Me, the adoptive mother. Maybe she was worried about hurting *my* feelings by showing she cared about this man she had never met.

"Sarah, are you afraid of hurting me?"

"Yes," she admitted. "I don't want you to feel bad, especially about Denise."

I had repeatedly told Sarah over the years not to feel bad about having feelings for Denise. *I* had feelings for Denise. How could *she* not?

Sarah had recently begun some small correspondence with Denise, too. I knew we were moving towards the day we would all meet. I hoped, however, I could keep it from happening for at least a few more years, until she was more emotionally mature. Eighteen was my earliest target date.

"Daddy and I know how connected to us you are, Sarah." Robin and I were lucky we had never felt jealous of Denise. "Enjoy it. You don't ever have to apologize."

NOT EXACTLY AS PLANNED

Denise had brought a beautiful, healthy baby into the world. She'd planted genetic seeds we were all watching come into bloom. She was the woman who chose to pass her child into our loving hands. That the relationship we maintained with Denise all these years worked so well was for all of us a blessing.

"Mom, when I'm older, I want to meet my birth dad and Dylan," she said. She picked the picture up again. "Do you think you'll be able to find them for me?"

We had been talking on and off for years about what it would be like when Sarah finally met Denise. But meeting her birth father had never come up before. It would undoubtedly be another significant relationship for her. I just had to look at Michael and Andrew to know.

"I'll do everything I can, Sarah. I'm not sure why, but in my heart, I honestly believe your birth father will be happy to be found." We didn't bother going back to the math. It no longer mattered.

Getting photos of Sarah's birth dad gave us the kick we needed to get a card and send our pictures to Denise and a note from Sarah:

> *Hi!*
>
> *Well, I'll just tell you what's up in my life. Well my best friend is Molly and we both go to a great school. I love sports and I am very physical. I have just noticed how much I look like you and my birth dad. I'm into baggy jeans and tight shirts. See the necklaces in the pictures? I never take them off. My room is always a mess (like a normal teenager's room!). On my wall I have pictures of hockey players, music people and art work.*
>
> *That letter really touched me. I cried and cried. I have a dog and love him so so much. Yeah, I have zits but I'm proud and try to look my best every day. With*

books I like mysteries or sometimes historical fiction.
With music I like PennyWise, NOET, *Offspring, Rancid,*
Bob Marley and more. I am not "popular" but I have
my own group of friends and that's what's important.
Eye heart (love) U.
P.S.: *My grades in school are just fine.*
　　Love, Sarah

There is a belief in Judaism that at the moment of birth you are touched by an angel on your philtrum, the indented area above your lip. At that moment, you forget everything there is to know in the world, knowledge you possessed while still in the womb. Your mission in life thereafter is to reaccumulate the knowledge and wisdom you forgot at that moment. You do this by being part of the world, forming relationships and learning from your experiences.

Sarah was fulfilling her mission. She took in everything going on around her. She could size up both people and situations, knowing if either one meant trouble. It gave her a natural wariness. For all her protective shielding, Sarah was tender, vulnerable and kind. During her early teens, Sarah wrote a poem that included the lines:

I'm strong as a bull,
Tender as my mother's heart.

She was all of that, and more.

13.
Michael's Song
Toronto, 2000

IT WAS MAY 2000. Robin and I woke with the same uncertainty as every morning, but the stakes were much higher. It was the day of our son's *bar mitzvah*. Would we get Michael out of bed, dressed, pilled, breakfasted, out the door and onto the ferry without turning the house into a war zone, damaging everyone's spirit along the way?

Michael had spent the previous evening at our friend Barbara's house baking two beautiful braided *challahs*. He went to bed knowing that when we woke him in the morning, it would be B-Day, the day he would become a *bar mitzvah*. All he had to do after breakfast was put on his new white shirt, navy blue pants and matching jacket. Daddy would do his tie up. Michael didn't know, but before we left the house, I would present him with my father's velvet and embroidered bag. In it was the silk *tallit* I had been saving for him since my dad's death six years before.

I ached thinking about my father, wishing he were with us. What pleasure and pride he would have had seeing his baby daughter pass on his *tallit* to her son in a gesture of *d'or v'dor*, from generation to generation. I knew on this, his grandson's *bar mitzvah* day, he would say to me, through his tears and gentle smile, "You've done a beautiful thing, Linda."

When Michael got home from Barbara's the previous night, he came upstairs to our bedroom as he had done every other night for the past year. I'd devised a half-hour routine to help him learn his *maftir*, the week's *parsha* (passage) reading from the Torah that he would sing using melodic chants. Not only did he have to read Hebrew, he had to read a special liturgical Hebrew in which the usual vowel sounds were removed and letters were written in a unique script.

Once Michael came out of his extended angry period with us over Kira, he regained his desire for cuddling. We were lucky. It was the last and only hold we had on him. Knowing this, I incorporated good doses of physical affection as a component in his nightly practice, something I learned from reading about *rebbes* of yore. When teaching Torah to young pupils for the first time, they slathered honey on each child's slate board. They wanted to make sure the boys enjoyed the moment and developed a sensory connection to the sweetness of Torah study.

In our version of this *yeshiva* practice, Michael came upstairs to our bedroom every night and climbed onto the bed with us. We smothered him with constant physical attention, including back rubs and hugs while he went over and over his lines. To our amazement, he had been remarkably agreeable about the study. So much so, we tried adding an extra dose of affection when we asked him to do a chore, look after his hygiene or clean up his room. It never worked. Michael still would not do anything he did not want to do.

On some level, Michael wanted to do his studying. He wanted to become a *bar mitzvah*. He couldn't tell us why, nor could we figure out why. His desire could have been anything from spiritual to financial. If the latter, we told ourselves, Michael wouldn't be the first *bar mitzvah* boy to do it for the money he'd receive from family to celebrate his accomplishments.

Robin and I repeatedly told Michael how proud we were of the fine job he was doing each night. We were. As Michael's memory was so poor, he often forgot his lines from one practice to the next. It left us worried about how he would do standing in front of a crowd of possibly 200 people, a number that included our invited guests as well as members of the synagogue's congregation there for the weekly *Shabbat* service. We remained unsure whether Michael would actually stand before the congregation and perform his *maftir* or run off the *bimah* instead, so we only invited family and friends who knew Michael well enough to understand if he decided to bolt. It would spare Robin and me some degree of angst, embarrassment and backstory, about what might or might not turn out to be a happy occasion.

The morning proceeded with remarkable ease. We were able to get Michael to bathe and wash his hair. It was clear, though, getting him to brush his teeth was not going to happen without Herculean force. We let it go rather than mess with the gods.

Sarah wore a lovely floral blue dress, bought for the day, and I a 1940's-inspired powder-blue suit made for the service. Mother and daughter decided to wear straw hats to top off our outfits. I pinned a Carmen Miranda-style brooch of bright red cherries to my brim for a dose of sartorial whimsy. I thought of my mother as I pinned it on. She too would have dressed beautifully for the occasion.

Both Robin and Michael looked like a million bucks in their suits and ties. We Rosenbaum-Christmases were a handsome, regular, everyday-looking family. The kind our politicians always like referring to as Average Canadians. No one would guess otherwise.

A few minutes before walking out the door, I stood at the dining-room table and told Michael that I had something special for him, warning him it wasn't a video game so he wouldn't be disappointed. I then presented my dad's *tallit*. He could tell by my tone it was special.

Sarah, Robin and I were teary-eyed watching Michael remove the *tallit* from the bag. With encouragement from Robin and me, Michael said the blessing for putting on the *tallit* that Dr. Greenberg had taught him. Michael then burst into one of his ear-to-ear grins that made him so endearing. It was impossible not to love the guy.

We were out of the house! As it was Saturday morning, many of our neighbours were also on their way to the boat with bundle buggies in tow. Going to St. Lawrence Market to buy groceries for the week was a Saturday morning ritual for many Islanders. Seeing us, they stopped to chat. Our outfits signalled that something was happening in the Rosenbaum-Christmas family household.

"You look so handsome today, Michael."

"I hear it's a big day for you, Michael. What's up?"

"You look great in that suit, Michael."

And to the neighbour who asked, "What's the special occasion?" Michael responded without skipping a beat.

"My *bar mitzvah*," he said, as if it was a regular thing for an Island boy to become a *bar mitzvah*. Robin and I laughed. In the community's 150-year history, Michael was undoubtedly the first, but hopefully not the last, Island child to become a *bar mitzvah*.

When we reached the dock, we hooked up with the Island friends whom we had invited to the service, including Barbara and her family as well as Lynn, Don and Andrew. We all made a beautiful, self-congratulatory sight. Seldom do our women friends wear such stylish hats, suits, dresses and heels. Seldom do our men friends wear suits and ties. But there we all were, waiting for the boat to pull in, dressed in fashionable *bar mitzvah* regalia. Everyone greeted us with hugs and kisses. They showered Michael with attention, praise and familial teases. Everyone gave Robin and me reassuring nods. They knew what was hiding under our snappy façades. One friend whispered, "It's a miracle you've come this far, enjoy it."

The mood on the boat was pure cheer. Michael was lapping it up. I was beyond happy that he felt so good. He was usually reclusive and uncomfortable with people and didn't like to be touched by anyone other than Robin, Sarah and me. He would normally retreat when in a group, preferring the quiet of his own company or the chaos of Andrew's. He certainly didn't tolerate being the centre of attention.

Not so today. He was more than willing to let everyone lavish him with recognition. I couldn't possibly explain why. Once cityside, we drove up to the synagogue at the north end of the city. Michael opened the car door and got out. I could now breathe.

We talked with the rabbi before entering the sanctuary for one last note of guidance. I gently reminded him to please use Michael's full last name when referring to him. I might have been mistaken, but in our last meeting I thought he referred to Michael using only one of the two names in the double-barreled moniker. And it wasn't Christmas.

I could understand if there had been such an omission. Beth Tikvah synagogue was Conservative, meaning it followed Judaic practices and doctrine closer to the traditional Orthodox observance-spectrum than to the more relaxed and progressive Reform. It required a few compromises on our part. Because Robin was not Jewish, the rabbi told us he could not be given the honour of reading from the Torah or opening the ark, which would typically be given to Jewish friends and family members. However, Robin would be allowed on the *bimah* with Michael, me and Sarah to receive the traditional blessing of the family.

My sister Barbara was appalled. She felt Robin deserved more. He'd *shlepped* Michael to Sunday school for years. He'd practised Michael's *bar mitzvah* lines with him each night. He had been an equal partner in making this *bar mitzvah* happen. He had supported me in my dream, every difficult step along the way.

I could understand my sister's position. Like me, she knew the statistics. Not about *shlepping* kids to Sunday school, though. Rather, about the enormously high rate of divorce among families with special needs children. Many lesser mortals, usually fathers, give up on their marriages because the hardships of raising their children created unbearable (to them) stress on the marital relationship. Therefore, how could Robin, who had given his loyal all, be denied full honours during the service?

I was less appalled. Over the years, I had learned to pick my battles regarding Michael. I had had my share, with schools, hospitals, social services, government bureaucracies, funding agencies. Everything I'd fought for came with a price, some higher than others. The compromises required for the *bar mitzvah* weren't unacceptably high to me. Beth Tikvah had allowed Dr. Greenberg to start a special needs Sunday school at the synagogue. Members of the synagogue's brotherhood stewarded the program. They honoured the students at the end of every academic year with a special ceremony, offering each child a present, recognition and respect. Parents, including Robin, were given opportunity to bathe in their child's accomplishment.

My blond, blue-eyed son with fetal alcohol syndrome and the last name of Christmas was becoming a *bar mitzvah* in their synagogue and they treated him with dignity. They had recognized the desperate need in the community for someplace for children like Michael to go, and they had served our family generously. So what if they mumbled the last part of Michael's name? So what if they wouldn't allow Robin to read from the Torah? Robin didn't *want* to read from the Torah. He didn't know *how* to read from the Torah. He didn't *care* about opening the ark. It had no resonance or history for him. If it did matter to him, it would matter to me, too. But Robin had told me repeatedly he didn't care and I believed him.

And what were my options, anyway? No hip, progressive, egalitarian *shule* had given us what Dr. Greenberg and this synagogue had.

We entered the synagogue's beautiful wood-panelled chapel where the service would be held. It was a special place, evocative of older European Jewish sanctuaries, warmed by its golden illumination, carved ornamentation and stained-glass windows. The *bimah* was decorated with wrought-iron railings, wooden pews and an ornate, hand-carved ark, the *Aron Hakodesh*.

The ark is the centre of any Jewish place of worship. It is set against the eastern wall of the synagogue to hold the congregation's Torahs and sacred texts. Beth Tikvah's *Aron Hakodesh* had been trucked down from the small northern Ontario town of Kirkland Lake in 1980 when the Jewish population decreased and the synagogue there was forced to close its doors. Before finding its home in Kirkland Lake in 1927, the ark was part of a Romanian synagogue in Montreal that also had to close its doors.

Robin, Sarah and I stood at the back of the chapel to greet guests and help them get comfortable. A lot of help in that department was still required even though I'd sent out a *"Bar Mitzvah 101"* primer along with the invitation, intended to help guests, particularly non-Jewish ones, feel more at home in what, for many, would be their first time in a synagogue.

I hoped my self-written guidebook, *Coles Notes to Michael's Bar Mitzvah*, would help unlock a few of the mysteries of traditional ways. Like should a non-Jewish man wear a yarmulke? Should women cover their heads, too? Can they wear pantsuits? Do we clap? Can we take pictures? Who wears a *tallit*, and why? How come my prayer book opens back to front? And, most importantly, what are Michael and the rabbi saying up there, anyway?

Our guests were stunned upon entering the chapel. Good stunned. They remained standing at the entry, looking around, taking in the ark, eternal light, Lions of Judah and the warm, beautiful glow. I was overjoyed seeing how moved they were by the sanctuary's powerful, transcendent other-worldliness.

The arrival of guests provided an excellent distraction from gnawing worry about Michael's intentions for the day. We were still wondering whether he would bail out at the last minute and go into hiding. It was a scenario we had become agonizingly familiar with. There had been precedents. Graduation ceremonies, birthday parties, Passover *seders*, presentations at school. Michael willingly agreed to participate at those events. He went. He acted reasonably okay for a while. Then, at the magic moment, time for him to sit down at the *seder* table, recite a line or blow out the candles, he cleverly disappeared without a trace, leaving us all agog and confused. Hey, fooled once again! Really, why should his *bar mitzvah* day be any different?

But Dr. Greenberg told us he was sure Michael would follow through. He had no doubts. He loved our kid. We loved Dr. Greenberg.

Magic hour was approaching. Michael went off with Dr. Greenberg to get ready for their entrance directly onto the *bimah*. Robin, Sarah and I walked to the front pew and took our seats. My oldest sister Barbara, nieces and nephews from Detroit and my sister Sharon and her daughter Tori from Virginia were seated around us. The pews were filling up. I turned around in my seat to see everyone. I inhaled their reassuring glances and two thumbs-up gestures.

Robin and I held hands and reaffirmed both our pride and fears to one another. Within minutes, we'd know one way or other if Michael would become a *bar mitzvah*. I was acutely aware of my parents' absence amongst us in the pews and began to shed a tear. Their absence did not detract from the beauty of the moment. Rather, it added a grace note of sadness to it. It was a reminder to me that even the good things in life seldom come completely untarnished.

The rabbi and cantor walked onto the *bimah*. The cantor took his seat while the rabbi walked across the floor. He bent down and picked up a little footstool, which he then placed in front of the table where the Torah would be read. Robin and I smiled at one another. We realized the stool was to make Michael tall enough to see the top of the table to read from the Torah. Then Michael walked onto the *bimah* with Dr. Greenberg. Though he looked so handsome in his navy blue suit and with his beautiful blond hair, he appeared nervous, small and vulnerable, as ever. He looked out at the congregation until he saw us. He smiled. I gave an appropriate, quiet little wave to him rather than the inappropriate gung-ho arm-waving one I would have preferred.

Several male congregation elders began assembling on the *bimah* around the rabbi, signalling the service was about to begin. Michael still had plenty of time to bail.

The rabbi walked up to the lectern at the front of the *bimah* and looked out at the filled chapel. He welcomed everyone to the *Shabbat* service, then announced that today, Michael Asher Rosenbaum-Christmas would become a *bar mitzvah*. The rabbi told us what page to turn to in the prayer book and began the service by leading the congregation in responsive prayer.

I kept staring at Michael to see if I could tell what he was thinking. I couldn't. Dr. Greenberg had assured us he would remain next to him throughout the course of the service. Yet I kept myself busy, staring, squeezing Robin's hand, thinking of my father. I kept turning around in my seat to find reassurance in familiar faces. In between, I prayed and sang joyously like one of the regular congregants.

Sooner than we expected, the rabbi explained that the Torah would be brought out from the ark. Michael would be asked to read his portion along with other verses he studied. Robin and I looked to each other, knowing the hour of reckoning was nigh. The Torah was laid down on the table. The handwritten parchment scroll was rolled open to the week's *parsha* (passage), and the spot where Michael's passage began. The rabbi smiled at Michael and signalled for him to come forward.

The room became celestially quiet. For a brief moment, it felt as if I was not the only one who had stopped breathing.

I saw Dr. Greenberg look at Michael. He signalled that they would walk together up to the Torah.

Michael rose and walked forward. He picked up the *yad* — the long, heavy, solid silver Torah pointer with carved index finger at its end. It was used to help readers follow their Torah lines without touching the delicate parchment with their fingers. My friend Barbara's family had inherited this German-made *yad* from her late uncle, and had lent it to Michael for the occasion. Michael paused, then looked up at Dr. Greenberg who gave the signal to begin.

Months before the day of the *bar mitzvah*, Robin and I had agreed that it would not matter if Michael recited rather than sang his *maftir* in the melodic cantillation he studied. It wouldn't matter if he lost his place, forgot his lines, mispronounced the Hebrew or needed Dr. Greenberg to accompany him. He had already shown dedication to study. He theoretically understood the responsibilities inherent in the rite of passage. He had accomplished more than anyone, including him, had dared to dream. The performance would be icing only. Ah, but what beautiful, rich, divine icing it would be, we thought.

Dr. Greenberg placed Michael's *yad* on the Hebrew word where he was to begin his recitation. Michael took a deep breath. The room fell into deeper silence. No movement, no sound. With the nod from Dr. Greenberg, Michael opened his mouth. He began to sing the melodic, ancient chant passed down to him. I heard audible sighs of relief in the congregation. Like me, my women friends were shuffling in their purses to dig out hankies. The room was again filled with sound. Michael, in a proud, solid voice, took his place as an adult member of the Jewish community.

I looked behind me and saw a congregation filled with smiling, tear-stained faces, like mine. This kind of miracle does that to you.

Michael continued to chant with ease and fluidity. He always looked to Dr. Greenberg for encouragement and support and always received it. Robin, Sarah and I were in Jewish nirvana. Not only did Michael perform, he performed beautifully. He looked so proud of himself.

Before the service was finished, the rabbi asked Michael to come forward to stand beside him. He placed his hand on Michael's shoulder and spoke to him about the life lessons to be learned from Moses' years of wandering in the wilderness after the Jews' exodus from Egypt. He then raised his hand and held it over my son's head as he recited a blessing recited at my wedding:

> *May the Lord bless you and protect you.*
> *May the Lord shine His face upon you and be gracious unto you.*
> *May the Lord lift up His countenance on you and grant you peace.*
> *Amen.*

I asked myself if there were words to express such joy that I was feeling, a joy I had never before known. The answer came quickly. There were, or I should say, was. It was one Yiddish word, most often used by Jewish parents in relation to an accomplishment of their child. It was called *nachas*.

Michael's party the next day was equally joyous, but in a different way. Robin and I hosted a glorified bagels, cream cheese and lox sit-down brunch for our guests in a former synagogue, now a community centre, in the neighbourhood I moved into when I first came to Toronto.

We hoped Michael would stick around for the meal, festivities, speeches and dancing. We were clear though that he would most likely come and go as he needed. We let him know that the fenced-in outdoor patio attached to the social hall was the perfect place to hang out if he wanted. We would keep an eye on him, along with the smokers, through the large picture window. While he did indeed spend time out there bursting balloons with Andrew, he surprised us once again.

Michael joined Dr. Greenberg and me at the head table set up in front of the room as we blessed the *challahs* he and Barbara had baked the night before. During the course of the party, he let people kiss him, hug him, touch him, shake his hand. He beamed every time he saw a present come his way. He appeared to listen to the speeches honouring him, including the delightful one Sarah delivered lovingly to her big brother.

Michael even allowed guests to seat him on a chair that they boosted above their heads into the air, while dancing around the room to traditional Jewish music. During a candle-lighting ceremony, Andrew, along with other guests, was invited to light a candle on the cake for Michael. As Andrew came forward to the head table, we played the song Michael requested, "He Ain't Heavy, He's My Brother."

The final surprise of the day came when our friend Annie asked Michael to sit near her and several other Islanders at the front of the room by the piano. They had worked up a Yiddish musical tribute, including early-twentieth-century chestnuts like *Bei Mir Bist du Schoen* and *Oyfen Pripichik*. In the tradition of Yiddish theatricality, they hoped to gesticulate dramatically towards Michael as they sang, if possible. And possible, it was. Michael sat grinning through the whole performance, beaming from beginning to end.

Who says miracles don't happen anymore? Michael allowed people to celebrate him, teach him, fete him, honour him and raise him high, closer to heaven.

At party's end, I looked around the room, past the few remaining friends, flowers and leftover food. I was finally able to absorb the meaning of the words so beautifully handwritten in calligraphy by Robin onto the two banners he had hung around the room for his son that morning:

Henai ma tov uma naim,
shevat achim gam yachad.

How good and sweet it is when brother and sister dwell
together in peace.

The other banner quoted the nineteenth-century Rabbi
Nachman of Breslav:

We all have a song, and how beautiful it is when sung
together.

14.
Adapting to More Realities
Toronto Island, 2002

T O OUR RELIEF, Michael stopped asking to meet Kira for a long stretch after the *bar mitzvah*. Kira hadn't requested a meeting either, so we managed to sashay around the whole issue rather than into it. But when Michael hit fifteen, the ranks were closing in. Both Andrew and Michael were insistent that Michael meet Kira. The time had come. As before, we needed help figuring out how to minimize possible, more likely probable, damage.

Sometimes, but by no means always, social service professionals are worth their weight in gold. The adoption counsellor we saw to develop a reunion strategy was one of the good ones. Robin and I first met with her alone to provide the necessary background for a meeting we'd have later with her and Michael. We also took the opportunity to express our fears and concerns about Kira.

Michael was willing to get together with the counsellor. It signalled to him that the time was getting closer for his meeting with Kira. He couldn't really understand why we had to go through what seemed to him unnecessary rigmarole, but he didn't have any choice. The adoption counsellor thought it essential he come to a session so she could gently probe his feelings and expectations about meeting his birth mother. Like us, she was afraid Michael would be vulnerable to Kira's whims and was likely expecting nothing less than a Fairy (God)mother who would whisk him into The Sublime, away from the cruelty of everyday life, and us, his same-old, same-old family. Who knew what fantasies he and Andrew had concocted?

The counsellor greeted Robin, Michael and me warmly, making a particular effort to reach out to Michael. She immediately asked Michael questions.

"Michael, how are you feeling about meeting your birth mother?"

"Good."

"Do you have any questions or worries that we can help you with?"

"No."

"What do you think it will be like to meet her?"

"I don't know."

She told Michael that she had met with dozens of other adopted children before they were introduced to their birth parents. She explained that it's a very emotional time for everyone, and sometimes the birth parent and child don't "click." "But," she added, "that doesn't mean it will be like that for you and Kira. I want you to understand that if this happens, it doesn't mean you've done anything wrong, or that Kira doesn't care about you. It's just that these meetings are hard for some people."

Since it was clear Michael wasn't going to share any thoughts, she added more sobering ones of her own.

"Michael, it's important you understand that Kira made the decision to put you up for adoption at birth. She didn't feel she could raise you. She wanted you to have a loving home with parents who could take care of you. So your mom and dad are your parents. The parents you live with are your real family."

When she could sense how that had sank in with Michael, she added, "Andrew has a different relationship with Kira. She decided to keep him when he was born and raise him. That's why he lives with her sometimes. But that can't be the same for you. Kira's not your mother. She is your birth mother."

On the surface, it appeared Michael understood. He didn't seem upset by what the counsellor said, but we were never really sure what was actually going on inside Michael's head.

Even if he couldn't follow everything, it felt like the cards had been set out on the table. We also made sure that Michael understood that Kira was now living with her boyfriend Kenny, and Kenny and Andrew spent a lot of time together.

Robin, Michael and I walked out of the meeting feeling good. We would have one more session together. The counsellor thought it important to see how Michael was managing with what she had explained to him. If she felt he was ready, I would call Kira, and arrange a meeting. We expected that to be the following week. Michael couldn't wait.

Robin headed home with Michael after our session. I stayed in the city and was in a downtown art supply store when I realized my cell phone had been off for hours. I turned it on and saw messages and missed calls from Lynn. There were too many. I immediately wondered if something was wrong. I knew I should call her back immediately.

"What's up?" I asked when Lynn answered. "I haven't listened to your messages yet, but figure it's important."

"Kira died this morning," Lynn said. "Her boyfriend Kenny found her body. Can't say for sure, but it looks like an overdose, probably alcohol and Tylenol 3s."

I could only think about Michael. He would never meet his birth mother. She could never reassure him of her love. Shit.

A few days later, as we were leaving the house for the funeral, I turned to Michael. "Kira's body will be on display in an open casket, Michael. Some people find it helpful to look, some don't. When we get there, you can decide what feels best for you."

Once at the funeral home, I took Michael's hand and walked with him into the room that held Kira's coffin. We stopped about five feet away from it.

"Close enough, Michael?" I think he sensed that I would not be going any closer.

He stood for a few seconds, then walked up to the casket.

Standing alone, he looked in, then back at me and said, "I just want to see what she looks like."

Seconds later, he answered his own question. "A lot like me, Mom."

It was the first and last day he would ever see Kira.

For months afterwards, the mood at home was sombre. Though Michael said nothing, we were all acutely aware of his loss. Also his anger. He and Andrew further bonded. They once again clung to each other, wanting nothing to do with the rest of us. Michael plastered more photos of Kira all over his bedroom wall. Andrew and Kenny mythologized Kira as if she were Mother Teresa. They decided that it was her sorrow about Andrew living mostly with Lynn and Don that had killed her. How could we counter? We couldn't.

I kept thinking of the words written by American playwright Langston Hughes. "What happens to a dream deferred? Does it dry up — like a raisin in the sun?"

It saddened Robin and me greatly that we didn't know what words, if any, might bring comfort to Michael. We so badly wanted him to understand that with time and willpower, the human spirit often soars above its sorrows. So while respecting Michael's pain, we carried on with our family life, slowly bringing Michael back into our folds. Kira couldn't assure him of her love, but *we* could. I believed that had to count for something.

We were standing outside at Holy Sepulchre Cemetery, standing in the cool air, waiting for the ceremony to get underway. I leaned into Robin. "He looks so much older today," I whispered, nodding towards Michael, dressed in the dark navy suit he first wore at the funeral six months before.

We shivered as drones of "Amazing Grace" reached a crescendo and echoed through the cemetery. A piper broke through the mist, dressed in tartan kilt, gillie brogues and white rabbit sporran. When the hymn was finished, he lowered his bagpipe and joined the twenty mourners circling Kira's newly erected tombstone.

We had come to Holy Sepulchre to bury the ashes of Kira Obe-Hilton, dead at thirty-seven from an overdose. Her husband Kenny had selected the tombstone we stood beside. He had also chosen the Catholic priest who began a lengthy spiel about resurrection and Kira's relation to it. Finally, he stopped and Kenny ceased the high-pitched wailing from his wheelchair.

Most of the small group that had assembled was now headed back to the parking lot. A handful remained. We were Kira's family — of sorts. On one side there was Don (Kira's father); Lynn (Don's second wife and stepmother to Kira); and Andrew, twelve (Kira's son). On the other side there were "us." Robin; Michael, fifteen (Kira's son); Sarah, thirteen; and me. We were the family "of sorts.'" Our lives were bound to her by blood.

While we stood by the monument, two women and a man walked towards us and introduced themselves as members of the Toronto Métis Association. Kira's grandfather on Don's side was Six Nations Mohawk.

"We are about to begin a ceremonial smudge," one of them said. "We invite you to join us as we send Kira's soul back to the Creator."

I nodded, aware that our participation was as much for Michael as it was for Kira.

Bernard instructed us to form a circle around Kira's tombstone. Then he walked into the centre. He pulled a wooden matchbox from his pocket, struck a match against its side, and lowered the flame onto tightly woven blades of dried sweetgrass in the palm of his left hand.

Everyone's gaze moved upward with the smoke, everyone's except mine. Mine remained riveted on Bernard. The man radiated both energy and calm. He was tall and remarkably handsome, with deeply carved, angular features. His long, shiny black hair was pulled back into a lush pony tail. He was dressed casually in chinos and plaid shirt. The multicoloured *ceinture fléchée* tied around his waist was, I presumed, a sartorial nod to his Métis forebears.

I'd seen him before, but I couldn't think where. Eventually, it came to me. He was in a book of full-page sepia photographs by Edward Curtis that my sister Sharon gave me on my fifteenth birthday in 1963. Curtis, fearing that North American Indians were on the verge of extinction, set out in the early 1900s on an odyssey across the continent to document this.

Now there I was, more than thirty years later in Toronto, Canada, standing with a man who could have leapt from the pages of Curtis's book. And he was asking me to participate in one of the fundamental rites of his people, Kira's people, a thread of my son's ancestral bloodline.

Bernard walked directly towards me, extending his right arm.

"Wave this eagle feather above your head, into the winds," he directed. "It will help send Kira's soul back home."

I raised the feather and made figure eights as instructed, then quickly passed the feather to Michael, wondering if he'd do as Bernard said. The answer, as always, was a crapshoot. I sighed with relief when he raised the feather. He then passed it on to Robin who handed it to Sarah until everyone in our circle had completed the task. Andrew was the last to wave his mother's soul into the sky.

Seeing Michael crying, I wanted to fold him in my arms, but I knew that at fifteen, he was too old to take comfort in that. He had lost his desire for physical affection from his parents. So I imagined the cemetery's huge alabaster cherubs and archangels that hovered above us swooping down, clutching Michael upwards from the ground, gently folding him in their wings, making him feel protected, the way I felt as a child wrapped in my father's *tallit*. When I would sit next to him at *shule*, he would extend his prayer shawl beyond his shoulders until it covered mine as well, engulfing me tenderly in his real and metaphorical warmth.

Catholic, Jewish, Mohawk, Scots. This ridiculous mélange of religious icons and cultural metaphors was stirring the simmering stew I was carrying inside. I wrestled with how Kira's missteps had affected each member of our family. I still held so much anger towards her, for lying, for harming Michael, for seeming not to care, for dying before Michael could meet her, dying before he could ask what he needed to know — did she love him?

Yet, I looked toward the darkening sky with a grateful nod, asking Kira's god to safeguard her soul. Robin, who clasped my hand in his, felt the same way. We loved our son, the son that Kira had given life, the son still grieving for the mother he never knew, the son who would never ask the question he had prepared for their first meeting, "Why couldn't you raise me?"

I began sobbing. What if my tears never stopped? This is something that serious criers like me fear: that once we let ourselves go, we may never come back. Shouldn't we know by now that crying, like life and a good story, has a beginning, a middle and an end?

Yes, perhaps I should have known. But it's hard when I never know where the story is taking me next. I kept crying.

In the months following Kira's memorial, we could see that Michael was growing into a nice-looking young man. We were all happy that he had reached five-foot-two, the maximum height the endocrinologists predicted from bone scans taken when he was diagnosed at six with FAS. He remained wiry, had strong muscles and a nice lean look. His hair was still thick and blond, and in recent years, with the arrival of facial hair, he had grown a scraggly moustache and beard. Naturally, I preferred him clean-shaven. I was his mother. He was never without T-shirt and jeans. As we feared, Michael's body had become badly scarred on his arms, shoulders and chest from his skin-picking. Miraculously, his face had been spared.

Michael always said he didn't care how he looked, but Robin,

Sarah and I would swear he was noticeably proud strutting around in the brown leather jacket we bought him for his sixteenth birthday. He topped it off with the best smile in the whole wide world, the one Robin described when he was born as able to launch a thousand camera clicks.

The relationship I had with my son was different than what I had with any other person. There were holes in it everywhere. I tried to patch them with both love and *rachmones*. The best definition I ever found for this Yiddish word was from American writer Burt Alpert in his book *Rachmones: The Passion of Hebraic Empathy, A History:*

> *Rachmones, I remember as having been the single word that probably carried the greatest import in my early life. While comparable in its sense to pity, sympathy, empathy, compassion, mercy, tenderness, fellow-feeling and caring, Hebraic rachmones embraces a wider perspective than any of these. One of my favorite song lines has the perfect explanation of rachmones when it assures the listener that, "When something's wrong with my baby, something's wrong with me."*

Michael never said hello when he came into the house unless I reminded him to, nor did he think of saying goodbye. I knew he was connected to me because he always appeared visibly upset if I hurt myself, stumbled or was sick; he sometimes let me hug him on request and laughed at my goofy jokes.

He had never wished me happy birthday, never gave me a Mother's Day card, or asked me how I was. He didn't know what I did for a living, the colour of my eyes or my favourite foods. Though he was of normal-range intelligence and had a good vocabulary, his memory was extremely poor, especially with anything sequential. He didn't remember the names of his grandparents, was hard pressed to come up with the days of the week or know what year it was. Though I always tried to engage him, I never had a conversation with my son.

At sixteen, Michael had quit school, having completed only part of Grade Nine. Our fears had come true. Entering high school overwhelmed him, academically and socially. The classes were bigger. Teachers demanded more independence. Home-room was gone. We hired tutors, dragged him to Homework Club, met continually with teachers and the principal. Nothing worked. Michael began refusing to go to school and eventually stopped altogether.

Basically, Michael had shut down. Though he talked about neither, leaving school and losing Kira had left their mark. He stayed in his room playing video games. He wandered around the house a lot, bored, looking for something to do, but never finding it. I found it painful to watch. He was able-bodied and ostensibly capable of doing physical and mental tasks required for many jobs, but we couldn't convince him to work. He said he never would. He didn't attend family events or join us at the dinner table. He still wouldn't brush his teeth, wash his hair or change his clothes except under duress. People always told me this would change when he became interested in girls. That had already happened, and still, the hygiene didn't come.

Sadly, many of the predictions made at SickKids at the time of his fetal alcohol diagnosis had come to be. We had entered the future, the one we were trying to nullify, the one projected by FAS experts. Michael had difficulty handling money and telling time. He didn't think things through or reason well. Generally, he didn't learn from past experiences or understand the consequences of his actions. He repeated mistakes — some-times even though he knew what he had done was wrong. His impulses usually overshadowed reasoning, but he always regretted doing something "wrong."

Michael couldn't remember things like appointments. He didn't interact with other people appropriately. He couldn't read people's faces, moods or subtleties. He wouldn't take his medication on his own. He had trouble dealing with everyday tasks, buying food or filling out forms. He could read, though he seldom chose to. He could print, but not write.

He did, however, like to watch nature shows on the Discovery Channel, canoe and go on occasional hikes. During vacations with us, he had learned how to downhill ski and scuba dive, both real accomplishments. He proudly taught himself to skateboard, which he would do in nice weather. He was comfortable in the woods, perhaps more comfortable than anywhere else. He talked about having a cabin in the wilderness someday. The idea appealed to him because he wouldn't need money and no one would ask him to do anything.

At sixteen, Michael was no longer aggressive as he was as a child. Though not particularly interested in or conscious of other people's well-being, he had become a gentle soul. There was a sweetness about him. He never said a bad thing about anyone nor would he do anything mean-spirited. He and the family dog, Bear, shared lavish physical attention on one another. The dog meant the world to him.

Like Sarah, Michael was irreversibly lodged in my psyche. He was with me wherever I went, no matter what I was doing. I tried to keep some of my feelings about him below my emotional radar or my eyes would start to tear. I think my friends knew this and sometimes wondered whether or not to ask in any detail how Michael was doing. They were afraid of causing me anguish by talking about him. And I suppose they were right, because sometimes my first reaction was to say, "Don't ask..." But I *did* want them to ask. He was my son. I was touched they were interested or cared. I didn't want to be one of those mothers who pretended the wayward child didn't exist. I was only sorry that I seldom had anything new or positive to report. I got tired of hearing myself talk about the same stuff over and over, time after time, year after year.

When people I wasn't close to asked how Michael was, I usually said, "He's fine, thanks for asking." I relayed more detail with family and close friends. I would often break down if we talked for long or they asked probing questions about problems we still hadn't found solutions for and wondered if we ever would. I wore Michael's heart on my sleeve. It's just the way I was.

It's natural when mothers get together that the talk turns to their kids. I seldom joined in except to talk about Sarah, and I felt weird talking about Sarah and not Michael, though I often did. Sarah deserved it. But most people's issues, concerns, worries and pleasures were completely different from mine. There was little I could add to a casual conversation about school, homework, curfews, part-time jobs, girlfriends or after-school activities. I didn't want to hijack a conversation by introducing something weighty.

When Michael's differences were beginning to surface in the early years, I shared some of my concerns. Most people automatically compared his issues to those of their own kids. They dismissed my worries, probably inadvertently. They said, "My kid's like that, too," or "He's going through a stage."

Yes, what he was doing was similar to their children, but there was a major difference. It was a question of degree, and Michael's not-so-healthy behaviours were at the extreme end of the continuum. Their kids grew out of things. Michael didn't. But perhaps those were points that only I could know.

At first I felt hurt, angry and lonely. Nobody's listening! It was hard to open up and too often when I did, it was a mistake. I never wanted sympathy. If I ever said anything, it was because I felt the need to talk or to seek advice. I never knew if people were trying to be comforting and helpful by always putting on positive spins, but I think a few people simply did lack empathy. I quickly learned to become careful about who it was I spoke to about Michael. I also learned to protect myself from judgment.

Barbara, Ellie, Sybil, my sisters and other close friends figured out early how to show interest, lend comfort, advice and concern. They also knew how to share the small, fleeting moments of *nachas* we had that so much needed to be celebrated. They also knew I loved hearing about their kids, and how truly happy I was when they were doing well.

I did, however, have limits as to how long I could hear other people, more distant from me, talk about their children's accomplishments, especially if they didn't know how lucky they were or took their blessings for granted. Nor could I listen too long to certain extended complaints, like when someone's kid got into Princeton but not Harvard. I could muster only so much sympathy for what they felt were life's cruelties.

Sometimes I had fantasy conversations with Michael in my head. In these delusionary moments, I came up with a question or a story that unlocked him from within and we began to talk. He told me what he was doing, how he was feeling, what he thought, what he hoped for, what made him happy and what made him sad. We laughed and joked and finished with a hug.

I kept trying to make that conversation really happen. I knew it was crazy. It meant I hadn't completely accepted that I would never know more about what my son was thinking or feeling. It also meant that I hadn't yet fully accepted him for who he truly was.

I believed there must be things that could hold Michael's attention other than computer games. I also believed that there were people like him he could be friendly with. I believed there was someone out there besides Robin, Sarah or me who would love him and take care of him one day. I believed one day he would brush his teeth, wash his hands, change his clothes and possibly take out the garbage.

Michael still loved being with Andrew and another buddy on the Island. Yet, even with them, Michael didn't really talk, or when he did, he often relied on false bravado for conversation. Nor would he hang with them for long. He retreated back to his room after short periods of interaction because after a while, he hadn't a clue what to say or do next. After taking a breather, he'd often go back for another dose of sociability, but this also lasted only a few minutes before he retreated once again.

When Robin was asked how his son was, he always answered by saying "He's Michael." It meant he doesn't really know, but Sarah and I always smiled hearing Robin say this. Michael being Michael elicits our tenderness. Clearly, he had a gift. We didn't know exactly what it was, but it came with him the first day Robin and I held him in our arms, and it hadn't left since.

A gift that begets love is undoubtedly a blessing. It had ensured our devotion, a devotion that nevertheless had come at a cost to our family. Robin, Sarah and I have paid dearly in our family life. It happens sometimes; you pay a price for love.

I had no doubt that the cocoon of love that enveloped me upon our first meeting, over time, had made me steadfast during our struggles to help Michael find his place in the world.

People often said, "I don't know how you do it," in regards to raising Michael. I was never sure how to respond. I didn't know either. We were the people who had chosen not to adopt a child with disabilities when we were first thinking about adopting. I guess I learned "how to do it" like anyone else would. I muddled through, did my best, pushed a little more than most people have to, drew upon everyone and everything I could to help me along, kept talking, had a few breakdowns, took meds, crossed my fingers, prayed, hoped for good luck, cried, laughed, read mysteries, watched romantic comedies and pushed on.

What exactly were the options?

I played my hand with everything I had. I didn't want to become like my father. I learned a hard lesson watching him. Burned by his losses in the Detroit riots, his world view and belief in humankind evaporated with the lighting of a match. He died a depressed, bitter man. It was awful to watch and awful to realize that I could do nothing to change that. I vowed not to let that happen to me. It's a cruel legacy to leave to your children, one I knew too well.

While for the most part I remained a positive person, there were three so-called positive beliefs I thoroughly rejected. They were:

God only gives you as much as you can handle.
Suffering makes you stronger
There's a reason for everything.

I've met too many walking wounded out there. Let's start with parents of other children with FAS, broken people who couldn't handle what came their way. They readily admit they'd given their lives and marriages to their kids. Then we could move onto victims of tsunamis, concentration camps or the Cambodian Killing Fields. Whoever's spouting that sunshine crapola hasn't had a look around lately or cracked a history book.

Though I barely knew my father's mother, and of course never knew my mother's, I believed I was learning what these grandmothers must have known. Life came with hardships and struggle. You protect, look after and fight for your family. Everybody's got something. What made me and so many other privileged, starry-eyed North Americans of my generation think we were exempt? Crosby, Stills, Nash and Young told us, "We are stardust, we are golden." Were we? Perhaps it is the folly of every generation's youth, not only mine, to think so.

I was coming closer to accepting that Michael's capacity for functioning in the world was severely diminished. Quite likely, he would never live on his own. Both Robin and I had given up the usual expectations and dreams most parents have for their children, all except for one. Despite Michael's seeming lack of interest in people, I knew he was lonely. A mother knows these things. My son was deeply lonely. I needed to think Michael could one day find comfort, pleasure and love.

We needed to do something to help Michael function better in the world, and if at all possible, become part of it. He needed other people in his life beyond our family.

It was a cold January morning. Once Robin picked up a car cityside, Robin, Sarah, Michael and I would drive 200 km into the snow-covered hill country around Collingwood, Ontario. Our destination was "The Farm," a residential treatment program where we were taking Michael to live during the coming year.

The mood around the house before we left felt like the morning of Michael's *bar mitzvah*. On the surface, it looked like we were each doing our routine morning *toilette*. Really, we were doing *pirouettes* on tiptoes, once again hoping not to offend the gods.

Our jitters were showing. Each of us knew that soon, one of us would blow his or her volcanic top before walking out the front door. If there really was such a thing as waking up on the wrong side of the bed, that's where our feet went *kerplunk* at the sound of the seven o'clock wake-up alarm that morning.

"Will you go get Michael up?" I asked Robin, the moment my eyes popped open.

"No you, why me? I have to catch an earlier boat than you to pick up the rental car. You've got more time." His tone wasn't friendly.

"You *know* we'll have a better chance if you do it," I said.

"I've got to catch the 7:30."

He figured that was the end of the conversation. Neither of us wanted the chore of getting Michael out of bed. Robin was saying that since he had only fifteen, maybe twenty minutes before he had to leave the house to catch the boat, it made sense for me to wake Michael. Sarah, Michael and I could catch the later boat. Therefore, I should be the one to get Michael ready.

Not so simple, Robin. "Why didn't you explain this last night when we set the alarm? We could have factored everything in. We could have woken up earlier so you could get Michael up and we'd all leave the house together. Now, I've got to get him dressed, finish packing him, get myself organized and get him and his suitcases out the door and to the boat. Alone. You left it all for me. You're ducking out."

"I didn't want to talk logistics last night." Of course not. He didn't want to get into a fight. The one we were now having.

"So leaving it for this morning would make it different? The only difference is that last night you couldn't walk out once you told me."

We'd been awake for less than five minutes and were already fighting. We were so anxious about today's trip to Collingwood, we'd once again forgotten that we should be comforting each other rather than giving grief.

The decision to send Michael "away" was tearing us apart. It had been long in coming, though Robin and I seldom acknowledged or discussed it. It was a possibility we each tucked into the back-pocket of our minds — just in case. At the same time, we were praying that just in case never came. Over the years, we had heard successful stories about other difficult kids who had been sent to The Farm. Many came home after a year or so with their behaviours sufficiently changed that they could successfully live with their families again.

Options like The Farm had always been crucial to both Robin's and my mental health when things were particularly rough. We always needed to know that if one day we "reached our limits" and couldn't "take it" anymore, there was something left to do. With mild shame, we quietly squirreled away options.

The Farm, run by the Hincks Dellcrest Foundation, was a structured, live-in treatment centre on a hundred-acre working farm in the Georgian Bay area of Ontario. It took roughly twenty or so "hard to serve, at-risk" youth through the age of sixteen. Kids having trouble with school, family and, of tentimes, the law were selected to live there with professional staff. They went to an on-site school, did chores, grew crops, raised sheep, poultry and livestock. The staff, who lived there around-the-clock, taught, parented and helped the kids develop life skills, improve their behaviour, manage their anger and build self-esteem.

Three years ago, we had put Michael's name on The Farm's waiting list, just in case. Michael loved animals and being in the country. Maybe, if worse ever did come to worst, this might be a good thing.

We never seriously expected to send him, though. Michael's therapist had concerns. "If Michael weren't adopted, it might be okay," she told us after one of his sessions. "But adopted children have severe problems with 'abandonment' and 'rejection.' Being sent away from home can be counterproductive."

The Farm's experience underscored her point. Their "success rate" was lower with adopted children. One more option door firmly closed, we thought.

But things got progressively worse at home. Michael completely shut down. After quitting school, he would do nothing all day but play video games, no matter how hard we tried to motivate him to do other things. We tried taking him places he would normally enjoy, doing things with him we used to all enjoy together. Taking the video games away didn't change a thing. He sat in his room, stared at the ceiling or slept, punched holes in the walls and picked at his skin. He created physical chaos in the house, emotional chaos in the family.

I was worried that Michael was depressed, still mourning Kira. We spoke to the doctors and a therapist, but nobody knew for sure because Michael wouldn't open up. We tried different meds, but it was the Ritalin we still mainly relied on. He was the same Michael, but age and hormones were in play. He was a teenager. As a teenager he became more threatening in stature when angry. Sadly for us all, Michael had, as we expected, lost all desire for physical warmth with Robin and me. Up until then, it had been our most successful form of communication. With that now gone, there was little he wanted from us. Not unnatural for a teenager, but we were Michael's only real link with the world of others. Now that too was gone.

For the ten years since his diagnosis, we'd tried our best to do all the things we thought we should do. Various therapies, special camps, tutors, social skills programs, therapists, tough love, soft love, plain love.

We hadn't been perfect. The best I could say in our favour was that we'd never wavered in our love and always made sure he knew that. Yet, if you asked either Robin or me what, in our opinion, had the most positive effect on Michael over the years, we'd both probably still say "meds and physical maturation." It made us wonder, sadly, if anything we did ever really mattered.

The words "I'll never do that" bounced in my head that day driving to The Farm, like smug, gremlin-style boxers pummelling me with miniature fisticuffs. I'd mumbled those words under my breath ten years before when the doctor at SickKids told us a family had decided to send their child with fetal alcohol syndrome away. "I'll never do that," I had smugly mumbled to myself.

The little monsters were repeating over and over in my brain, "I'll never do that" "I'll never do that" "I'll never do that," as I went into Michael's room, sat down beside him on his bed and said as calmly as I could, "Good morning, Michael. It's Thursday. Daddy's just gone into the city to get the car for us. Today's the day we go to The Farm."

Robin was just plain on-edge nervous and scattered before leaving for the boat. He was rushing around madly, dropping things on the floor, losing things, barking at everyone.

Sarah didn't say much. She kept looking to me for comfort. Part of her hated the idea of her Mikey leaving. Not much different from the way both Robin and I felt. There was another part to each of us, though. We wanted to know what home life would be like without Michael. We each had had enough for a while.

And Michael? How was he feeling about it all? Who knew?

We'd taken Michael to The Farm for several visits. He had met the staff, hung with the animals, walked the property. We'd presented his move there as positive, like going to camp. It's not a punishment, we reassured him. It's an opportunity to be in the country, with animals, learn skills. They'll take you camping, skiing, snowshoeing, rafting. You'll have opportunities to meet girls, learn useful skills and go to a school made for kids with learning disabilities. You'll get to drive a tractor. We'll call and visit often. You'll come home for visits. The staff are wonderful.

We encouraged him to talk about his feelings about being away from home, but he never said anything other than "Riding the tractor could be fun." We let him know it would be tough for us to be without him.

Robin and I said everything to Michael short of the complete truth: we were sending him away because we were frustrated, exhausted, losing heart, in a state of crisis. We didn't tell him "We're hoping other people can teach you things you need to know to live without us someday." We didn't say that we were afraid we hadn't done very well as parents, or that there was too much tension in the house. I never said, "Having you at home has been a serious strain on Daddy's and my marriage and rough on Sarah. She needs us all to herself for a while."

And over and over we said, "We love you."

After we arrived at The Farm, we helped Michael unpack, make his bed and hang Metallica posters in his room until it was the designated time to leave.

We hugged and kissed Michael goodbye. We didn't look back as we walked solemnly to our car through the heavy snow.

Sarah was in the backseat crying, a condition usually monopolized by me. For some reason, I was not. When I tried to comfort her, Sarah made it clear she didn't want to talk; she was putting in her iPod earbuds to listen to Ozzie Osbourne's "Dreamer," a song she found comforting: *I'm just a dreamer, I dream my life away. I'm just a dreamer, who dreams of better days.*

She planned to remain plugged in for the whole trip. Robin was concentrating deeply on the snow-covered road he was finding difficult to drive. He didn't want to talk about anything, either. Nor did I. What was there to say? In my case, I could usually find something, but not right then. I was experiencing everything I expected to feel, including guilt, sadness and worry. But there was something new mixed into the equation. I felt remarkably free and unburdened, as if I had shed a clay water jug that I'd been balancing on my head during a sixteen-year journey to a well.

The countryside we were driving through had gentle rolling hills dotted with grazing sheep and snow-covered apple orchards. I liked the sense of peace and order on the farms we passed. My eye was drawn to the neat, symmetrical row of trees, *allees*, lining both sides of the road leading up to their front entrances.

Though it was mid-winter, the landscape made me think about my garden back home. I began forming pictures in my mind's eye of formal gardens I'd seen during our travels in Europe. I was envisioning the grand properties with clipped hedges and geometric pathways around palaces, palazzos and castles in France, Italy and England. The kind I'd always found a bit stuffy. The kind where people, the silly beasts, were trying to control nature. Such gardens were the polar opposite of the gently informal cottage garden in my front yard on the Island. No one could have been more shocked than I was — for the first time in my life I could see something good in those seriously structured landscapes.

What was happening to me?

"What's so funny?" Robin asked, hearing me quietly chuckle. "I was thinking about our backyard and wondered how it would look as a formal garden."

"A formal garden on the Island? Like Versailles?"

"Exactly."

The next morning, my first day home without Michael, I got up early, took the boat into the city and went shopping for new garden books. The dozens I already owned wouldn't do. I needed ones with pictures of moss-covered lion-spewing water fountains, tightly clipped hedges, intricately designed knot gardens and oversized urns dripping with ivies and ferns. That night, reading one of my new books, something delightful caught my eye.

I turned to Robin. I remained utterly dependent on him for anything that required spatial and mechanical sense or involved an instrument other than pen or pencil.

"Will you look at these then tell me if you think you could make one for the garden?"

He took the book, studied it momentarily then laughed aloud. "Sure. Why not? It might take thirty years to get a bush large enough, but sure, I could clip a shrub into the shape of a partridge or giant aardvark. I could even make a kingfisher for you."

"Now there's an idea," I said. "A kingfisher."

Several weeks later, I saw an ad in *The Toronto Star* newspaper about a contest they were sponsoring. A free makeover in the backyard garden of the person who writes the best hundred-word essay explaining why they think they should be chosen for the reno. It was perfect. I carefully worded my essay and sent it in. I thought I was a shoe-in. I had had a history of good luck with newspaper ads in my life.

Help! I Want My Backyard Back
   I turned our backyard garden over to our children when they were young, for sports and creative

acts of destruction. Now that they have grown into surly, rebellious teenagers, I'm ready to reclaim my turf. I request your help to turn the yard into a calm oasis, totally different from the more free-flowing, cottage-style garden in our front yard here on Toronto Island. My desire for a mini-Versailles reflects a need for more order and control during this period of parenthood. I am now attracted to straight paths, formal geometric borders and clipped hedges. I want orderly plants that stand at attention in tidy little rows where I tell them to.

If such a garden ever came to be, the children would be invited by invitation only.

Perhaps for afternoon tea.

I never heard a peep back from the newspaper. I was disappointed, but didn't let that stop me. I called Penny, my Island gardening buddy.

"How about coming for coffee? I need to talk to you."

"I can tell this means trouble," she said, "but whatever it is, I'm up for it."

And so, the frenzy began. I never doubted for a second that building the garden, with all the unimaginable demands, which included hauling bricks, stones and cobbles to my carless Island, was therapy for my soul. I needed to nurture beauty, put my energy into building something concrete, stable and orderly; something that would bring me joy, comfort and solace. I needed Constructive (or was it Construction) Horticultural Therapy.

Months later, I invited friends and family to join Robin and me in the new garden. Sitting on the new stone terrace, we sipped tea under our cherry tree, the area that we now called Tuscany. Tuscany was only a few feet from Versailles, complete with our new circular pond, lavender border and topiary chicken.

15.
My Family Finds Itself
Toronto Island, 2003

MICHAEL HAD BEEN AT THE FARM for almost a year. We all missed him, but there was no denying it. Home had been more peaceful, our emotional life more stable.

When neighbours asked "How's it going without Michael?" we'd say something along the lines of "It's hard having him away from us." But to those in our inner sanctum, we could be less circumspect. "It's good having him gone for a while. We're all more relaxed."

The year had been a time of healing. Robin and I barely bickered, had more fun. We travelled together, took Sarah to Paris. We invited people over to our house more often. I had dinner parties again. Sarah relished all the attention we lavished on her. I got back to reading literary fiction.

I was reclaiming myself during the year, probably more in need to do so than Robin or Sarah. I longed to see myself as someone other than a mother of a disabled child . Though that was not the image I presented to the rest of the world, much of my identity had turned to raising Michael. I had lost bits and pieces of Linda over the years.

On a sunny August morning while Michael was still away, Sarah and I were rifling through family photos on the table under the cherry tree in the backyard. Golden orange Baltimore orioles were flying past, heading to our next-door neighbour's feeder. Our dog Bear was lounging sleepily at Sarah's feet. I knew what a treasure this jewel-like moment with my daughter was.

"Grandma looks so beautiful in this picture," Sarah said, holding up a yellowing photo with ragged white borders. "Look at her long curly hair, and that bathing suit! She looks so happy. How old do you think she was?"

I took the photo into my own hand and stared at my mother. I had seen this picture before, but never looked with such concentration. "She couldn't have been more than eighteen or nineteen," I said. "But I'm not really sure. You're right about how beautiful she was — and happy." I knew so little about my mother's youth, I realized. I assumed this was taken before she met my father. I wondered if she really was as happy and carefree as she looked. Was it before her mother got sick or was she, like me in my unhappy hours, pretending?

I hoped she really *was* happy. I thought back to the day that my anger towards her began to dissipate, the first time I actually saw joy on her face. "Sarah, have I ever told you how much you helped me with Grandma?"

"What do you mean?"

"My relationship with Grandma was really different than the one we have," I said. "We weren't always close." I had never told her about the "I love you" moment between her and my mother in Florida. I didn't think she needed to know the problems I had with my mother, nor did I want her to see her grandma in a bad light.

"I knew Grandma loved me, Sarah, but she wasn't good at showing it," I said. I described the long-ago birthday when she jumped up from playing Lego with Michael, ran up to my mother and announced "I love you."

"Grandma said it back to you, Sarah, and that was a pretty special moment. I'm not sure I had ever heard her say those words before."

Naturally, Sarah was shocked. "I love you's" were tossed easily to one another in our family, and she didn't remember the time in Florida. Even if she had, she most likely wouldn't have had any idea how momentous it was.

"You unlocked Grandma's heart, Sarah. My relationship with her improved from that day on. The following week she told me she loved me, too. I owe you for that. I've never thanked you."

We talked a bit more about my mother, then Sarah asked, "Why do you think it was so hard for Grandma to say I love you?"

"I don't really know," I said. "I've thought it might have something to do with her own mother. Maybe *she* never said, 'I love you' to Grandma, either. "

I continued looking at the photo of my mother on the beach, smiling and flirtatious with the camera. She really did look carefree. But I knew looks could deceive. What was going on with her mother at home during the time of the photo? How old was my mother when they sent my grandmother off to Eloise? It was time to clean out the last bit of cobwebs in my family tree.

"Hi, Steve. It's Linda Rosenbaum. We had spoken a while ago about my grandmother in Eloise. You offered to help me should I decide to look for her records."

The offer was still good. The first step would be to find out if the records even existed. "I'll get back to you."

Steve had made essential contacts at Wayne County Probate Court while researching *Annie's Ghosts*. A longtime investigative reporter and editor for the *Washington Post*, Steve's sleuthing eventually revealed who to speak to and what specific files to ask for.

Two days later, Steve called back. "They've located a file of Esther Koenigsberg. It must be your grandmother. They were used by the judge to have your grandmother declared insane."

Declared insane? Though this was the legal word used for all mental illnesses that required hospitalization, nothing short of a Molotov cocktail was exploding in my brain upon hearing it. Up to that moment, I had assumed my grandmother was what we today call clinically depressed. Based on the little we knew, my sisters and I thought she never recovered after one of her sons died. Hearing the word insane, even though the legal term might have embraced the diagnosis of depression, made me worry there might be something more.

Being depressed made sense. Never recovering from such a tragedy made sense. Being depressed wasn't the same as being declared insane, though, at least not the way we think of insanity today.

"There may be very little in the files. Don't get your hopes up, but if you're lucky, you may at least get a diagnosis."

Since they wouldn't be medical records, I didn't expect much. I wondered whether I could possibly trust anything doctors said in the files, anyway. Psychiatry was in the Dark Ages then. We still were, but we'd come a long way. Nevertheless, I wanted to find out whatever I could. Once I had made the decision to look for her records, I became determined to make my grandmother a real person, not just a story I trotted out on occasion.

Steve explained that I needed to contact the Wayne County Probate Court's office in Detroit's City-county building. I called Detroit the next day and got the ball rolling. I sent in my fifty dollars, then tucked thoughts of my mother and grandmother away. Having worked in a bureaucracy, I didn't expect anyone to be in a rush to fill my request. My grandmother had been dead more than forty years.

A week later, a large manila envelope arrived in the mail. Wayne County Probate Office was typed in the upper-left-hand corner. I was home by myself and didn't know whether to look at the records alone or wait for Robin to come home. Sarah was in school, but even if she were home, I didn't know if the records contained anything I'd want to share without vetting it first.

I poured myself a cup of coffee and sat down at the dining-room table. I pulled out the envelope's contents and quickly leafed through a thick wad of thirteen printed forms with signatures, stamps and information that had been hand-typed into the printed pages.

I stopped abruptly on one of the last pages in the packet. I saw my mother's handwriting. It was unmistakable. It was her signature, the one I had seen her use all her life — signing thank-you cards, sick notes to my teachers, letters to me away at school. She had a very distinctive handwriting. It read: Belle Rosenbaum, daughter, age twenty-four.

Was she twenty-four when her mother was sent away? I searched on the sheet for a date. August 8, 1935, it said. But when I looked more closely at the sheet, I realized it wasn't the first date listed in my grandmother's committal papers. The page I was looking at was a review of her condition. She was *re*committed on this date. A quick look through other pages revealed that my grandmother had been committed in 1931, four years before. My mother was *twenty* when Esther Koenigsberg, her mother, was sent to Eloise. The photograph of my mother on the beach that Sarah and I were looking at would have been taken around that time.

I was heartsick for my mother. Children don't send a parent to an institution without trying every other option first. To commit had to be a last resort. So what had my grandmother been like leading up to this date? How many years had the family been living with her while she was ill? I had to presume many. Otherwise, how do children reach the conclusion: "We have no choice. We have to have our mother committed."

I was crying by that point, wondering if I should have waited for Robin to come home before looking at the papers. It was such a personal sorrow, though. Who else could possibly understand my layers and layers of feeling, going back to the day in 1956 when I answered the phone and the woman on the other end said, "Belle Rosenbaum, please. I'm calling from Eloise Mental Hospital."

On other pages of my grandmother's records, I found a

diagnosis: *paranoid schizophrenia*. So painful to read, I kept trying to determine whether the term was meaningful, made up to fit some bureaucratic guidelines needed for a committal at that time, or ersatz scientific musings of doctors who didn't really understand mental health as we do now.

What added to my confusion was this: they were quoting my grandmother in English, explaining what she was saying, stressing her incoherency, her loss in train of thought, her confusion. What language had my grandmother used to speak to the doctors or nurses? Wouldn't she have been speaking Yiddish, her mother tongue? Had she learned English while in America? I was doubtful. So many women in her generation hadn't. She was fifty-six when committed, according to the documents. She had come in her thirties to America. She took care of a brood of thirteen children and never worked outside the home.

I couldn't imagine that my grandmother was English-speaking. So if not, were doctors really able to understand what she was saying, even with a translator? I had no one to ask.

I read on. "Her thoughts are dominated by thoughts of persecution, centering on her own family and at times including the whole Jewish race."

"Voices distrust and suspicion."

"She attempted suicide a year ago, and threatens to kill her grandchildren because they are unkind to her."

"Constantly afraid of people — especially afraid of men, thinking some one is going to raid her home. Refuses to live in a home where men present. Refuses to live in Detroit because 'people' here are going to raid her home."

"She says she must die to satisfy the people in America so there can be peace. She is rambling and incoherent in her speech."

"At some time or other she or her husband had some conflict with the Federal Government by making prune whisky."

Awful, awful stuff. I didn't want to believe any of it. I wanted to think my grandmother was saying "I'm gonna kill those grandchildren of mine" as hyperbole, as mothers do when they're sick to death of their ungrateful offspring. I wanted to believe the prune whisky business was a real altercation with "authorities." This was Prohibition time. *Slivovitz*, what they called "prune whisky" in the records, was a common drink of Jewish immigrants. Maybe my grandfather, though dead at the time of her committal, really had been caught making it home years before. And the term "prune whisky" didn't sit well with me either. No one would translate *slivovitz* into prune whisky. It's *slivovitz*.

But I couldn't pretend the records were a sham, as was my first instinct. And why should I? My mother and aunts wouldn't have had my grandmother committed unless something was so wrong that they absolutely couldn't take care of her. Whether it was 1930s psychiatry or not, the words I read had to mean something: "*She cannot meet the vicissitudes of everyday life, and requires institutional care. Recommendation: committal.*" The papers, dated 1931, then again in 1935, 1938 and 1939 were signed by five of my grandmother's children, including my mother.

Reading all this, I momentarily feared that I might be betraying my mother's wishes and grandmother's privacy. Yet, by uncovering these documents, I was pulling my grandmother's life out from the shadows, bringing a mythical grandmother, lost to time, history and secrecy back into the family where she belonged. She had to be part of someone's memory, if only mine.

I wanted to tell my mother, as I so often had with my own children, "Everything's all right. It's okay." Her mother was sick. As I had said to Sarah's birth mum when we first spoke on the phone. "Who's to judge? Why does fate send someone one way, the next another?" We are all dealt hands. At that moment, with my grandmother's records spread out on the table in front of me, I realized my mother and I were very much alike in some ways. Life threw us each a curveball. We weren't sure what to do or how to do it. We were both flying by the seat of our pants, trying to do the best we could for our children, not knowing exactly what that was.

The records about my grandmother exposed something else about my mother, giving me a probable explanation for why she criticized her daughters so much about our looks, our grades, our boyfriends, our careers. She cared deeply how the rest of the world saw us, and by extension, herself. Perhaps she had never been able to completely free herself from the shame she felt about her mother.

It was time for another piece of family history to be put in place.

Robin and I had always told Sarah that we wanted her to wait until she was at least eighteen before meeting Denise. That day was now three weeks away. She was eighteen and ready. Denise let us know early on that when Sarah was ready, she would be too.

It was eighteen years that Denise and I had been speaking on the phone, exchanging letters or, more recently, emails. I made sure she heard when Sarah lost her first tooth, bought her first hockey skates, kicked a winning goal in soccer and saved her brother Michael from falling into a dangerously big hole.

Since she was fifteen, Sarah had been communicating directly with her birth mother through emails, and every once in a while, spoke to her on the phone. If Denise was calling me and Sarah happened to pick up, she spoke to her on the phone. When it first happened, Sarah immediately pressed the phone into my hand, too nervous to speak, but that soon changed.

Sarah had a strong desire to meet Denise when she was thirteen, but I had suggested she ask Denise for pictures of herself instead, and somehow, that sidetracked the immediate urge. For many years, a large picture of Denise was prominently displayed in Sarah's bedroom, just as Kira's once was in Michael's.

We started making plans for the reunion, all agreeing it should be at Denise's home in Kitchener, a city roughly one and a half hours outside Toronto.

As with Michael, we spent time talking to Sarah about her expectations of the meeting, any hopes or dreams she harboured. It wasn't the same as it was for Michael, though, because Denise wasn't an unknown. We knew so much about her, even the sound of her voice. She knew about us, too. We just hadn't yet met. Nevertheless, this was a major, possibly life-altering event, as was the phone call I received from Denise eighteen years before: "Hi, I'm calling about the ad in the newspaper." To which I had responded, "What ad?"

Michael was coming with Sarah, Robin and me to meet Denise. He had been home from The Farm for several years by this time. We were again the Rosenbaum-Christmas family of four. The year away from us had been as good for Michael as it had been for us. He liked being in the country and taking care of animals. He thrived on the outdoor activities, including winter camping and snowshoeing. Though there had been a treatment aspect to the The Farm's program, we didn't see major changes upon his return. His mood was good though, he was less preoccupied with Kira and seemed to have a confidence we hadn't noticed before. He still wasn't back in school and had not started to work. He was more willing to open channels for both, he said, and was showing a real interest in woodcarving. The idea of a remote cabin in the woods, however, remained more appealing than any of these other options.

It felt good having Michael home. He seemed like he wanted to be there, too. As before, however, worry about his future gnawed away at us. At twenty, his ability to look after himself remained markedly limited.

As we piled into the car, I wondered if the trip to Denise's might be painful for Michael. He'd been so close to meeting his own birth mother, but because of her death, he never did, never would. I worried this might make him sad or jealous. "Mike, will it be hard for you to see Sarah meet Denise since you didn't get to meet Kira?" I asked.

"No," he said. I thought our young man of few words was finished, but he then added, "I'm happy for Sarah." I thought back to the days at SickKids when Dr. Roberts told us we had to "model" emotions for Michael so he could learn words for what he was feeling. Over the years we had been saying things like "You must be feeling angry, Michael," when someone bullied him at school. "You must be sad, Michael," when Kira died. "You must be proud, Michael," when he learned to ski. On his own, right then, he said he was happy for his sister. He probably was. He didn't have a mean bone in his body.

I didn't say much on the drive out to Denise's. I had learned over the years, and particularly on the drive back from The Farm, that I didn't always have to rescue my family from uncomfortable feelings. Sure, everyone was nervous, but we'd survive. Anyway, I knew that once we were at Denise's I was going to be commandeered into active duty to keep everything moving along nicely.

We drove up to the small, wood-sided white house where Denise was living. "You walk in first, Ma," Sarah said, virtually shoving me at the door of Denise's small basement apartment, at the back of the house.

I knocked, and Denise came quickly to open the door, dressed casually, in jeans and a T-shirt. She said hello in her husky voice, then gave me a hearty laugh and spontaneous hug. I moved in quickly to make room for Sarah who was standing directly behind me. Denise gave her an even bigger bear hug. When they eventually pulled apart, they just stared at each other for what seemed forever, but was more likely just a few intense seconds.

Denise ushered us into her living room and led us to seats on her cushy couch. A huge television on mute was playing in the corner of the small room. Photographs of Sarah were hung on a wall alongside other family members.

Denise brought out bowls of corn chips, salsa, guacamole and a plate of homemade brownies and placed them on a coffee table in front of us. We sat in the living room for almost two hours, chatting, looking through photo albums, rereading old letters and telling stories about the past eighteen years. We kept looking for physical resemblances between the two. Denise's hair was much darker and skin more olive, but we all agreed that Sarah had Denise's prominent cheekbones and square jaw.

There was no shortage of laughter or tears. After a few hours, we were all emotionally exhausted.

Before we arrived, I told Sarah I would make sure that she and Denise had time alone. She said she wasn't sure if she'd need it, but I wanted her to know it was fine, just in case. After a half hour there, Denise asked Sarah if she wanted to go for a little walk together. Sarah looked at me before answering, and I, of course, nodded. They came back shortly after a brief trip to a nearby Tim Hortons. They were delighted to have discovered they were both aficionados of Timmy's and the Toronto Maple Leafs.

Sarah had been noticeably careful about my feelings during the whole lead-up to the meeting. "You don't have to worry, Mum, I know who my mother is," she said. She was equally sensitive when we were with Denise. She often gave me glances, nudges or little touches, letting me know she wasn't forgetting about me. I believed she was making sure I wasn't jealous or hurt. Of course, I could have been wrong. Maybe those reassuring gestures had been for her, reaffirming my presence to help her feel more stable in a difficult situation. She had two mothers in the same room, after all. I sensed a deep kindness in Sarah that day.

The end of the visit brought the unburdening of the last Rosenbaum-Christmas secret! We told Denise what Sarah's full name was. We could have done it before, of course, but at some point over the years we decided we wanted to be with Denise when she heard that the daughter she gave birth to on Christmas day was Sarah Ellen Rosenbaum-Christmas.

"Come on! I can't believe it," Denise said, shrieking, shaking her head back and forth. "What were the chances? Talk about a Christmas miracle. Does Oprah know?" We all had a good laugh, though we had been laughing about it for the last eighteen years. Denise was just catching up.

Yep, our Sarah Christmas, born on Christmas, and as she used to say... "raised Jewish." We left Denise's all agreeing that Sarah was our shared joy to the world.

Days after returning from Kitchener, our dog Bear bit someone. Robin and I agonized over the decision of whether to put him down. Ultimately, we knew we would never forgive ourselves if Bear bit again.

We told the kids. They were devastated and tried to convince us otherwise. But they could tell the decision was firm. Both cried. Michael was inconsolable.

We called our vet. He told us to come in the next day. "It will be peaceful for Bear. He won't be in any pain, we promise you." We were told we could hold him in our arms until the end.

"I'll take him tomorrow morning," Robin offered.

"I'll go with you, Dad," Michael said, much to our collective surprise.

There was no way I could take Bear, let alone hold him in my arms those last moments. Having made the decision with Robin to put him down was enough for me. For the first time in my life, I pulled out my mother's old warhorse. "Too sensitive," I said. "I just can't do it."

Sarah, at that moment, was her mother's daughter. "Me too," she said. "Too sensitive." Through tears, we laughed. Like the poem Sarah wrote in her early teens, "I'm strong as a bull, tender as my mother's heart," right then, she was her mum.

Our friend Lorraine offered to accompany Robin. Lorraine

and her partner Mary had a special, loving "auntie" relationship with our frisky, playful poodle. Every summer, they took him for a week to a northern Ontario island retreat, the occasion dubbed as Bear's Big Adventure.

After the boots and jackets went on the next morning, Michael attached Bear's leash and walked out the door with Robin. Sarah and I looked out through the living-room window, sobbing.

Lorraine was waiting at the boat. Good thing, because according to Robin, Michael just broke down. "I can't do it, Dad," he said, handing Robin the leash. He then walked home, straight into his bedroom, closing the door. It was hard to see him suffer like that, but I took comfort knowing Michael was clearly in touch with his feelings, as painful as they were.

"They had a quiet, candle-lit room for us," Robin said on his return. "We held Bear in our arms while they gave him the shot. We petted and talked to him while he slipped away." To the children, he added, "He died peacefully. It couldn't have been better."

I thought we needed a doggie wake cum *shiva*. Judaism had taught me how helpful, almost necessary rituals are during major life events, so I thought we should all gather round the table to celebrate Bear's life in as many ways as we could think of.

Sarah and I baked poppyseed cookies with our doggie cookie cutters, producing a big batch of spotted hounds. We lit white candles on the dining-room table on which sat framed photographs of Bear, his collar, a few pieces of kibble, a ball and a ratty old favourite chew toy.

It was time. I made the announcement: "Okay, everyone, let the games begin."

No one, not even Sarah, raised her eyebrows with a "There goes Mum being a camp counsellor, again."

On an empty wall near us, I had taped a large sheet of blank white poster paper. I took a pack of multicoloured markers, and on the left-hand side of the paper, printed each letter of Bear's name, each one below the next, with lots of space between each letter. B-E-A-R, vertically.

"We're going to take each letter of Bear's name, one by one," I said, "and shout out a word that describes Bear, starting with that letter, like *brown* for B. Then I'll write it on the paper next to the letter. We might come up with words we wanted to explain, like *barking*, because Bear had a sixth sense, knowing to bark at the neighbour we all agreed was our least favourite.

Everyone chimed in, shouting out words like, "bratty," "endearing," "affectionate," "rambunctious" (ironically, all making me think of Michael as I wrote them down). Michael's words were particularly noticed: argumentative, rambunctious, effervescent. Each was precise, clever and spot on. We had no idea he had the vocabulary — emotional or verbal.

Just then Michael, yelled out an "R" word. "Rascal! Bear was such a cute little rascal," he said. We laughed at Bear's rascally moments, including theft of an entire rib roast from the kitchen counter. I kept looking at Michael. He was sharing stories, smiling, eliciting loving responses from everyone. Michael was part of the group, no small thing.

There is a passage in the Torah's *Book of Numbers* describing God taking a census of the Jews expelled from Egypt, still wandering in the desert, far from the Promised Land. "And the people ... shall pitch their tents, each person by his or her own family camp, and each person under his or her own flag."

That's what Robin, Michael, Sarah and I were doing, I thought, that day and always. We were wandering in the desert, far from the Promised Land. Though oftentimes lost or directionless, we came together as one. Each of us in our family camp, each under his or her own personal flag.

Epilogue: Wolf Howling at Moon
Toronto Island, 2013

I SIT ON THE RED OTTOMAN by the fireplace, leaning towards the flame, rubbing my hands together to increase the warmth. Winters are cold on Toronto Island. I seldom sit still this time of year unless I make a fire.

I hear children laughing in the background. I know the sound should make me happy. It doesn't. I'm tempted to cover my ears.

"Come here," Robin says to me. "I've got one of us returning to the Island after bringing Michael home from the hospital ... and his fifth birthday party ... the kids digging up the dinosaur bones..."

My husband is nearby, transferring old videos of the children to DVDs. I've been listening to the sounds, of good times, all morning.

An abrupt cut in the soundtrack. I hear a clarinet. Unmistakably Klezmer. Michael's *bar mitzvah*.

"I'm good," I say to Robin, using the expression our twenty-three-year-old daughter Sarah recently taught me to replace "no." Robin laughs hearing me say it, but I can tell he's not sure why.

I lie. "I'm happy sitting over here for now. I'll come look at the videos later." I know he doesn't get it. I don't want to see the videos. Too bittersweet.

I don't need to see the videos to remind me of the sunny day in May when we brought our first child home from the hospital. And I can still picture Michael's birthday party, five years later, in the grassy fields of a nearby meadow. For our Treasure

Island theme, Robin and I had given Michael and neighbouring children yellowing maps left behind by once-roaming pirates. Hand-drawn sketches led them to buried gold doubloons and to "dinosaur" bones bought cityside from a butcher at St. Lawrence Market.

Then the diagnosis, the following year, 1993. Michael was six.

In the nineteen years since learning Michael had fetal alcohol syndrome, we've tried our best. Michael, now twenty-five, has become a lovely, soft-spoken young man, kind of heart. Also a school dropout, unable to keep a job or function in the world without helping hands. He lives in a group home during the week, with us on weekends.

"Mum, I want to show you my new carving," says Michael. He has come out of his bedroom to join me by the fire. "I'm starting an owl, in the round."

Five years ago, Robin signed Michael and himself up for woodcarving classes.

"Maybe this will be it," Robin and I continually said to one another before each attempt to help Michael find something of interest, to build confidence, bring a little joy.

After one year of classes, his large bas-relief *Wolf Howling at Moon*, carved from a thick piece of basswood, was finished. Third Place, Canadian Woodcarving Competition, Novice Category. The next year, *Pike Swimming Through Waves*, Third Place, Ontario Woodcarving Championships. This year, *Bear Upstream with Salmon*, Second Place, Ontario Woodcarving Championships.

I walk with Michael to his bedroom. What I see is a chunky block of wood clamped to his desk, a few edges chipped away. Yet, similar to Michaelangelo who saw the *Pietà* within a block of Carrara marble, I know that when Michael looks at his piece of wood, his heart, hands and eyes are envisioning an owl within, wings spanned, eyes fierce and glaring, waiting to take flight.

"I can't wait to see what you're going to do," I tell Michael. Then, to my surprise, add, "How about taking a short break? Dad has some videos he'd like us to see."

Acknowledgements

In early days, I took a rough draft of *Not Exactly As Planned* to writer Merilyn Simonds, asking whether my unpolished manuscript was meant to see the light of day. Fortunately, Merilyn saw the story I wanted to tell hiding within. She believed it was an important story to tell, but more importantly, she believed I could tell it. I just needed to find my "voice." Merilyn taught me until I did.

Editor Renate Mohr helped shape the story and bring more honesty to it. Detecting holes in the narrative, she encouraged me to confront events needing to be told.

I put down my manuscript for several years, filing it away in a folder titled "Book, Unfinished." Then Beth McAuley of The Editing Company stepped into my life. My "Manuscript Whisperer" gently nuzzled me back into the ring, with calm voice, skill and keen enthusiasm. Beth wasn't going to let go of me until the manuscript was published. Her faith in both me, and the book, meant the world to me.

Editor Jessie Hale, working at The Editing Company at the time, also provided much-needed encouragement and strong editing skills.

In addition to early proofreading, Eagle Eye Ellen Eisenberg, aka Miss Needle-in-a Haystack, brought errant information to my attention that interfered with the flow of the story. Besides gratitude for her work and devotion as a friend, I owe her a large pack of sticky notes.

A big thank you to Allyson Woodroofe for her stellar skills on the cover design. I could happily look at fonts and layouts with her for days on end. We almost did. And to Lynn Cunningham for following us through the design process with her watchful eye and ever-constructive comments.

I am grateful to all who encouraged me to write the book, read early versions and provided useful feedback. They include Barbara Kopitz, Barbara Dresner, Sybil Faigin, Bonnie Buxton, Penny Lawler, Frank Meyer, Lorraine Filyer, Bob Eisenberg, Ellen Eisenberg, Lindalee Tracey, Lynn Cunningham, Steve Luxenberg, Stuart Ross, Rabbi Elyse Goldstein, Amy Marcus and my husband, Robin Christmas. My sister Barbara Kopitz, like no other, pushed me to carry on, no matter what external or internal tide was pushing back. She believed in me, and this book, from day one, and hasn't stopped yet.

Another big thanks to Lynn Cunningham and Andrew Hild for allowing me to include stories about their lives throughout the book.

I am grateful to Andrea O'Reilly, publisher of Demeter Press, for publishing my book and guiding both it, and me, through all the hoops to make this happen. Angie Deveau has also been an important support at Demeter.

An acknowledgement wouldn't be complete without a group hug to the unsung hero parents — particularly mothers — of children with disabilities and special needs who might not have thrived without their love and devotion. It's tough out there.

Of course, my biggest thank you goes to Robin, Michael and Sarah, for giving me the go-ahead to share our family's story, and to tell it *my* way. I hope you can feel the love for each of you oozing from (almost!) every page.